FABULOUS FINDS

THE SOPHISTICATED SHOPPERS GUIDE TO FACTORY OUTLET CENTERS

IRIS ELLIS

Writer's Digest Books

CINCINNATI, OHIO

Fabulous Finds: The Sophisticated Shopper's Guide to Factory Outlet Centers. Copyright © 1991 by Fabulous Finds, Inc. Printed and bound in the United States of America. All rights reserved. No part of this book may be reproduced in any form or by any electronic or mechanical means including information storage and retrieval systems without permission in writing from the publisher, except by a reviewer, who may quote brief passages in a review. Published by Writer's Digest Books, an imprint of F&W Publications, Inc., 1507 Dana Avenue, Cincinnati, Ohio 45207. First edition.

95 94 93 92 91   5 4 3 2 1

Library of Congress Cataloging in Publication Data

Ellis, Iris.
     Fabulous finds : the sophisticated shopper's guide
to factory outlet centers / Iris Ellis. — 1st ed.
          p.   cm.
     Includes index.
     ISBN 0-89879-481-1
     1. Outlet stores — United States — Directories. 2.
Outlet stores — Canada — Directories. I. Title.
HF5429.3.E45   1991
381'.15'02573 — dc20   91-24825
                                                          CIP

Edited by Bill Brohaugh
Designed by Kristi Kane Cullen
Maps drawn by Suzanne Whitaker

ABOUT THE AUTHOR

Iris Ellis identified factory outlet retailing as a retail concept in 1969. She collected information about the field and began publicizing it. Her first book, *SOS Directory*, published in 1972, sold 30,000 copies in the first thirty days after it became available. Shoppers had been waiting for the alternatives Iris described and detailed in *SOS Directory*.

Iris is a national spokesperson on the consumer's behalf. She has given speeches, training sessions, and consulting services to numerous retail organizations. Her new book, *Fabulous Finds*, along with valuable customer input, will guide the factory outlet industry to provide desirable locations, prices, and retail philosophies. Iris knows that retailers cannot exist without customers and that customers need to make their opinions heard. She wants *you* to take that opportunity with *Fabulous Finds*.

Iris lives and works in Jacksonville, Florida.

TABLE OF CONTENTS

FABULOUS FINDS IS YOUR GUIDEBOOK TO ADVENTURE!

To all nonstop shoppers:

The purpose of *Fabulous Finds* is to tell recreational shoppers about *real* factory outlet shopping and to describe other attractions to visit in nearby areas. With *Fabulous Finds*, you can shop the greatest specialty retail outlets in the U.S. and Canada and avoid the centers and stores that waste your time.

Each segment of *Fabulous Finds* focuses on a *factory outlet shopping center*. Factory outlet centers are fun to shop but hard to find. The real ones are hidden away just off a highway, thirty or forty miles from a metropolitan area; are tucked in a tourist town; or are located in an "outlet town." Some so-called "factory outlet centers" are located just outside the suburbs, but are usually a mix of discounters, off-pricers and overexposed outlets. A *few* bargains are mixed in with many questionable items and that is *not* a fabulous find.

Outlets are expected to offer discounts of 30-70 percent below regular retail prices. The outlet concept was created by manufacturers who wanted to eliminate the middleman. (See the introduction to the Pennsylvania chapter for a historical aside about how this concept began in Pennsylvania, and how women were the driving force.) The only time an outlet store's prices are in competition with a local department store is when the department store is having a sale. Outlet stores say that every day is sale day in the outlet centers.

How can you tell the difference between an outlet and an off-price store? An outlet store has the manufacturer's label and is owned by a manufacturer. They may mix in accessories and a few outside labels, but if the mix of labels becomes obvious, the manufacturer is also an off-price merchant.

Off-price stores belong to an enterprising company that sends good buyers to manufacturers to buy out job lots of merchandise. The job lots are purchased at ten to twenty cents on the dollar and the savings are passed along to the customer.

Over the years, customers have voiced a definite preference for shopping a true outlet concept. Mixing outlet and off-price merchandise tends to obscure the credibility necessary for the factory outlet concept to succeed. (Later in this book, we have included some surveys: Fill them out so we know how you feel about mixing the outlets with the off-pricers.)

To qualify for this book, a town or area must have a *true* factory outlet center. States and towns are listed alphabetically to help you look them up as you follow travel maps. Several factory outlet centers are sometimes clustered in an outlet town and when they are, they will be listed alphabetically. In most cases, there will be only one factory outlet center per town or area.

Listings are excerpts of information submitted by factory outlet personnel. The listings are *not* ads. Some are embellished with customer comments. The next edition will include more comments from shoppers. Editorial discretion has determined what has been listed, how much description has been used, and whether a store or center has been omitted because they diluted the outlet concept. Factory outlet stores and centers are growing rapidly; therefore, the information will change. Information is as up-to-date as possible when *Fabulous Finds* is sent to the printer. Maps were drawn based on maps and directions supplied by the factory outlet developers. (Note: If shopping center promotional people failed to supply the full tenant list, we couldn't print it for you. If you see that any listing in *Fabulous Finds* is incomplete or is not current, please suggest to the retailer or the shopping center management that they supply information on their outlet stores or centers. It will help *Fabulous Finds* give you the kind of information you need to plan your vacations and day trips.)

We also describe other man-made and natural attractions in or near the area to increase your possibilities for pleasure when you visit the outlet center. The recommendations for restaurants and overnight accommodations will help your adventure be an outstanding experience. These recommendations come from people just like you, and you are invited to share *your* experiences with others by writing to *Fabulous Finds*. (When making your recommendations, we don't want to hear about national chains, please. They're easy to find.)

Use the forms and questionnaires on the final pages of *Fabulous Finds* to share your opinions and experiences with readers of subsequent editions. We want to know what you think about *Fabulous Finds*, about the centers and stores that you visit, and about restaurants, lodgings and attractions that are special. *Fabulous Finds* seeks the unusual and exceptionally enjoyable experience in shopping, eating and adventuring. Any store, restaurant or lodging listed in *Fabulous Finds* must be great by today's standards. Time is too valuable to shop, eat or sleep in undesirable environments. Let us know what you liked—and what you didn't. Your positive comments will be printed in the next edition. Your negative comments will be taken seriously when deciding what not to include in the next edition. This is your direct line to manufacturing retailers—tell them what you will support.

Tear out the "referral tickets" in the back of the book to refer a particular center to your friends and neighbors when they are planning a trip. Each ticket will have enough information on it to direct your friends to a great shopping experience, and you can keep your directory at home where it belongs.

This directory is for you, our customer—please tell us if you like it, and if you have fabulous finds that are new to us. Your imagination and creativity put this book's predecessor, *SOS: The Save on Shopping Directory* on the *New York Times* best-seller list. But the concept for *SOS Directory* became obsolete when working women no longer had time to drive across town or to a neighboring town to shop a terrific factory outlet store. Instead, working women scheduled minitrips and vacations to have some time away from the double duty of career and homemaking. The appeal of minitrips and vacations was a change of pace for the modern woman. And so was a factory outlet center where travelers and tourists could indulge a penchant for recreational shopping. *Fabulous Finds* serves the *total experience* of our customers when they are planning a getaway.

Your comments, recommendations, suggestions and ideas helped shape *SOS Directory*. Sharing experiences through this publication will enable our customers have satisfying experiences in their minitrips and vacations. With the help of experienced adventurers like yourself, *Fabulous Finds* can make traveling enjoyable, eliminate unsatisfying experiences, and point out the best in every trip.

Tell everyone—shopkeepers, shopping center representatives, waitresses, hotel clerks—that you found their establishment in *Fabulous Finds*.

And happy shopping.

FABULOUS FINDS
IN
ALABAMA

Alabama is a collection of many cultures and influences. Alabama is where to go for forested mountains, bright white sandy beaches, rolling grasslands and green fields that stretch for miles. Alabama offers great natural sights such as the caves of DeSoto, Sequoyah and Russell, where excavations by the National Geographic Society have uncovered evidence of Indian campfires from ten thousand years ago. The Highlands, in northern Alabama, is an area of craggy canyons, rushing rivers and emerald green lakes. The Highlands' river-worn rocks, cascading waterfalls, natural rock bridges and hardwood forests are refreshing, as are the vast caves carved out by thousands of years of the water's flow.

Cathedral Caverns, about five miles northwest of Guntersville, boasts the world's largest cave mouth and inside is a magnificent stalactite and stalagmite forest and frozen waterfall. Start planning now to play in Alabama at their year-round attractions and annual festivals.

☞ **FOR MORE INFORMATION**
For comprehensive information on Alabama's numerous attractions, call 1(800)ALABAMA (inside Alabama, call (800)392-8096). Take your fishing gear when you go to Alabama. For information on fishing in northern Alabama's Big Seven Lakes, write to Alabama Mountain Lakes Association (P.O. Box 1075, Decatur, AL 35602). For state parks, write Division of

State Parks, Alabama Dept. of Conservation and Natural Resources (64 N. Union St., Montgomery, AL 36130). For restaurant and accommodations information in Alabama, write the Alabama Hotel and Motel Association (Suite 254, 660 Adams Ave., Montgomery, AL 36104).

Fabulous Finds in . . .
BOAZ

Boaz is an outlet town located on beautiful Sand Mountain. Several outlet centers have developed in the general area.

Comment from Del Tinsley, "It takes a full two days going flat out to cover all of Boaz. It's got everything! A $188 Benetton coat for $65! A $26.95 pair of Nike water socks for $17.95. Belgian chocolates for $4.99 that cost $8 in Belgium!"

LOCATION: US 431, 70 miles northeast of Birmingham, between Huntsville and Gadsden. Call (205)593-9306 for information and directions.

BOAZ OUTLET CENTER

Genuine factory-owned-and-operated stores full of their own merchandise.

STORES: **Aileen.** Every woman wears something from Aileen.
Bass Shoes. Shoes like you used to use.
Burlington, Oneida. Silver, crystal and gifts.
Campus. Men's casual clothing.
Captree. Junior's ready to wear.
Carter's. Children's wear.
Clothes Works.
Corning Factory Store. Cookwear to tabletop and more.
Cosmetics. Full line of temptation.
Devon. Large-size ladies' clothing.
E.J. Plum Socks. Socks for everyone.
Farah. Men's wear.

Fashion Flair. Izod and more.

Fieldcrest Cannon. Towels, spreads and sheets.

Fuller Brush. Feedback invited on this unique outlet.

Full Size Fashions. Women's clothing.

Gitano. Youth-oriented casual clothing.

Gitano Kids. Casual wear for kids.

Hanes Activewear. Underwear and underclothing.

Henson. Lingerie and nightwear.

Jack Winter. Women's wear.

Jaymar. Men's suits and accoutrements — upscale.

Jerzees Benetton. Same as full-price Benetton.

Jockey. Underwear.

Judy Bond. Blouses and women's clothing.

Kids Port USA. Children's wear.

King Arthur Jewelry. Trimmings.

Kitchen Collection. Appliances and cookware with lots of goodies.

Kitchen Place. Cooking and serving pieces.

Knits by K.T. Kenneth Two knits.

Leather Loft. Designer luggage and leather goods.

Little Red Shoe House. Men's and women's shoes.

Manhattan. Men's and women's casual and career wear.

Munsingwear. Underclothing and more.

Mushrooms. Comfortable shoes.

Old Mill. Women's petite, missy and junior apparel.

Old Mill II. Can you believe two stores in one complex?

Oxford Brands. Men's, women's and children's wear.

Polly Flinders. Smocked dresses for little girls.

The Ribbon Outlet. Ribbons and crafts.

Royal Doulton. Elegant china and gifts.

Sergio Valente. Youth-oriented weekend wear.

Ship 'n Shore. Nice ladies' wear.

Shoe Bar. Women's shoes.
Shoe Outlet. Shoes and accessories.
Socks Galore. Take home a bag full.
Sports Wearhouse.
Swank. Belts, jewelry and more.
Toy Liquidator. Toys at deep discounts.
Toys and Gifts. The name says it all.
Van Heusen. Men's and women's wear.
Wallet Works. Leather goods — office to
    personal.
Welcome Home. Wood, brass, glass and more.
WestPoint Pepperell Mill Store. Linens,
    bedding and a small section of ready-to-wear
    items.

BOAZ FACTORY STORES

Factory-owned-and-operated stores, all in one
complex, with savings up to 70%.

STORES: Liz Claiborne Outlet Store, Mikasa,
OshKosh, Stone Mountain, Craftsmen's Guild,
Calvin Klein, Dansk, Barbizon Lingerie,
Samsonite Luggage, Allen Edmonds, Dansk
Table Top, Farberware Cookware, Bugle Boy,
J.G. Hook, Leslie Fay.

FASHION OUTLETS

An upscale development in this outlet city, with
some impressive factory outlet retailers. Take
checks, charge card and cash because you will
always regret the great buy that got away if the
cash flow dries up. Negotiate with your traveling
companions to go their own way, roll up your
sleeves, wear slip-on shoes for fast changes . . .
and shop till you drop. This is where recreational
retail got its name.

LOCATION: Call for directions, (205)593-4606.

STORES: harvé benard, J. Crew, Anne Klein,
Polo/Ralph Lauren, JH Collectibles, Bruce Alan

Bags, Benetton, Nilani, Eagle's Eye, Nike, Nettle Creek, Specials, Sportswear Systems, Damon, Shoe Place, Bags 'n Things, Bon Worth, Blue Denim, Factory Connection, L&S Shoes, Kids, Book Warehouse, Rolane, No-Nonsense Factory Store, Ruff Hewn.

VF FACTORY OUTLET COMPLEX

Vanity Fair (VF) and a group of stores clustered together, including Reading China & Glass, create a minicenter you won't want to miss.

LOCATION: In the center of Boaz. Call for directions, (205)593-2930, (205)593-8014 or (800)747-7224.

STORES: VF Outlet Store, Evan-Picone Factory Store, Banister Shoe, Prestige Fragrance & Cosmetics, Jantzen/Kay Windsor/Heron Cove, Black & Decker, The Jewelry Outlet, Jonathan Logan Outlet, Etienne Aigner and Misty Harbor,

DIRECTIONS

From Birmingham—I-59 North to Gadsden, Hwy. 431 North to Boaz, left on Dyar Blvd. to VF Factory Outlet.

From Huntsville—Hwy. 431 South to Boaz, Right on Hwy. 168 South to first red light. Turn left to VF Factory Outlet.

From Chattanooga, TN— South on I-59 to Collinsville. West on Hwy. 68 to Hwy. 168 South to Boaz. Left at first red light after Hwy. 431 to VF Factory Outlet.

From Atlanta, GA—I-20 West to Anniston. Hwy. 431 North to Boaz. Left on Dyar Blvd. to VF Factory Outlet.

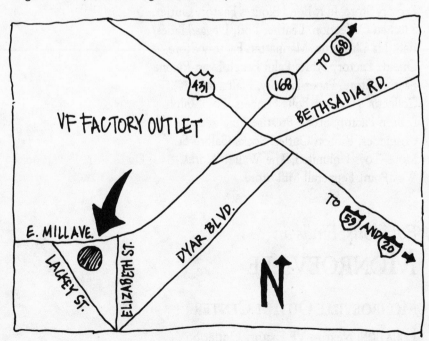

The Paper Factory, American Tourister, Reading China & Glass.

Fabulous Finds in . . .
FOLEY

RIVIERA CENTRE

The most elegant stores in Alabama.

LOCATION: 2601 S. McKenzie St., Hwy. 59 S., Foley, AL 36535. In the beaches tourist area.

STORES: Aileen, American Tourister Factory Store, Banister Shoe Outlet, Calvin Klein Outlet, Captree/Vanderbilt Fashions, Dansk Factory Outlet, Danskin Factory Outlet, Gilligan & O'Malley Factory Store, Gitano Factory Store, harvé benard, J.G. Hook Company Store, Jerzees Factory Store, Judy Bond Blouses Factory Outlet, Kitchen Collection, Leather Loft, L'eggs/Hanes/ Bali, Liz Claiborne, Manhattan Factory Store, Oneida Factory Store, Palm Beach/Evan-Picone Factory Store, Paper Factory, Pfaltzgraff Collector's Center, Polly Flinders, Polo/Ralph Lauren Factory Store, Prestige Fragrance & Cosmetics, Ribbon Outlet, Socks Galore & More, Toys Unlimited, The Wallet Works, WestPoint Pepperell Mill Store.

Fabulous Finds in . . .
MONROEVILLE

MONROEVILLE OUTLET CENTER

LOCATION: Next to VF Factory Outlet on Drewry Rd.

STORES: Munsingwear, Banister Shoe (US Shoe), Old Mill, Phillips Van Heusen, Jonathan Logan, Manhattan, Health-Tex (Kids Port), Monroeville International Jewelers, Socks Galore & More, Evan-Picone, Clothesworks — Jack Winter, Russell Mills, Hanes/L'eggs/Bali, The Shoe Outlet, Campus Sportswear, Swank, Aileen, Oxford Brands, Toy Liquidators, Prestige Fragrance & Cosmetics, Full Figure Fashions, Captree Fashions, Little Red Shoe House (Wolverine), Corning Glass Works.

VF FACTORY OUTLET

This is a true factory outlet offering merchandise direct from the factory under a pricing structure that offers real value on brand name products throughout the year. Unlike off-price outlets, which often mark up the prices in order to discount without losing money, all VF Outlet merchandise is priced from the start at half off the suggested retail.

LOCATION: On Drewry Rd., (205)575-2330.

WANTED
New information about factory outlet shopping centers — dead or alive. Tell me if you enjoyed your shopping experiences and why.

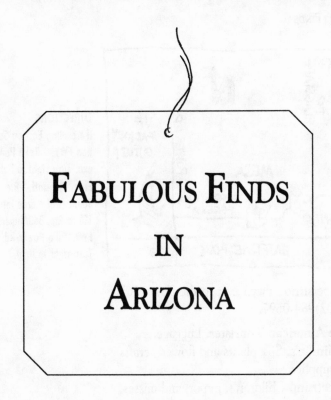

FABULOUS FINDS

IN

ARIZONA

"Has anybody ever seen it all?" asks the Arizona office of tourism (1480 E. Bethany Home Rd., Phoenix, AZ 85014; (602)255-3618). Arizona claims some of the U.S.'s most compelling natural attractions in its five tourist regions, including the Grand Canyon of the North Canyon Country and the massive cliffs of the Indian Country that sheltered ancient tribes. Hogans squat near towering rock arches; prehistoric cliff dwellings pock canyon walls; villages are tucked into caverns. Travel through huge forests of the giant Saguaro, state flower of Arizona. Pitch camp beside a clear blue stream, visit a ghost town or old fort, or tour the state's many gold mines. Arizona indeed has it all, from deserts and wooded mountains to shopping!

Fabulous Finds in . . .
MESA

VF FACTORY OUTLET CENTER
LOCATION: In Superstition Springs at the corner of Baseline and Power Rds. Take Rte. 10 to Rte.

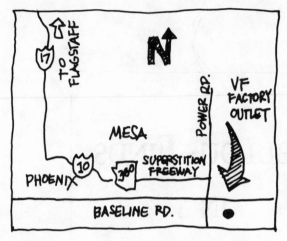

DIRECTIONS
If traveling East on Superstition FWY. — Take Power Rd. exit. Turn right to light.
From Flagstaff — Rte. 17 South (will merge into Rte. 10) to Rte. 360/Superstition FWY. Take Power Rd. exit. Turn right to light.

360 (Superstition Fwy.) east to the Power Rd. exit; (602)984-0697.

STORES: American Tourister. Luggage.

Aunt Minnie's. Silk plants and flowers, crafts and supplies.

B.I. Spectrum. Children's, junior, and misses sportswear.

Banister. The 40 brand shoe outlet.

Bon Worth. Ladies' apparel.

Corning Factory Store. Corningware, Visions, microwave cookware.

Fieldcrest Cannon. Towels, sheets, blankets, and bed and bath items.

The Lenox Shop Factory Store. Fine china, silverplate, candles.

Mushrooms. Shoes — Cobbies, Mushrooms, Red Cross and Selby.

The Paper Factory. Party goods and decorations, office products.

Prestige Fragrance & Cosmetics. Cosmetics and related items.

Reading Bag Co. Handbags and business cases.

Royal Robbins. Classic outdoor clothing made with natural fibers.

The Tanner Factory Stores. Quality ladies' wear.

VF Outlet. Men's, women's and children's clothing.

Van Heusen Factory Store. Men's and women's apparel.

The Wallet Works. Wallets, clutches, key cases and accessories.

Windsor Shirt Co. Men's and women's sweaters, men's shirts.

Your Toy Center. Fisher-Price, Mattel, Coleco, Playskool and more.

Fabulous Finds in . . .

SEDONA

OAK CREEK FACTORY STORES

LOCATION: Hwy. 179, Oak Creek Village. This center opened July 1990. Call (602)284-2150 for directions and information.

STORES: Adolfo II, Aileen, Anne Klein Outlet, Bass Factory Outlet, Book Warehouse, Bruce Alan Bags, Etc., Capezio Factory Direct, Corning/Revere Factory Store, Fragrance World, Going South Home Accessory Outlet, harvé benard, Izod/Gant, Maidenform, Mikasa Factory Store, Old Mill, Oneida Factory Store, The Ribbon Outlet, Socks Galore & More, Swank Factory Store, Toy Liquidators, Van Heusen Factory Outlet, The Wallet Works, Welcome Home, The Yogurt House.

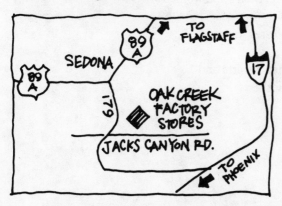

DIRECTIONS
On Hwy. 179 at the Village of Oak Creek.

Fabulous Finds in . . .
TUSCON

VF FACTORY OUTLET CENTER

LOCATION: VF Commerce Center, 5120 S. Julian Dr., Tucson, AZ 85706; (602)889-4400.

STORES: **American Tourister.** Business cases, totes and travel accessories.

Aunt Minnie's. Silk plants and flowers.

B.I. Spectrum. Fashion sportswear made in the U.S.A.

Banister. The 40 brand shoe outlet.

Bon Worth. Contemporary ladies' apparel.

Corning Factory Store. Cookware, microwave and thermal accessories.

Mushrooms Factory Store. Shoes.

The Paper Factory. Office products and party decorations.

Polly Flinders. Hand-smocked dresses up to 60% less than retail.

Prestige Fragrance & Cosmetics. Cosmetics and related items.

Reading Bag Co. Brand name handbags and business cases.

VF Factory Outlet. Men's, women's and children's apparel.

Van Heusen Factory Store. Men's and women's brand apparel.

The Wallet Works. Briefcases, luggage, handbags and gifts.

Windsor Shirt Co. Women's shirts and sweaters, men's sportclothes.

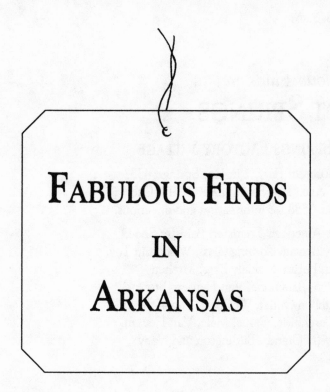

FABULOUS FINDS

IN

ARKANSAS

Arkansas has long been known for producing nostalgic mountain crafts such as dulcimers, quilts, baskets and brooms. At five retail shops operated by the Ozark Foothills Craft Guild, you can still find these items along with an astonishing variety of contemporary crafts. Each shop carries items made by Arkansas craftsmen only. Ozark Foothills Craft Guild shops are in the following locations: Eureka Springs (501)253-7072; Heber Springs (501)362-6222; Hot Springs (501)321-1460; Little Rock (501)371-0841, Mountain View (501)269-3896.

If you stop in Murfreesboro, about one hour southwest of Hot Springs, visit the Crater of Diamonds state park. If you pay the entry fee, you can keep all the diamonds you find. The park boasts that twelve hundred diamonds were found in 1988; in 1975 one lucky soul found a diamond that weighed sixteen carats.

☞ **FOR MORE INFORMATION**
For a free vacation planning kit, call (800)NATURAL, or write to Arkansas Vacations (Dept. 1465, 1 Capitol Mall, Little Rock, AR 72201).

Fabulous Finds in . . .
HOT SPRINGS

HOT SPRINGS FACTORY VILLAGE

LOCATION: Off Hwy. 7 in Hot Springs; 4332
Central Ave., Hot Springs, AR 71913. Call
(501)525-0888 for information and directions.

STORES: American Tourister, Banister Shoe,
Cape Craftsman, Corning Glass, Wisconsin Toy,
Jonathan Logan, Mainely Bags, Kitchen
Collection, Bass Shoe, Van Heusen, Brown
Shoe, Ribbon Outlet, Westport, Top of the Line,
Book Warehouse, Casual Male, Van Heusen,
Brinkley (N Grand), Burlington and many
others.

FABULOUS FINDS

IN

CALIFORNIA

A state of superlatives — from sandy beaches to jagged coastlines, spectacular mountains to desert valleys — California is a land for all tastes! Natural beauty and adventure potential lure vacationers and retirees. Vintage wines and towering redwoods; the timeless charm of the San Francisco Bay Area; the Shasta-Cascade — a paradise for sportsmen and nature lovers; the high sierra, boasting majestic peaks and the deserts with stunning contrasts from rugged dunes to miles and miles of miles and miles . . . this is just an introduction to California.

California is a vacation kaleidoscope laden with a multitude of natural and man-made wonders. It is a land of paradoxes and contrasts. Within 150 miles (as the crow flies) are both the highest and lowest points in the lower forty-eight — Mount Whitney, at 14,494 feet and Badwater in Death Valley National Monument at 282 feet below sea level.

Choose your vacation adventures from bed and breakfast inns, snow skiing, driving tours, water sports, guest ranches, health spas, hiking and camping — whatever you desire; California is a year-round playground.

☞ **FOR MORE INFORMATION**
The California Office of Tourism (Suite 200, 1030 13th St., Sacramento, CA 95814) can provide travel information for whatever California destination you desire — there are lots to

choose from. Also try The Best of the Californias, California Dept. of Commerce (Suite 600, 1121 L St., Sacramento, CA 95814; (916)322-1394) for additional information.

Fabulous Finds in ...

BARSTOW

If you have any money left after you've been to Las Vegas, spend it here and you'll have something to take home.

LOCATION: Between Los Angeles and Las Vegas in the middle of the Mojave desert. Take the Lenwood Rd. exit off the 15 Fwy., just south of Barstow.

STORES: The Lenox Factory, Barbizon Lingerie, David Brooks & Robert Scott Outlet, General Housewares, Bugle Boy Factory Outlet, Fieldcrest Cannon, Leather Loft, Evan-Picone/ Gant, Hanes Activewear, L'eggs/Hanes/Bali, Oneida Factory Store, Fragrance World, Izod/ Ship 'n Shore/Monet, Toys Unlimited, ACA Joe, Anne Klein Outlet, John Henry and Friends, OshKosh B'Gosh, Book Warehouse, Black & Decker, Eagle's Eye Company Store, Corning/ Revere Factory Store, Rawlings Sporting Goods, Welcome Home, Big Dogs Sportswear, Johnston & Murphy, Swank, Capezio Factory Direct, Bruce Alan Bags, Designer Brands Accessories, Levi Outlet by Most, London Fog, Gitano, Socks Galore, Aileen, Banister Shoe, The Ribbon Outlet, The Wallet Works, Leading Designer Outlet, The Paper Outlet, Sergio Tacchini, Reebok Factory Outlet Store.

Fabulous Finds in ...

CABAZON

DESERT HILLS FACTORY STORES

LOCATION: Off I-10, 20 miles west of Palm Springs.

STORES: WestPoint Pepperell, American
Tourister, Corning, Van Heusen/Bass, Palm
Beach, Prestige Fragrance & Cosmetics,
Maidenform, Leather Loft, Izod, Paper Factory,
Wisconsin Toy, US Shoe Corp, Royal Doulton,
Ribbon Outlet, Socks Galore, Amity Leather,
Aileen, Hawaiian Cotton, Benetton, Gitano,
Oneida, Bugle Boy, Kitchen Collection, Cape
Craftsmen, Apparel America, Wicker Factory,
Lots to Love and more.

Fabulous Finds in . . .
GILROY

PACIFIC WEST OUTLET CENTER
LOCATION: Exit at Leavesley Rd. from Rte. 101.
STORES: Socks Galore, Nike, Maidenform, Van
Heusen, Wallet Works, Liz Claiborne, Aileen,
American Tourister, Anne Klein, Argenti,
Barbizon Lingerie, Capezio, Carole Hochman,
Crisa Factory Store, Hanes Active, harvé benard,
He-Ro Group Outlet, I.B. Diffusion, J.G. Hook
Company Store, Jones New York, Jordache,
Leather Loft, L'eggs/Hanes/Bali, Manhattan
Jewelry Manufacturers, The Ribbon Outlet, Toys
Unlimited, Welcome Home and others.

Fabulous Finds in . . .
LOS ANGELES

Outlet shopping takes on a new flavor on the
west coast. Fashion goods importers are concen-
trated in Los Angeles. Many manufacturers are
actually importers, seeking out the cheaper labor
costs in foreign countries. (The Eastern fashion
manufacturers had established brand names that
were famous before importing became the thing

17

to do.) A manufacturer's store is a factory outlet regardless of where the stitching takes place — in the U.S. or China. These manufacturers have the same distribution problems that make a factory outlet store necessary.

THE COOPER BUILDING

In the heart of the garment district in Los Angeles, the Cooper Building is the outstanding example of importers and manufacturers opening outlet shops in the heart of a city. Tenants turn over constantly, and shopping is a hassle, but if you're a bargain hunter, your life will not be complete until you take a friend and visit the Cooper Building. You'll find shoes, apparel, cosmetics, jewelry and who knows what else, but you'll *never* forget the experience. Hang on to your purse and be prepared to shop five or six floors . . . maybe more depending on who has opened a store here.

LOCATION: 860 S. Los Angeles St., Los Angeles, CA 90014.

OTHER SHOPPING

Another small group of stores in downtown Los Angeles may provide fun shopping.

LOCATION: 1717 Figueroa

STORES: Esprit, Camp Beverly Hills, Camp Beverly Hills and several other stores offer shopping for the opportunist.

Fabulous Finds in . . .
PACIFIC GROVE

Mild coastal weather, natural beauty and abundant attractions make the Monterey Peninsula California's fourth most popular tourist attrac-

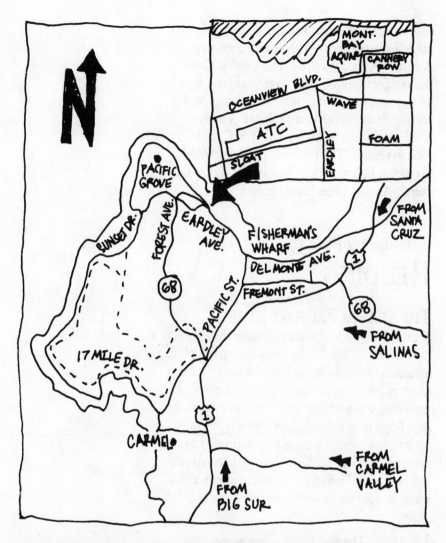

tion. Pacific Grove, on the peninsula, home of American Tin Cannery is hailed as "America's last hometown," as a tribute to its Victorian charm and friendly residents.

AMERICAN TIN CANNERY

LOCATION: One block past Monterey Bay Aquarium on Ocean View Blvd. (408)372-1442.

STORES: Van Heusen Factory Store, Corning Factory Store, Women's Fashions, Dynasty Imports, Royal House, Joan & David Designer

DIRECTIONS

Easy access from Scenic Rte. 1, Pacific Grove Exit. Follow signs to Cannery Row and Aquarium. American Tin Cannery (ATC) is one block past Aquarium on Ocean View Blvd. Parking available behind ATC, off Eardley Ave.; and on Foam St. between Hoffman and Prescott Streets.

Outlet, Prestige Fragrance & Cosmetics, Bass
Shoe, Banister Shoe, Carter's Childrenswear,
Athletic Outlet, Westport Ltd. Outlet, Crisa
Factory Store, Jindo Furs, Skyr Company Store,
The Housewares Store, Royal Doulton, Oneida
Factory Store, harvé benard, Mr. Z Jewelers,
Maidenform Outlet Store, The Toy Club,
Ribbon Outlet, The Back Shop, Wallet Works,
Magnolia, Polly Flinders, Barbizon, Leather Loft
Stores, Aileen, Cape Isle Knitters.

Fabulous Finds in . . .
REDDING

THE SHASTA FACTORY STORES

Shasta county is a recreational haven. Mt. Shasta
rises 14,162 feet and offers snow skiing, camping,
hiking and fishing. Shasta Lake, located ten miles
north of Redding, has more than 370 miles of
shoreline, a third more than the San Francisco
Bay. I-5, which runs straight through Shasta
county, is a major thoroughfare between Los
Angeles and Seattle, WA. The Redding/Ander-
son area would make a convenient stopover for
travelers touring between these two major U.S.
cities.

LOCATION: The Redding/Anderson area is on
I-5 north of Sacramento. The Shasta Factory
Stores are approximately eight miles south of
Redding on a highly visible location directly
adjacent to I-5 at Hwy. 217 and Sheets Rd.;
(916)378-1000.

STORES: Aileen's, Levi, Duffel, Banister, Kitchen
Collection, Full Size Fashions, harvé benard,
L'eggs/Hanes/Bali Factory Outlet, Sports
Outlook Shoes & Apparel, Westport Ltd.,
Designer/Brands Accessories, The Ribbon
Outlet, totes, Wallet Works, Book Warehouse,

Toy Liquidators, Home Again, Cape Isle, Van Heusen, Bass, London Fog, Mikasa, Gitano, Oneida, Corning, Campus, Leather Loft, Fragrance World, Whims.

Fabulous Finds in . . .
SAN DIEGO

SAN DIEGO FACTORY OUTLET CENTER

LOCATION: 4498 Camino de la Plaza, San Ysidro, CA 92073; (619)690-2999. Store hours vary; call for current information. (See map on following page.)

STORES: Mikasa, Nike, Black & Decker, Corning/Revere, Bass Shoe Factory Outlet, Fashion Flair, Prestige Fragrance & Cosmetics, Toy Liquidators, The Wallet Works, Banister Shoe, Van Heusen, The Paper Outlet, The Ribbon Outlet, Black Hills Gold.

Fabulous Finds in . . .
SAN FRANCISCO

San Francisco is a manufacturing and importing town and has its factory outlet and clearance district somewhat similar to the Lower East Side in New York City.

LOCATION: Most of the outlets are located near Second and Third with cross streets — Townsend, Brannan, Bryant, Harrison. You will be in a factory district, so be prepared to walk and walk. You will find some spectacular buys beyond belief if you just mosey along, cherry picking the best buys. Go by car or cab — this district covers miles.

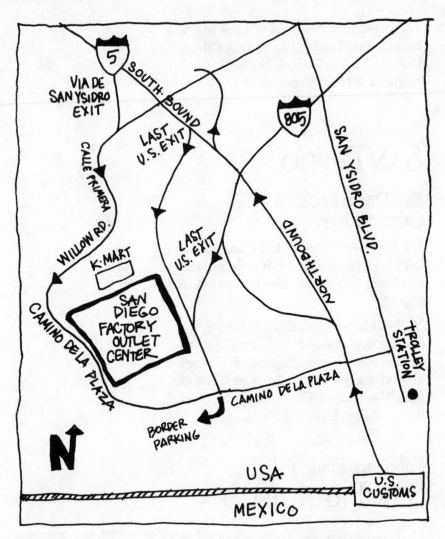

STORES: Stores come and go, but here are a few that could be permanent.

Coat Factory Outlet Store. 1350 Folsom St. between Ninth and Tenth.

Esprit Factory Outlet Store. Illinois and Sixteenth.

Fritzi Outlet. 218 Fremont.

Gunne Sax Factory Outlet. 35 Stanford Pl.

Joanie Char Outlet for silk and wool. 777 Florida Ave.

Lilli Ann Outlet. 2701 Sixteenth St.

Sprint. 45 Bryant.

DIRECTIONS

Southbound—Take I-5 or 805 toward the international border. Take the "Last U.S. Exit" and make a right onto Camino De La Plaza. Go 2 blocks and look for the Center on right.

Fabulous Finds in . . .

SANTA NELLA

Fabulous shopping with fast food restaurants, family restaurants, gas stations and Pea Soup Andersen's Restaurant, serving 2,400 meals daily. That's a lot of food.

LOCATION: On the California Turnpike—I-5 at Hwy. 33.

STORES: Stop, eat, gas up and shop at these factory-direct stores: Book Warehouse, Scott Brooks & Harvey, Designer Accessories, ACA Joe, Toy Liquidator, Fragrance World, Welcome Home, Aileen, Generra, Banister Shoes, Bass Shoe, Van Heusen, totes, Hanes/L'eggs/Bali, Adolfo, Westport, Gitano, Swank Accessories, Ribbon Outlet, Socks Galore, harvé benard, Crystal Brands, Andersen, Fieldcrest Cannon.

Fabulous Finds in . . .

VACAVILLE

THE FACTORY STORES AT NUT TREE

LOCATION: Nut Tree and I-80, between Sacramento and San Francisco.

STORES: WestPoint Pepperell, Prestige Fragrance & Cosmetics, Leather Loft, Converse, Corning, American Tourister, Van Heusen, The Paper Factory, Toy Liquidators, Polly Flinders, Banister, harvé benard, Palm Beach, Royal Doulton, Cape Craftsmen, Ribbons, Pfaltzgraff, Kitchen Collection, Oneida, Eva Dicore, Gant, The Shoe Outlet, Evan-Picone, Capezio, Aileen, Crisa, Diamonds Direct, Hawaiian Cotton, Royal Cathay, Lots to Love, New York Express and more.

WANTED
Your gems. The true shopping aficionado will always know about a few great little stores in the middle of nowhere that have wonderful buys. Researching for these little "gems," as we did for *SOS,* is expensive but you can make the difference if you think of *Fabulous Finds* when you shop.

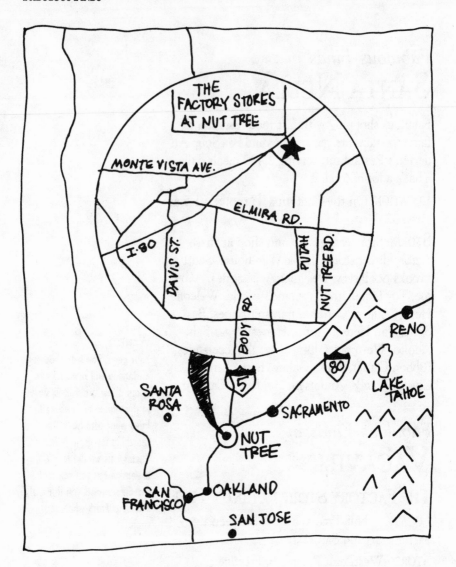

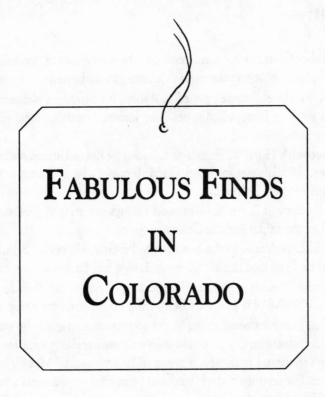

FABULOUS FINDS IN COLORADO

Colorado has been known for years for its grand old hotels, many of which were built in the mid- to late-nineteenth century to accommodate gold rush spectators. Several of the more famous of these structures have been renovated to their original grandeur and are well worth a visit by the modern traveler. Here are a few comments from history about some of the grand hotels that you might want to visit on your next fabulous finds trip to Colorado:

William Jennings Bryan addressed crowds in front of the New Sheridan Hotel in Telluride in 1903. The New Sheridan is no longer new, but it is still the New Sheridan.

When the Beaumont Hotel in Ouray was built in 1886, it was the first hotel in the U.S. with alternating current.

When President Grant visited the Teller House in Central City in 1873, a pathway of silver bricks was laid for him to walk on.

When the Grand Hotel (now named the Grand Imperial) opened in Silverton in 1883, it came to be known as the "home of the silver kings."

The slogan of Durango's Strater Hotel was once "Three square meals a day and clean sheets every morning," but a printer's error made it "One clean meal and three square sheets every morning."

The Tabor Grand Hotel (also known as the Vendome) in two-mile-high Leadville played host to numerous celebrities in its heyday.

When the Hotel Jerome opened in Aspen, it boasted an elevator operated by a series of handpulled ropes. The Jerome remains a focal point in Aspen.

Georgetown's Hotel de Paris was founded by Louis Dupuy, a chef par excellence. With his elegant hotel, Dupuy brought a bit of France to rugged nineteenth-century Colorado.

The Hot Springs Lodge at Glenwood Springs sits on land that was once an island in the middle of the Colorado River.

Personal experiences in the Beaumont, the Grand Imperial, Strater Hotel, Hotel de Paris and the Hot Springs Lodge will be forever memorable.

The Great Boulder Mountain Tour Co. (479 Arapahoe, Boulder, CO 80302; (303)449-8148) can provide touring information for these areas.

The San Juan mountain range in the southwest corner of the state is spectacular. Silverton, Ouray and Mesa Verde are excellent vacation spots. About two thousand years ago, a group of Indians picked Mesa Verde for their home. For centuries, they lived and prospered on the mesa and in its canyons. When they abandoned their homes, they left a matchless concentration of cliff dwellings and personal possessions behind.

Colorado National Monument, with eighteen thousand acres of towering monoliths and savagely beautiful rock formations, is one of the world's great natural wonders. The spires, cliffs, canyons and mesas are breathtaking.

John Wesley Powell, after journeying down the Green River in 1869 said, "Its walls and cliffs, its peaks and crags, its amphitheaters and alcoves tell a story of grandeur that I hear yet." See for yourself in northwest Colorado. Most of the wild and rugged canyons of northwest Colorado are best explored by raft trips, not all of which are wild and woolly. Some river rats prefer a leisurely float past the scenic wilderness. Colorado is an explorer's paradise. The discovery of rich veins of gold in 1859 touched off a rush to the Rockies that continues; today's rush is to view the mountains' majesty and to see a unique land.

☞ FOR MORE INFORMATION

Contact the Colorado Tourism Board, (Suite 267, 5500 South Syracuse Circle, Englewood, CO 80111; (303)779-1067) or the Office of Tourism (Suite 500, 1313 Sherman, Denver, CO 80203) for complete travel information.

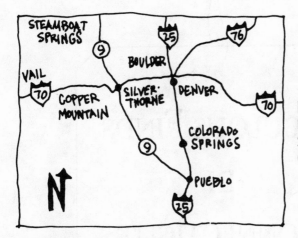

DIRECTIONS
Located on I-70 West at Exit 205. Look for the Silverthorne Clock Tower.

Fabulous Finds in . . .

SILVERTHORNE

SILVERTHORNE FACTORY STORES
Extraordinary values for the whole family.

LOCATION: Located on I-70 west at exit 205. Call (303)468-9440 for directions.

STORES: Evan-Picone, Jindo Furs, Toys Unlimited, Capezio, harvé benard, Prestige Fragrance & Cosmetics, The Ribbon Outlet, Wallet Works, Socks Galore, I.B. Diffusion, American Tourister, Welcome Home, Bass Shoe, Van Heusen, Maidenform, Gitano, Royal Doulton, Liz Claiborne, Adolfo II, Aileen, Anne Klein, Banister Shoe, Barbizon Lingerie, Cape Isle Knitters, Carole Little, Corning/Revere, Galt/Sand, Geoffrey Beene, Great Outdoor Clothing, Hanes Activewear, He-Ro Group Outlet, J. Crew Factory Store, JH Collectibles, Jones New York Factory Store, Leather Loft, Leather Trendz, L'eggs/Hanes/Bali, Members Only, Nike, Oneida Factory Store, Pfaltzgraff, Sassafras, Silverheels Jewelry and a small café.

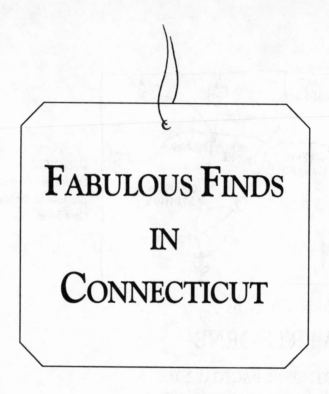

FABULOUS FINDS
IN
CONNECTICUT

The *Connecticut Vacation Guide* says: "Stay a while, relax and get acquainted. Sail our waters, climb our hills, track our history, relish our diversity. Connecticut will put you in touch with America's beginnings. More than three centuries come alive in historic places all around the state. Spinning wheels and wide fireplaces, rope beds and handhewn beams show you the way it was. Connecticut has history everywhere. Supplies for George Washington's ragged army were organized in Governor Jonathan Trumbull's tiny store in Lebanon. Mementoes of the patriot Nathan Hale and the feisty Israel Putnam, who ordered the troops at Bunker Hill not to fire 'until you see the whites of their eyes' . . . all are available in this historic state."

Connecticut is a haven for the arts. At the turn of the century, American impressionists took a look at the sunlight in the countryside and founded colonies in Old Lyme and Greenwich. Summer shows are held in the galleries they founded.

Connecticut is proud of its inventiveness. The insurance industry, the pay telephone and the submarine are all part of the productivity that was born in this state. Inventive Connecticut Yankees like Sam Colt, Eli Whitney, Charles Goodyear and Seth Thomas met necessity with creativity.

☞ **FOR MORE INFORMATION**

Contact the Connecticut Tourism Office (210 Washington St., Hartford, CT 06106; (203)566-2496) and ask for additional information such as antique dealers, factory outlets, horseback riding, package tours, vacation property, state parks and forest recreation areas, summer arts calendar; you can plan your trips around free information.

Fabulous Finds in . . .

BRANFORD

BRANFORD OUTLET CENTER

LOCATION: Near East Haven, off I-95 at exit 51 (north) or exit 53 (south) to Rte. 1.

DIRECTIONS

From New York (75 miles) — Take Rte. 95 North to Exit 51 (Frontage Rd.). Keep right off exit and road will turn into Rte. 1. Branford Outlet Center is located on the right, approximately 2 miles from the exit.

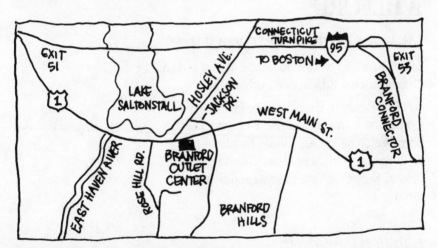

STORES: Van Heusen, Aileen, Accessory Factory, Manhattan Factory Outlet, Chaus, Prestige Fragrance & Cosmetics, Petals, American Tourister, Leather Loft, harvé benard, Anne Klein, Crazy Horse, Bass Shoe, 3D Bed and Bath, Athletic Outlet, Mainely Bags, Just Coats 'N Swimwear, Mighty-Mac, Stephanie Kay Ltd., Royal Doulton, Toy Liquidators, Banister Shoe, Crystal Works, Classic Fashions by Micki, Towle Silver, Head over Heels, Divineyard Fashion, Great Footwear, Paper Factory and a restaurant.

From Hartford (39 miles) — Take 91 South (toward New Haven) to Rte. 95 North to Exit 51 (Frontage Rd.). Stay right off the exit and follow the same directions as above.

From Providence, RI (105 miles) — Take 95 South to Exit 53. Take a left off the exit and follow to Rte. 1. Take a right onto Rte. 1 and the center is 1 mile on the left.

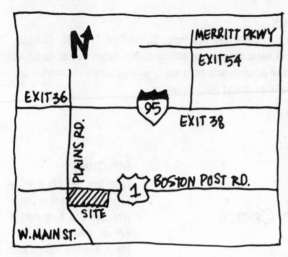

DIRECTIONS
Take Exit 36 off of I-95. We are at the corner of U.S. 1 Boston Post Rd. and West Main St.

Fabulous Finds in . . .
MILFORD

MILFORD FACTORY OUTLET CENTER

LOCATION: I-95 to exit 36, at the corner of U.S. 1 (Boston Post Rd.) and West Main St.

STORES: Banister Shoe, Prestige Fragrance & Cosmetics, Van Heusen, harvé benard, Leather Loft, Welcome Home, Classic Fashions, Oscar de la Renta, Hathaway Shirt, Olga Lingerie, Crystal Factory, Micki Designs and Separates, totes.

Fabulous Finds in . . .
MYSTIC

After you shop at the Mystic Factory Outlets, visit Olde Mistick Village and Mystic Marine Life Aquarium.

MYSTIC FACTORY OUTLETS

LOCATION: Off I-95 at exit 90 (Mystic Seaport) to Coogan Blvd. For further information, call (203)886-1886.

STORES: Dalton Ladies' Fashions, Manhattan Factory Outlet, Factory Handbag Store, Quoddy Crafted Footwear, Swank Factory Store, Van Heusen Factory Store, Aileen, Campus Factory Outlet.

Fabulous Finds in . . .

NORWALK

NORWALK FACTORY OUTLET

LOCATION: 11 Rowan St. For information, call (203)838-1349. Exit 16 off the I-95 Connecticut Turnpike.

STORES: American Tourister, B&B Sweets, Bed 'n Bath Outlet, By the Yard fabrics, Dress Barn, Fashion Shoe Outlet, Gentlemen's Wearhouse, Head over Heels, Royal Doulton Shoppe, S.M.O. Men's, Sneaker Town, Top of the Line Cosmetics and Fragrances, Van Heusen Factory Store, Way Station, Designer's Only featuring Adolfo II, Intimate Eve, Micki's Designer Separates, Old Mill, Quoddy Crafted Footwear, S.M.O. Women's, Bag & Baggage, Company Store, harvé benard, Just Coats 'n Swimwear, Manhattan Factory Outlet, Red Horse.

FABULOUS FINDS IN DELAWARE

Delaware calls itself a "small wonder." With beautiful beaches, renown museums, historic sites and superb places to dine and stay, it offers style and substance. Read this inspired prose from a state brochure:

"The sky is filled with clouds of birds and the air vibrates with the sound of beating wings. Thousands of geese, ducks and other migratory wanderers rest in Delaware's beautiful Bombay Hook National Wildlife Refuge. A trip down the picturesque Route 9 may bring you closer to nature than you've ever been before. Call (800)441-8846. Catch the next flight!"

And try this: "*Off-season beach!* Delaware beaches have a secret few people seem to know about . . . they don't disappear between September and June. Only the crowds do. Imagine a fine seafood dinner in a cool breeze. Imagine having the whole Delaware Bay to sail and fish in . . . alone. Or the entire Atlantic Ocean. Imagine staying in a gracious hotel at a hefty off-season discount. Imagine our beaches in the spring and fall . . . the perfect place to get away from it all."

Or this: "Some of Delaware's most welcome visitors come complete with fins and gills. A variety of both fresh and saltwater sport fish can be caught from either shore, dock or deep water. They are biting somewhere in Delaware all year long."

☞ **FOR MORE INFORMATION**
Contact the Delaware State Travel Service (99 Kings Hwy., Dover, DE 19903; (800)441-8846)
for how to find unforgettable experiences.

Fabulous Finds in . . .

REHOBOTH BEACH

OCEAN OUTLETS
FACTORY OUTLETS

If the foregoing description sounds just right
for entertaining the family while you shop,
call (302)227-6860 for center hours and plan
to shop to your heart's content.

LOCATION: On Hwy. 1 at the entrance to
Rehoboth Beach Resort.

STORES: Aileen, American Tourister,
Banister Shoe, Bass Shoe, Cape Isle Knitters,
Corning/Revere Factory Store, Fanny Farmer
Outlet Store, Glass Resort, harvé benard,
Islandgear, Izod/Lacoste/Ship 'n Shore,
Kentmere Fine Fabrics, Kitchen Collection,
Leather Loft, Lots of Linens, Oneida,
Prestige Fragrance & Cosmetics, Ribbon
Outlet, Sports Fans, Toy Liquidators, Van
Heusen, Westport Ltd., Wicker Outlet and
a candy kitchen, bakery, deli and Pizza
Works. Then take the ferry to Cape May and
Atlantic City, New Jersey.

FABULOUS FINDS

IN

FLORIDA

We'll let the state of Florida do all the talking here:

"History comes to life in northeast Florida, where memories of pirates sailing the Spanish Main intermingle with the taste of modern-day hospitality in the deep South. St. Augustine, the nation's oldest permanent city, just south of Jacksonville on picturesque Hwy. A1A, will fascinate you with landmarks like the nineteen-foot-thick walls in the Castillo de San Marcos.

Northwest Florida is an outdoorsman's paradise, blessed as it is with rolling hills, mist-shrouded forests, crystal-clear springs and more than one hundred miles of sugary, hideaway beaches. Sportsmen will feel right at home in the half million acres of the Apalachicola National Forest where campsites, picnic areas and boat ramps open the doorway to nature in northwest Florida.

Explore the world of space travel, fish for large-mouth bass, or just soak up the sun along the east central coast of Florida. Dig your toes into the warm sand, go shelling on pristine beaches, watch fishermen on the wharves dress the seafood caught that afternoon that you'll have for dinner that night, dining to the roar of the surf.

Take a look at Florida's wild side — explore the mysterious Everglades

34

where water birds, 'gators and wild deer are part of nature's daily show. Island beaches offer some of the finest seashell collecting in the world. For a close look at the setting sun, sail for the horizon in late afternoon or visit Key West where the natives say goodbye to the day as the sun sinks into the ocean.

No place on earth has so many things in so many places to make so many people feel so good as Florida."

☞ **FOR MORE INFORMATION**

Write to Florida Attractions Association (P.O. Box 10295, Tallahassee, FL 32302; (904)222-2885), or Florida Department of Commerce (Dept. FRB, 126 Van Buren St., Tallahassee, FL 32301). Florida plays host to the world and knows how to serve up a super vacation. You can start with hotel referrals from Florida Hotel and Motel Association's Travel Directory (P.O. Box 1529, Tallahassee, FL 32302; (904)224-2888). For condos call (800)247-2999 or write to Florida Condo, 2203 Lyme Bay Dr., Orlando, FL 32809.

Fabulous Finds in . . .
FORT PIERCE

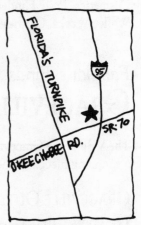

MANUFACTURER'S OUTLET CENTER

LOCATION: I-95, exit 65 at S.R. 70.

STORES: Russell Action Wear, Towle 1690 House, Bass Shoe Outlet, Fieldcrest Cannon, American Tourister Factory Outlet, Corning/Revere, Converse, Van Heusen Factory Store, Banister Shoe, OshKosh B'Gosh, Campus, Jonathan Logan, Kitchen Collection, Aileen Sportswear, Polly Flinders, Prestige Fragrance & Cosmetics, Toys Unlimited, Full Size Fashions, Manhattan Factory Store, Golf Outlet Center, Swank, Dexter Shoe Factory, Judy Bond, Gitano.

DIRECTIONS

We are at the intersection of I-95, Exit 65; and the Florida Turnpike, Exit 152 (State Road 70) in Ft. Pierce, Florida.

Fabulous Finds in . . .
FORT WALTON BEACH

FORT WALTON BEACH OUTLET CENTER

LOCATION: 127 Hwy. 98, west of Ft. Walton Beach City Hall.

STORES: Russell Sports, Van Heusen Factory Store, Converse Footwear, Carter's, Bass Shoe Outlet, Judy Bond, Prestige Fragrance & Cosmetics, Polly Flinders, Aileen Sportswear, Wallet Works, Clothes Works.

Fabulous Finds in . . .
GRACEVILLE

The VF and the Graceville Outlet Centers create a shopping mecca in the Florida Panhandle.

GRACEVILLE OUTLET CENTER

LOCATION: I-10 to Exit 18 at Hwy. 77S. and W. Prim Ave. Call (904)263-3207 for directions.

STORES: Oxford Industries, Full Size Fashions, Kids Port USA, Munsingwear, The Shoe Outlet, Swank, Manhattan Industries, Old Mill, Judy Bond, Clothes Works, Toy Liquidators, Cape Craft, Socks Galore, Aileen, Henson Lingerie, Gitano, Jewelry Exchange and more.

VF FACTORY OUTLET CENTER

STORES: VF Factory Outlet, Jonathan Logan, Corning, Prestige Fragrance & Cosmetics,

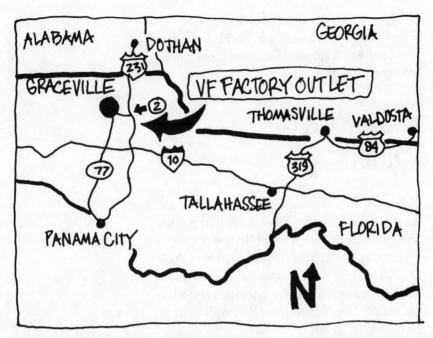

Banister, Clothes Hound, Wallet Works, Van Heusen, Mushrooms Factory Store.

Fabulous Finds in . . .
KISSIMMEE
KISSIMMEE MANUFACTURER'S MALL
LOCATION: On Hwy. 192 in Kissimmee. For information, call (813) 796-8760.

STORES: Acme Boot, Aileen, Amity Leather/ Wallet Works, Bass Shoe, Campus Sportswear, Fieldcrest Cannon, Frayne Fashions, Judy Bond, Just Kids, Manhattan, Nike, Polly Flinders, Van Heusen.

Fabulous Finds in . . .
OCALA
OCALA FACTORY STORES
LOCATION: Take exit 67 off I-75. If you get lost, call (904) 347-4455.

DIRECTIONS
From Dothan — Hwy. 231 South to Hwy. 2 West. At Graceville go south on Hwy. 77. Look for sign.

From Panama City — Hwy. 77 North toward Graceville. Look for sign.

From Valdosta — Hwy. 84 West to Hwy. 319 South. Go south on Hwy. 319 to I-10 West. Take Exit 18, drive north on Hwy. 77 toward Graceville. Look for sign.

From Tallahassee — I-10 West to Exit 18. North on Hwy. 77 toward Graceville. Look for sign.

STORES: Aileen, Bass, Banister Shoe, Book Warehouse, Euro Collections, Florida Surf Gear, Van Heusen, Welcome Home and more stores are opening soon.

Fabulous Finds in . . .
ORLANDO

Orlando is a destination city with Church Street Station, Disney World, Epcot, Universal Studios and Sea World. Church Street Station is a popular entertainment complex that began with Rosie O'Grady's Good Time Emporium and has grown with Cheyenne Saloon, which recaptures the legends of the Gay Nineties, the Roaring Twenties, and the Wild West.

Every child knows about Sea World but the magic is always there when Baby Shamu makes an entrance. Universal Studios is another new motion picture and television studio and tops on every visitor's priority list.

BELZ FACTORY OUTLET MALL AND ANNEX

Just minutes from Walt Disney World and downtown Orlando, the Belz Factory Outlet Mall has itself become one of the most sought-after tourist destinations in Florida. In one year, more than five-and-a-half-million customers visited the mall.

The mall is located just off famous International Dr., home to Wet 'N Wild, the Orlando Convention Center, and the Orlando Peabody, where ducks make a daily visit to the lobby to entertain guests.

A constant turnover in stores will guarantee an outstanding shopping experience. This is a mixed concept mall with outlet, off-price and dis-

PLACES TO EAT AND SLEEP: International Dr. is one long street built just to feed and lodge tourists. It would be impossible to list all the choices for entertaining and vacationing that appear in this area. Any referrals to restaurants and lodgings will be printed in the next edition of *Fabulous Finds.*

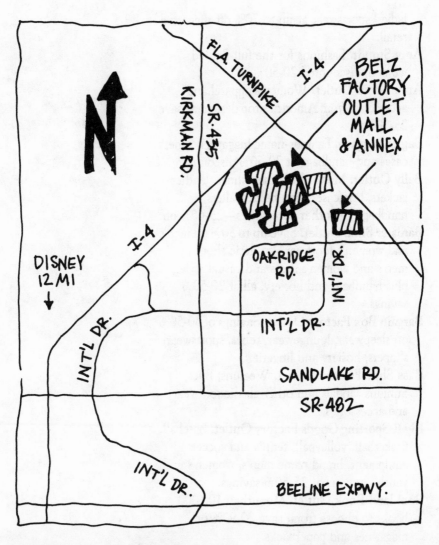

counters. Evaluate this mall and let me know how you like mixed concepts.

LOCATION: 5401 W. Oakridge Rd. From downtown Orlando, take I-4 west to the Kirkman Rd. exit. Exit left on Kirkman Rd. (435 S.) and left again on International Dr. If you are coming from Disney World, take I-4 east to the International Dr. exit and turn left again on International Dr. (at the light); (407)352-9600.

STORES: **Aileen Factory Outlet.** First-quality

DIRECTIONS

From Downtown Orlando — Take I-4 west to the Kirkman Rd. exit. Exit left on Kirkman Rd. (435 South). Take Kirkman Rd. to International Drive. Left on International Drive, then one mile ahead to Belz Factory Outlet Mall.

ladies' sportswear at up to 70% off suggested retail.

Amy Stoudt. Fashions for the full-figured women, discounted 20-50%.

Anne Klein Outlet. Women's apparel and accessories from America's top designers; save 25-50%.

Bag & Baggage. Famous-name luggage, business cases and handbags at 20-50% discounts.

Bally Outlet. Men's and ladies' shoes, leather jackets, briefcases, ties, belts, wallets, handbags and other accessories — 25-60% off.

Banister Shoe Outlet. Save up to 50% on men's and women's footwear — athletic shoes to men's and women's dress and casual styles, plus handbags and hosiery, all at 20-50% savings.

Bargain Box Factory Outlet. Savings of 30-50% on sleepwear, loungewear, robes, sportswear, slippers, hosiery and lingerie.

Bass Shoe Factory Outlet. Weejuns, Bucs, Sunjuns sandals and other classic footwear and accessories.

Big R Sporting Goods Factory Outlet. Baseball, basketball, volleyball, tennis and soccer equipment, brand name men's, women's and youth's apparel at 25-50% savings.

Bookland Book Outlet. More than 100,000 books to choose from; save 80-90% on magazines and paperbacks.

Brighter Side. Traditional and contemporary oil lamps and accessories, plus special outdoor models at up to 70% off retail.

Calvin Klein. Direct factory savings of 40-70% on casual sportswear for men and women.

Campus. Featuring men's regular sizes and big and tall, plus boys' 4-20; knit and woven shirts, shorts, slacks, sweaters and jackets.

Captree Factory Outlet. Junior and missy fashions at 20-60% off.

Carole Hochman Lingerie. Fashion intimate

apparel by Christian Dior, Carole Hochman, Sara Beth Lingerie and Lily of France.

Christmas World. Traditional and fashion color trees, themed displays, animated characters and exclusive ornament collection.

Converse Factory Outlet. 40-70% off athletic footwear and active wear clothing—savings on all children's shoes.

Cosmetic Factory Outlet. Up to 75% off name brand cosmetics, fragrances, makeup accessories, skin care and gift sets.

Crown Jewels. A large selection of the world's finest fashion.

Danskin Factory Outlet. Savings of 50% or more on leotards, tights, unitards, leg warmers, pantyhose and lingerie for dance and activewear.

Designer's Only featuring Adolfo II. Women's wear by Adolfo, Rafael, Donna Torn and Dressy Tessy at 25-50% off.

Dexter Shoe Factory Outlet. A manufacturer's outlet for leather, dress and casual men's and women's shoes, at savings up to 50%.

Diamonds Unlimited. America's largest outlet jeweler; manufactures thousands of fine diamond, gemstone and gold jewelry items.

Dress Barn. Famous fashion labels always 20-50% off.

Fieldcrest Cannon. Towels, sheets, pillowcases, bedspreads, comforters, blankets, bath rugs and sets, kitchen accessories, bed pillows, mattress pads, shower curtains and accessories for the bathroom and bedroom.

Fitz and Floyd Factory Outlet. World-renowned dinnerware, giftware and decorative accessories for the home; also giftware by Omnibus Collection International, fine crystal and brass.

General Shoe Factory to You Store. Factory owned-and-operated, selling Genesco and

many other famous brands at 20-50% below
the regular price.

The Genuine Article/OshKosh B'Gosh.
Savings of 20-50% on children's sportswear;
jewelry at 50% off.

Gitano Factory Store. Savings up to 50% on
casual and active sportswear, including tops,
pants, skirts, dresses, outerwear and
underwear.

Glasgo Knitwear Factory Outlet. First-quality
missy-sized casual ladies' apparel at 20-50%
off.

Good Deal Records and Tapes. Popular,
classical and jazz records and tapes; more than
10,000 compact discs in all categories.

harvé benard. Business and casual wardrobes,
men's and women's sportswear, suits, dresses,
coats, accessories and more available in every
size — 30-60% off.

Just Kids Outlet Store. Her Majesty girls'
sportswear, sleepwear, swimwear, slips and
panties; brand name clothing for boys,
children's accessories, tennis and jogging
shoes and hosiery for the entire family —
savings up to 50% and more.

Kitchen Collection. Exclusive factory outlet
store for WearEver cookware and Proctor-
Silex appliances — wide selection of first-
quality products, as well as selected
manufacturer seconds and closeout items at
savings of 20-70%.

Kuppenheimer Men's Clothiers. Men's suits,
sportcoats and slacks.

Londontown Factory Store. Owned and
operated by London Fog selling rainwear,
jackets, outerwear, leathers — all at half off.

Maidenform. Intimate apparel, bras, lingerie,
panties, sleepwear — save up to 60%.

Menswear, Inc., Fashion Sportswear. Better
men's clothing, sportswear, furnishings and
action wear.

Mikasa Factory Store. Tremendous selection of dinnerware, stemware, flatware, table linen, giftware; save up to 80% on internationally famous designs.

Newport, the Factory Store for Men. Save 35% and more every day on current season, first-quality coordinated sportswear, shirts, sweaters, active wear and outerwear.

Old Mill Ladies' Sportswear. Current, updated coordinates and contemporary separates; save 25-70%.

Petite Shop. If you are 5'4" or under and wear sizes 2-14; 20-50% discount.

Polly Flinder's Factory Outlet. Hand-smocked girl's dresses sizes newborn to 14, girls' and infants' dresses, shoes, panties, tights and sleepwear.

Prestige Fragrance & Cosmetics. 25-75% off suggested retail value on world famous, prestigious brands of men's and women's fragrances, toiletries and cosmetics.

Price Jewelers. An outlet owned and operated by a jewelry manufacturer—save 20-50% on Seiko, Citizen, Colibri and Cross.

Rack Room Shoes. Takes the pinch out of buying shoes—men's, ladies', children's fashion footwear and athletic shoes.

The Ribbon Outlet. 2,500 varieties of first-quality ribbons and trims, handcrafted gift items, selected craft supplies, novelty and seasonal items.

San Francisco Music Box Co. More than 800 musical gifts.

Shapes Active Wear. Exclusive factory outlet for famous-maker leotards, tights, active wear and swimwear for exercising and dance.

SneaKee Feet. Puma, Nike, Reebok, Adidas, athletic shoes and apparel, leisure wear and sporting goods.

Socks 'n Such. Athletic, dress and fashion socks.

totes Factory Outlet. Save 40-70% on totes and

associated brands—umbrellas, raincoats, bags, headgear for men and women—overstocks, closeouts, discontinued styles and colors and some irregulars.

Toy Liquidators. Thousands of brand name toys at less than manufacturer's original wholesale prices.

Van Heusen Factory Store. Current-season, first-quality men's and women's Van Heusen and Lady Van Heusen apparel at 30-60% off.

Waechtersbach. Solid and decorated dinnerware and many mugs, vases, bowls, etc., by Boda Nova.

Welcome Home. Manufacturers of early American decorative items from Ponderosa Pine; more than 500 items for the home— brass, pictures, glass, crystal, candles, at 40-60% savings.

WANTED
Interesting and unique lodgings, not chains—they are easy to find. Think of *Fabulous Finds* as the connecting link to thousands of other travelers and think what you would like to recommend to them.

OTHER STORES: Ruff Hewn, Capezio Shoes, Etienne Aigner, Knife Factory, Oneida Factory Store, OshKosh B'Gosh, Young Generations, Paper Factory, L'eggs/Hanes/Bali, No-Nonsense, Pinehurst Lingerie, Socks Galore & More, Swank, Wallet Works, Act I, Bike Athletic, Cape Isle Knitters, Crazy Horse, Guess Jeans, Ideas, Russell Mills Jerzees, Jonathan Logan, Koolers, London Fog, Old Mill Sportswear, Sergio Tacchini, Levi Specials, Prestige Fragrance & Cosmetics, Toy Liquidators, Barbizon, Aileen and dozens of other stores.

QUALITY OUTLET CENTER

LOCATION: On International Dr., one block east of Kirkman Rd. (435). From I-4 west, exit 435 S. From I-4 east, exit International Dr. and turn left at the traffic light. For additional information, call (407)423-5885.

STORES: American Tourister Factory Outlet, Book Warehouse, Corning/Revere Factory Store, General Housewares, Great Western Boot

Outlet, LJ's Fashion at a Discount, Leather Loft
Factory Outlet, Le Creuset Factory Store, Linens
'n Things, Mikasa Factory Store, Perfumania,
Petals Silk Flowers Factory Outlet, Royal
Doulton, Six Star Factory Outlet, Special Tee
Golf, Stone Mountain Handbag Factory Store,
T-Shirt Factory Outlet, totes, Villeroy & Boch,
Yes Brasil.

Fabulous Finds in . . .
PALM BEACH

PALM BEACH SQUARE
FACTORY OUTLET CENTER

Palm Beach Outlet Center is not a typical outlet
center. The decor dates to a time when developers built with 100 percent financing then suffered
foreclosures and, sometimes, bankruptcy. Elegant malls are on the block today for bargain
prices. The retailers here are open for business in
posh surroundings.

LOCATION: 5700 Okeechobee Blvd. in West
Palm Beach, between the Florida Turnpike and
I-95.

STORES: Adolfo II, Aileen Factory Outlet,
American Tourister Factory Outlet, Barbizon
Lingerie, Bass Factory Outlet, Bi Joux Jewelry
Outlet, Book Warehouse, Bugle Boy Factory
Outlet, Capezio Factory Direct, Corning/Revere
Factory Store, Crazy Horse, C.Y.A., Dexter Shoe
Factory Outlet, Fieldcrest Cannon, Gitano
Factory Store, harvé benard, Leather Loft, Olga/
Warner's, Polly Flinders, Prestige Fragrance &
Cosmetics, The Ribbon Outlet, Royal Doulton,
Secaucus Handbag Outlet, Toy Liquidator, Van
Heusen Factory Store, Welcome Home. More
stores coming soon.

Fabulous Finds in . . .
PANAMA CITY

MANUFACTURER'S OUTLET CENTER

LOCATION: 105 W. 23rd St. (one mile west of Hwy. 231) in Panama City.

STORES: Russell Mills, Pinehurst Lingerie, Country Set Sportswear, Judy Bond, Aileen, Sun Britches, Van Heusen, G.H. Bass, Clothesworks — Jack Winter, Carter's, Polly Flinders, Wallet Works.

Fabulous Finds in . . .
ST. AUGUSTINE

Enjoy the nation's newest retail concept in the nation's oldest city.

LOCATION: Exit I-95 at S.R. 16 (exit 95).

STORES: Adolfo II, Aileen, Barbizon Lingerie, Euro Collections (Bleyle of America), harvé benard, Island Gear, Jerzees, Jordache Outlet, Judy Bond Factory Outlet, L'eggs/Hanes/Bali, London Fog Factory Store, Secaucus Handbags, Stone Mountain Handbag Factory Store, Van Heusen Factory Store, Banister Shoe, Bass Shoe Outlet, Famous Footwear Factory Store, American Tourister, Book Warehouse, Corning/ Revere Factory Store, Distinctive Silk Flowers, Kitchen Collection, Prestige Fragrance & Cosmetics, Toy Liquidators, Welcome Home, WestPoint Pepperell Mill Store, Dexter Shoes, Bon Worth, Famous Brands Housewares, Westport Ltd.

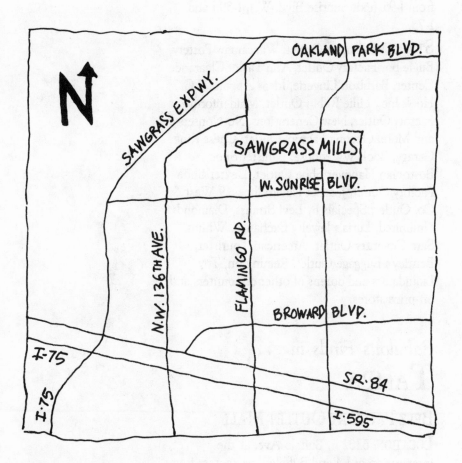

Fabulous Finds in . . .
SUNRISE

SAWGRASS MILLS

The "world's largest outlet mall." Explore Sawgrass Mills and you will discover the biggest selection of outlet, off-price and discount stores. Entertainment and ambience are part of the perks in Sawgrass Mills. Grade card time, please. Tell me what you like about retail and want to see in the future.

LOCATION: Flamingo Rd. and W. Sunrise Blvd. between Miami and Ft. Lauderdale. Accessible

DIRECTIONS
We are at Flamingo Rd. and West Sunrise Blvd. in Sunrise, Florida. Just 15 minutes from the Ft. Lauderdale International Airport and 30 minutes from Miami International Airport. From I-95, exit Sunrise Blvd. West. Easy access from I-595, I-75, and the Sawgrass Expressway.

from I-95 (exit Sunrise Blvd. W.), I-595 and I-75.

STORES: VF Factory Outlet, Waccamaw Pottery, Bugle Boy Factory Outlet, Ann Taylor Clearance Center, Barbizon Lingerie, Ideas Apparel, J.G. Hook Inc., Lillie Rubin Outlet, Maidenform Factory Outlet, New Generations, No-Nonsense and More, Obenna Factory Outlet, Chess King Garage, Book Warehouse, Banister Shoe, Bostonian Hanover Shoe Outlet, Dexter Shoe Factory Outlet, Joan & David Shoes, 9 West & Co. Outlet, Specials by Levi Strauss, Diamonds Unlimited, Luria's Jewelry Exchange, Whims/ Sara Coventry Outlet, American Tourister, Bentley's Luggage Outlet, Remington, Toy Liquidators and dozens of other discounters and off-price stores.

Fabulous Finds in . . .
TAMPA

BELZ FACTORY OUTLET MALL

LOCATION: 6302 E. Buffalo Ave. at the intersection of I-4 and Buffalo Ave., across from the fairgrounds at exit 4; (813)621-6047.

STORES: **Amy Stoudt.** Large size women's work, day-into-evening and weekend wear at 20-50% off.

Banister Shoe Company. Save up to 50% on men's and women's footwear.

Bass Shoe Factory Outlet. Save 25% and more on Weejuns, Bucs, Sunjuns sandals and other footwear and accessories.

Beacon Linen Factory Outlet. Closeouts, discontinued and slight imperfections manufactured by Fieldcrest Cannon—save 20-50% and more on towels, sheets, pillowcases, bedspreads, comforters, blankets, bath rugs/sets and kitchen accessories.

Big & Tall Casual Male. Clothes for the hard-to-fit man—brands from Girbaud, Bugle Boy, Williwear, Jordache, Harbor Bay, Mark Elliot and Introspect.

Carolina Pottery. Dinnerware, housewares, glassware, brass and porcelains, prints and frames, lamps and home furnishings, baskets, craft supplies, wicker furniture, silk flowers and even some pottery.

Converse Factory Outlet. 40-70% off complete lines of athletic footwear and activewear clothing—basketball, tennis, aerobics, training, walking, baseball and football shoes.

Designers Only featuring Adolfo II. Quality women's sportswear by Adolfo, Rafael, Donna Torn and Dressy Tessy at 25-50% off regular retail.

General Shoe Factory to You. Savings of 35-50%.

Gitano. Featuring the latest fashion in tops, pants, skirts, fashion jeans, swimwear, outerwear, shoes, underwear, handbags and accessories.

Goody's Shoes. Candies, Luciannos, Wimzees, Naturalizers and many more; tennis shoes by Brooks, Nike, Etonic; golf shoes and steel-toe work shoes, cowboy boots, children's and infants' tennis shoes.

Just Kids. Save to 50% and more on brand name clothing and accessories for boys and girls from infant, 2-14 and young junior sizes.

The Kitchen Collection. Exclusive factory outlet for WearEver cookware and Proctor-Silex appliances—first-quality products and selected manufacturer seconds and closeout items at savings of 20-70%.

Old Mill Ladies' Sportswear. Exclusive factory outlet for one of America's leading manufacturers of women's apparel—current

coordinates and contemporary separates at
25-70% savings.

totes Factory Outlet. Save 40-70% on totes and
associated brands: umbrellas, raincoats, bags,
headwear for men and women—overstocks,
closeouts, discontinued styles and colors and
some irregulars.

FABULOUS FINDS

IN

GEORGIA

Georgia is without a doubt the "carpet capital of the U.S." Write for a brochure from the Dalton Carpet & Rug Outlet Council (524 Holiday Dr., P.O. Box 99, Dalton, GA 30722-0099) or call (404)278-7373 for bargains in carpet and rugs. You will receive more than three dozen contacts and a map to help you get around. The best way to shop carpet is to bring your carpet smarts up to speed before you plan a trip. Contractors go to Dalton in a truck and bring home house-sized bargains.

Georgia has other attractions that may help to make a trip to or through memorable. The northwest corner of the state is rich in Indian history, including New Echota and the Vann House state historic sites. Georgia is also the birthplace of Sequoyah, creator of the Cherokee Indian alphabet. And Stone Mountain, in the same general area, is home to Stone Mountain Handbags.

Pick up some peaches and peanuts as you tour the state heading to the Georgia coast. Georgia reaches to the Atlantic Ocean with some world-class resorts and beaches—some for Presidential budgets such as Sea Island—but some are free. Remember Jekyll Island, St. Simons Island, Cumberland Island National Seashore and Tybee Island on the Savannah coastline.

Arts and crafts are *big* in Georgia. Stop at information centers for brochures for the section of Georgia that is your destination, or call (404)278-0168 for northwest Georgia or (404)493-5780 for state arts and craft information. Pecans are also big, and one of the best pecan buys has to be Adcock Pecans just one block east of I-75. Take Exit 18 at Tifton and turn on US Hwy. 82, or call (912)382-5566 for more information. You can also mail order.

For state parks and historic sites, call the Office of Information at (404)656-3530, and if you want to visit the home of the original Cabbage Patch Kids, call (404)865-5356.

☞ FOR MORE INFORMATION

Obviously Georgia has a lot to offer. Contact the Tourist Division (P.O. Box 1776, Atlanta, GA 30301; (404)656-3590) or (404)651-9461 for details. Other useful contacts: Guide to Georgia, 1655 Peachtree St., Atlanta 30309; (404)892-0961. Georgia Hospitality and Travel Association, Suite 625, 148 International Blvd., Atlanta, GA 30303; (404)577-5888 and for Atlanta pick up a copy of "Where" at your hotel or motel; (404)237-4435.

Fabulous Finds in . . .

BRUNSWICK

OUTLETS LTD.

LOCATION: Intersection of I-95 and Hwy. 341 at Exit 7.

STORES: Polly Flinders, Aileen, American Tourister, Socks Galore, Old Mill, Corning

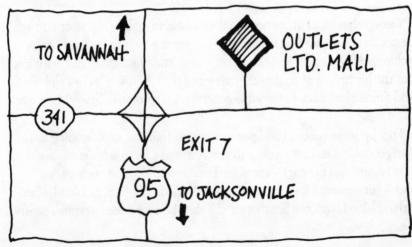

Glass, Judy Bond, Stone Mountain Handbags, Manhattan, Leather Loft, Prestige Fragrance & Cosmetics, Van Heusen, Oxford Brands, Necklace Factory, Bass Shoe, Bike Athletic, Book Warehouse, L'eggs/Hanes/Bali, Linen Factory, MacGregor Golf Factory, Old Mill, Oxford Brands, Pinehurst Lingerie, The Ribbon Outlet and others.

Fabulous Finds in . . .
BYRON

PEACH FESTIVAL OUTLET CENTER

LOCATION: At I-85 and US 49.

STORES: Van Heusen, Wisconsin Toy, US Shoe, Prestige Fragrance & Cosmetics, Manhattan, Aileen, Little Red Shoe House, Kitchen Collection, Health-Tex/Kids Port, Fashion Direct, Corning/Revere Factory Store, Welcome Home, Ribbon Outlet, American Tourister, Towle Silver, Jonathan Logan, Bass Shoe, Gitano, The Paper Factory, Dress Barn, Nilani, Specials/Levi's.

Fabulous Finds in . . .
COMMERCE

TANGER FACTORY OUTLET CENTER

Shop smart! Buy direct from nationally known manufacturers. Avoid the middleman and high department store markups. All stores in this center are owned and operated by each manufacturer.

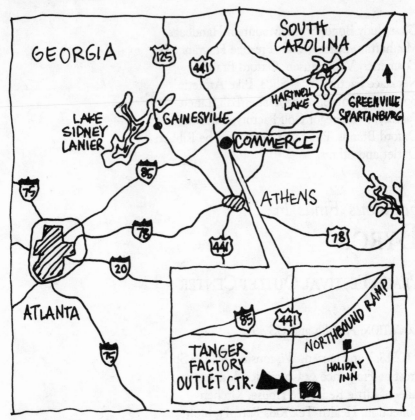

LOCATION: Take I-85 to exit 53 and look for the red roofs just off the exit. For information, call (404)335-4537.

DIRECTIONS
Take I-85 to Exit 53. Look for the red roofs just off the exit.

STORES: Absorba, Inc. Infants' and children's wear 30-50% off regular retail.

Adolfo II. Ladies' apparel by Adolfo II, Donna Toran and Dressy Tessy; save up to 70%.

Aileen. Knit casual and career dressing for women in a wide array of colors and styles in petite, missy and plus sizes and all at least 35% off suggested retail.

American Tourister. Full selection of luggage, business cases, travel accessories. They ship.

Banister. Capezio, Pappagallo, Mushroom, Liz Claiborne, Freeman, French Shriner, Reebok, Famous shoes at factory direct savings.

Barbizon Lingerie. 30-60% savings on fine lingerie.

Bass Shoe. Men's, women's and children's Bass shoes and accessories.

Black & Decker. Discontinued, blemished and reconditioned power tools, housewares and accessories.

Bruce Alan. Leather handbags, wallets, belts, attachés, luggage and leathergoods.

Bugle Boy Outlet. Savings of 30-70% on kids', boys', prep, girls', juniors', missy, young men's and men's contemporary sportswear.

Cape Isle Knitters. The finest cotton sweaters and knits for men and women.

Capezio Shoes.

Corning Factory Store. Huge assortment of overstocks, discontinued and cosmetic seconds of Corning Ware, Revere, Pyrex, Corelle, Visions and coordinated accessories, sets and open stock.

Farberware Inc. Brand name stainless steel cookware and kitchen electrics. They ship.

Fieldcrest Cannon. Made in the U.S.A., discontinued and irregular sheets, towels, bath rugs, blankets, comforters and more in a spectrum of colors to accent any decor.

Generra. Full collection of fashion sportswear for young men, juniors, boys and girls with savings of 30-60%.

Gitano. Top-quality sportswear, accessories, outerwear and more.

harvé benard. Business and casual wardrobes in men's and women's sportswear, suits, dresses, coats, accessories and more 30-60% off suggested retail.

Jerzees. American activewear, T-shirts, sweatpants, and leisure wear.

Just Kids. Name brand daywear, sportswear and sleepwear for boys and girls, newborn to size 14—Adrienne Vittadini, Cole for Kids, Her Majesty, Cole Minors, Lee, Calabash, Members Only, London Fog, Hush Puppies, Ocean Pacific and many more top brands.

L'eggs/Hanes/Bali. Slightly imperfects, closeouts and overstocks of brand name hosiery, underwear, lingerie, socks and more.

Liz Claiborne. Substantial savings on wear-now selections, slightly irregular merchandise including dresses and sportswear for misses and petite sizes, Claiborne men's sportswear and furnishings.

London Fog. Rainwear, jackets, outerwear and toppers for ladies; rainwear, outerwear and jackets for men at substantial savings.

Maidenform. Bras, panties, camisoles, pettislips, full slips, teddies, garter belts, control briefs and sleepwear.

Manhattan. Excellent shopping values for men and women direct from the manufacturers at up to 60% below retail prices.

Multiples Modular Knit. One-size-fits-all clothing.

Oneida Factory Store. A large selection of seconds, closeouts and discontinued stainless, silver-plated and gold electroplated flatware.

Oxford Brands Ltd. Brand name clothing for men and women at 30-70% off original retail.

The Paper Factory. Complete line of party goods and decorations, gift wrap and accessories, paper home and office supplies.

Reebok. Athletic and fashion footwear, apparel and accessories.

The Ribbon Outlet. More than 3,000 varieties of first-quality ribbons and trims.

Socks Galore. A sock-lover's dream with more than 60,000 pairs of designer socks for the entire family.

Specials by Levi Strauss. Levi's in men's, women's and children's sizes.

Top of the Line Cosmetics. Save up to 75% on nationally advertised brands of fragrances, cosmetics.

Toy Liquidators. Thousands of national brand toys—Mattel, Hasbro, Playskool, Tonka,

Fisher-Price and more at 70% off suggested retail.

Van Heusen. Dress shirts, accessories and sportswear for men and women.

Wallet Works. More than 150 different styles of men's and ladies' billfolds; luggage, leather handbags, portfolios and attaché cases.

Welcome Home. Collection of decorative home accessories and quality giftware reflecting current fashion trends.

Fabulous Finds in . . .
DALTON

DALTON FACTORY STORES PLAZA

LOCATION: just off I-75.

STORES: WestPoint Pepperell Mill Store, American Tourister, Banister, Book Warehouse, Bugle Boy, Cape Isle Knitters, Corning/Revere, G.H. Bass, Ideas, L'eggs/Hanes/Bali, Prestige Fragrance & Cosmetics, Rack Room, Van Heusen, Welcome Home, Westport Ltd., totes, Stone Mountain, Leggoons, Wisconsin Toy, Jonathan Logan, Genesco, M&M Nautical, Bon Worth, Bruce Alan Bags, East of Italy, Judy Bond, Cape Isle, Book Warehouse and others.

WANTED
Great restaurants—big or small, but not chains. When you eat in one chain, you've got the menu locked into your brain. Travelers are "strangers in town" and they need some objective guidance to good food and good service ... the kind that makes you want to tip!

Fabulous Finds in . . .
HELEN

The Helen Chamber of Commerce will send you brochures on where to stay, what to do, where to eat, and where to shop if you call (404)878-2181. You can shop a factory outlet complex while you enjoy an authentic Bavarian Alpine village.

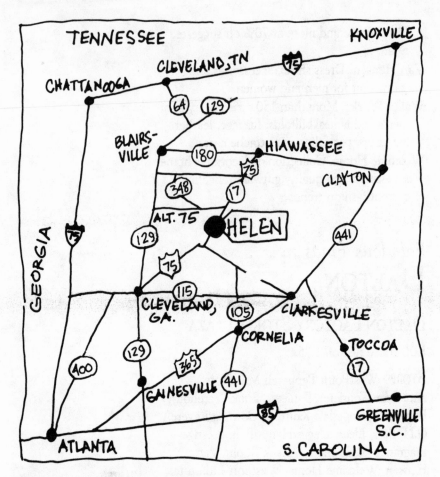

ALPINE VILLAGE OUTLETS

Joyce Becker of Dunwoody, Georgia, says, "I just moved to Dunwoody from Overland Park, Kansas and thought this outlet mall was great!"

STORES: Clothes Works, RevereWare Factory Store, Manhattan Factory Outlet, Kids Port USA, Orbit Factory Outlet, Aileen, Corning Factory Store, Banister Shoe Outlet, Fashion Flair, Van Heusen, Prestige Fragrance & Cosmetics, Ribbon Outlet, totes, Kitchen Collection, American Tourister, Little Red Shoe House, Gitano, Huckleberry's Patch, Old Mill, Toy Liquidators, Clothes Ltd., Bass, Leather Loft, Cape Isle Knitters and a winery.

Fabulous Finds in . . .
SAVANNAH

Savannah is a city of charm and beauty and the food is pure enjoyment. Your first stop should be the Great Savannah Exposition and information center. You will see 250 years of Savannah's history in a unique exhibition that features two major sight and sound theater presentations and a museum containing millions of dollars' worth of exhibits and artifacts. The spacious Exposition Hall displays a replica of the cotton gin, a restored Central of Georgia railroad engine, a spectacular model of the *S.S. Savannah* and other exhibits. Take time to see the restored riverfront and the homes with ornate ironwork. When "cotton was king" the money rolled through Savannah. If you want some tantalizing advance information, contact the Savannah Visitors Center (301 W. Broad St., Savannah, GA 31499; (912)233-6651 for their *Visitors Guide Map* and the brochure listing area hotels, motels and historic inns. Another call to (800)262-INNS will put you in touch with inns and guest houses. This description gives you an idea of the treat in store at a guest house: "Homey, nineteenth-century flavor fills this 1853 Federal townhouse with solid comfort. Well-stocked library, Chinese porcelains, art are among elegant touches. Private garden suites with master bedroom, living room with queen sleeper sofa, bath, full kitchen for one to four persons. Guest room rates: $30-65."

SAVANNAH FESTIVAL OUTLET CENTER

LOCATION: I-95 and S.R. 204.

STORES: American Tourister, Bass Shoe, Van Heusen, Manhattan, Clothes Works, Leather

Loft, Prestige Fragrance & Cosmetics, Ribbon
Outlet, Aileen, Wisconsin Toy, Kids Port USA,
Kitchen Collection, Corning, Levi Strauss,
Towle, Jonathan Logan, Dress Barn, Hartwell,
Orbit, London Fog, Springs Industry, Ship 'n
Shore and others.

Fabulous Finds in . . .
VALDOSTA

FARMHOUSE PLAZA

LOCATION: I-75 at Exit 2, Lake Park, GA;
(912)559-4175.

STORES: Royal Doulton, Knits by K.T., Leather
Loft Stores, Capezio and the Book Warehouse,
Barbizon Intimate Apparel, George Stafford
(Plantation Country Clothing).

DIRECTIONS
Take I-75, Exit 2, Lake Park,
Georgia. We are 14 miles
South of Valdosta.

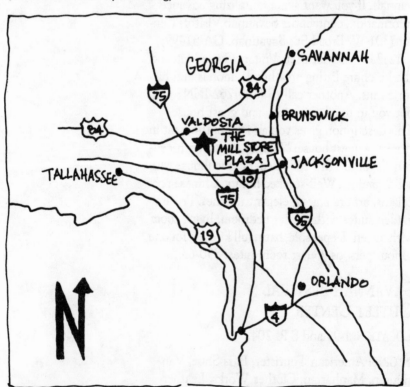

MILL STORE PLAZA

LOCATION: I-75 at exit 2, Lake Park, GA.

STORES: WestPoint Pepperell, Little Red Shoe House, Black & Decker, Aileen Stores, Dansk Factory Outlet, Converse Factory Outlet, OshKosh B'Gosh, Van Heusen Factory Store, Carter's Childrenswear, Londontown Factory Outlet Store, Corning Factory Stores, Kids Port USA, Famous Footwear, Clothes Works, Manhattan Factory Outlet, Warnaco/Olga, Stone Mountain Handbags, Kuppenheimer Men's Clothiers, Prestige Fragrance & Cosmetics, Cluett Factory Store, Jonathan Logan, Vassarette, Fostoria, Swank, Polly Flinders, Fashion Flair, Edwards Tobacco, Carry-alls Handbags & Luggage, Oxford Sportswear Outlet, Oneida, R. Russell, Gilligan & O'Malley Factory Stores, Gold & Diamonds Direct, Campus Factory Outlet, totes, Kitchen Collection, Semco, Evan-Picone, The Lenox Shop, Pfaltzgraff.

OTHER SHOPPING

Carolina Pottery has a brand new outlet center across the intersection from the Mill Store Plaza. Contact the center at P.O. Box 1610, Lake Park, GA 31636; (912)559-6177, for more details.

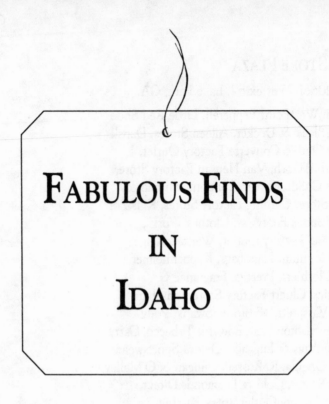

FABULOUS FINDS IN IDAHO

People come to Coeur d'Alene and northern Idaho for the natural beauty of the region and to take advantage of the numerous recreational activities. There are sixty lakes in a sixty-mile radius that feature lakeside golf courses, parks and marinas. Water skiers, sailors, fishermen and swimmers love these lakes, as well as the ski resorts, theme parks, and two new golf courses. The climate is cool in the winter and warm (not hot) in the summer.

Fabulous Finds in . . .
COEUR D'ALENE

THE COEUR D'ALENE FACTORY OUTLET CENTER

LOCATION: On Jacklin Ave. in Post Falls. Take I-90 to Exit 2 (Pleasantview). Post Falls, Idaho is located approximately twenty-five miles east of Spokane, Washington, and eight miles west of Coeur d'Alene, Idaho, on I-90 and in the "finger" of the state. For more information, contact the Post Falls Chamber of Commerce, P.O. Box 32, 510 E. Sixth Ave., Post Falls, ID 83854; (208)773-5016.

STORES: The following stores are currently committed to this center: Corning/Revere Factory Store, Van Heusen/Bass Shoe, Cape Isle Knitters, Sweatshirt Company, Duffel, Gitano, Banister Shoe Outlet, Fragrance World, Book Warehouse, Leather Loft Factory Store, Toy Liquidators.

FABULOUS FINDS

IN

ILLINOIS

Illinois has provided America with some of its great leaders in politics, the arts and commerce. Abraham Lincoln was, of course, Illinois's most famous citizen.

History records that the Illinois River was already used as an uncharted waterway by Indian canoes when the early explorers Marquette and Joliet traveled on the river in the late 1600s. Writing of his trip, Joliet noted that he was delighted with the easy passage from the Illinois and Des Plaines rivers into the Chicago River and Lake Michigan. It was he who first suggested the relative ease with which a canal cut through "but half a league of prairie" (less than three miles) could connect the water system of the Great Lakes to the Mississippi Valley.

Today the history of Illinois is well preserved in museums, displays and buildings. The great inventions, the works of art, the historic places are all maintained so that visitors can experience the spirit of Illinois's astonishing past.

☞ **FOR MORE INFORMATION**
Call the Illinois Traveline twenty-four hours a day at (800)252-8987 or the Tourist Information Center at (312)793-2094. Illinois Department of Commerce & Community Affairs, Division of Tourism, 620 East Adams, Springfield, IL 62701; (217)782-7139. Illinois Tourist Information

Center, Suite 108, 310 South Michigan Ave., Chicago, IL 60604; (312)793-2094. The Morton Arboretum, Lisle, IL 60532; (312)968-0074.

Fabulous Finds in . . .
CHICAGO

In larger cities you can always find unique items in museum shops; Chicago has the Art Institute of Chicago, the Field Museum of Natural History and the Chicago Historical Society. The Chicago Architecture Foundation (Glessner House, 1800 S. Prairie Ave., Chicago, IL 60616; (312)326-1393) has information on walking and bus and boat tours so that you can relish Chicago's magnificent architecture. The Chicago Convention and Tourism Bureau (McCormick Place on the Lake, Chicago, IL 60616; (312)225-5000) has a publication that will detail dining, shopping and entertainment.

STORES: Special retailers in this city are:

Crate and Barrell. 1510 N. Wells.

Lands' End. Several stores are located throughout the city.

The Marshall Field's Warehouse. Open to the public once a month for clearance on furniture and large items; 4000 W. Diversey.

Private Lives Warehouse. Ralph Lauren and Esprit at 40% lower than the competition.

The Spiegel Outlet Stores. Nine locations for overstocked catalog goods. If you are on the catalog mailing list, you know that they sell clothing and shoes and fashion goods.

Fabulous Finds in . . .
LAKE COUNTY

Gurnee Mills will open August 8, 1991 and will be a blockbuster retail operation. With 2.2 million square feet, Gurnee Mills is gigantic. Some of the stores will be outlet stores and a lot of the stores will be "value oriented" and different.

In addition to a gigantic shopping mall, a bank, hotel, restaurants and residential area are part of the development. The mall will have 15 anchors and about 250 other stores. Even though this mixed concept does not fit in with the thrust of Fabulous Finds, it is too important to leave it out. The quality of the stores, makes the difference. The developer isn't ready to release the names of their tenants yet but note the quality of a few retailers that they will discuss.

LOCATION: Gurnee Mills, at the intersection of I-94 and Grand Ave., is halfway between Chicago and Milwaukee with easy access by the Tri-State Tollway, and is just a stone's throw from Six Flags Great America.

STORES: Bed Bath & Beyond. A home decor chain specializing in bath decor and accessories is famous for its merchandising, displays, colorful towels, bath mats and linens.

Phar-Mor. One of the nation's largest deep-discount drugstore chains, sells health and beauty aids, over the counter and R drugs, video rentals and home and office supplies.

Sears Outlet. The clearance operation for Sears full line stores. The outlets are primarily stocked with catalog clearance and fill-in merchandise to complete product assortment for full retail presentation.

Waccamaw Pottery. One of the nation's leading retailers of housewares and home decor. A typical Waccamaw store is 100,000 square feet and features 21 departments full of housewares and home decor and discounted well below full price.

Other stores coming to this huge mall are Bigsby & Kruthers, Mondi, Designs by Levi,

Merry-Go-Round and 9 West. If you want to compare Gurnee Mills with Franklin Mills, look in the Philadelphia, PA section. If you get lost call 708/263-7500.

This is the only developer in this country who successfully mixes outlet and off-price. They do it by seeking out the off-price retailers that are unique and unusual . . . and they insist on the store giving a good value to the customer. Let me know what you think about the Mills stores being included in an outlet directory.

Fabulous Finds in . . .

ST. CHARLES

PIANO FACTORY OF ST. CHARLES

A former piano manufacturing plant converted to a factory outlet shopping center. Write to the St. Charles Convention and Visitors Bureau (P.O. Box 11, St. Charles, IL 60174; (312)377-6161) for other things to do in St. Charles along the Fox River.

LOCATION: On the west side of Chicago along the Fox River. The easiest route from Chicago is west on I-64 to St. Charles. Call (312)664-6873 for directions.

STORES: Carter's, Pfaltzgraff, Manhattan, Corning Glass, Van Heusen, New England Classics, harvé benard, Prevue Fashions, Top of the Line, Kitchen Collections, American Tourister, Dan Ray Lingerie, Leather Manor, Gitano, Aileens, Campus Factory Outlet, Jonathan Logan, Stephanie Kay Ltd. Factory Card Outlet, US Shoe, Housewares Outlet, Aunt Mary's Yarns, Temptation Jewelry.

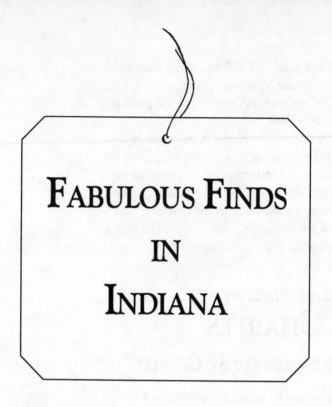

FABULOUS FINDS

IN

INDIANA

As they say in Indiana:

"Sample life where it's leisurely. Dangle your toes in the clear warm water of Indiana lakes. Swim. Sail. Fish.

"In the winter, thrill to the rush of a Pokagon toboggan ride. Skate. Snowmobile. Ski. Then warm yourself in front of a roaring fire. Settle back to the comforts of lake country.

"When you're longing for something more lively, head to the cities. Visit the museums, shops and restaurants. Amble along the old historic avenues. Whatever your interests, go ahead. Dive in."

Fabulous Finds in . . .
ANGOLA
VALLEY OUTLET CENTER

It's appropriate that this outlet center is located along one of the major trade routes used by early French fur traders as they bartered with the Indian tribes that once called these rolling woodlands home.

LOCATION: At the intersection of I-69 and I-80/90, Fremont, Indiana (46737); (219)833-1684.

STORES: Kitchen Collection, Aunt Mary's Yarns, Gitano, Corning Glass, Clothes Works, Little Red Shoe House, Old Mill, Kids Port USA, Van Heusen, Leather Manor, totes, Manhattan, Jaymar, Banister Shoe, Toy Liquidators, Warnaco, Socks Galore, Fashion Flair/Izod, Top of the Line Cosmetics, Salem China, Aileen, Cape Craftsmen, G.H. Bass and a restaurant and restrooms.

Fabulous Finds in . . .
EDINBURGH

EDINBURGH MANUFACTURERS MARKETPLACE FACTORY OUTLET

Edinburgh is a stone's throw from the Brown County/Nashville area, which features a variety

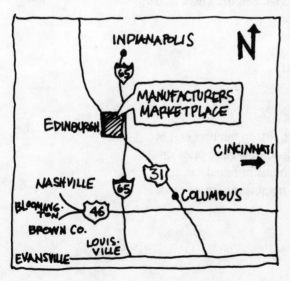

DIRECTIONS

We are located at the U.S. 31 and I-65 junction; Exit 76-B, Edinburgh/Columbus.

From Indianapolis—A short 32 minutes to savings.

From Louisville (80 miles)— Take I-65 North to Exit 76-B, just north of Columbus, Indiana.

From Cincinnati (130 miles)—Take I-74 West to Indianapolis, then I-465 West, then I-65 South to Exit 76-B.

From Evansville (200 miles)—Take Hwy. 41 North to I-65 East to I-65 North then Exit 76-B.

of attractions including recreation in Brown County State Park, seventh most visited in the nation. Arts and crafts, antiques and the Edinburgh Manufacturers Marketplace Factory Outlet Center will provide recreational shopping.

LOCATION: I-65 and U.S. 31, exit 76-B. Call (800)866-5900 for information.

STORES: Corning/Revere Factory Store, Bon Worth Factory Store, Stone Mountain Handbags, Aileen, Welcome Home, Toy Liquidators, Knits by K.T., Swank, Big and Better, Aunt Mary's Yarn, Kids Port USA, American Tourister, Kitchen Collection, Just My Size, Hanes Activewear, L'eggs/Hanes/Bali, Van Heusen, Bass Shoe, Farah Factory Store, Fieldcrest Cannon, Wallet Works, Paper Factory, Socks Galore, Gitano, Specials By Levi Strauss, Banister Shoe, Ribbon Outlet, Tool Warehouse, Book Warehouse, Ambassador Crystal, Cape Isle Knitters, Windsor Shirt, Fanny Farmer, Old Mill, Barbizon, Mackintosh of New England, Westport Ltd., Leather Loft, Nickels Company Store, Fragrance World, Manhattan, Little Red Shoe House, Maidenform, Ideas, Izod Fashion Flair, Evan-Picone.

Fabulous Finds in . . .
ELKHART

If you travel near Elkhart, fifteen minutes east of South Bend, you can negotiate a good price on a travel trailer. More than one hundred van conversions and fifty-six RV manufacturers are ready to wheel and deal.

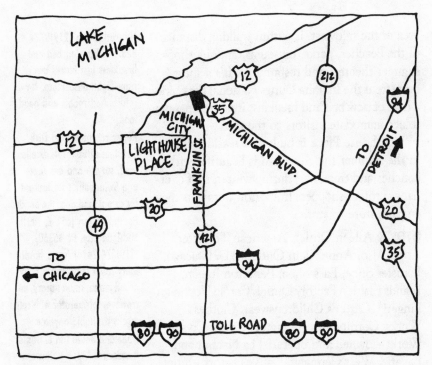

Fabulous Finds in . . .

MICHIGAN CITY

LIGHTHOUSE PLACE

Listen to this: "We envy you all the fun you'll have discovering LaPorte County for the first time. Here, an hour from crowded Chicago are wide open spaces and the water's edge of Lake Michigan and five inland lakes: with farmlands and orchards, small towns, large parks and the joy of being in uncrowded natural and beautiful surroundings." Sound good? Write to the Visitors Information Center (601 Wabash St., Michigan City, IN 46360; (219)879-6506) for information.

Indiana's Dune Country is vacationland for a couple of million people each year. They go for the beaches and for fishing, horseback riding and hiking.

Lighthouse Place, in a recently "discovered"

DIRECTIONS

Named for a symbol that is highly visible for miles around, Lighthouse Place is on the shores of Lake Michigan, close to Chicago. It's on the major east/west interstates serving the Upper Midwest.

PLACES TO EAT AND SLEEP

Personally recommended by Peggy Landsman, who works at Lighthouse Place: Creekwood Inn (Rte. 20-35 and I-94, Michigan City (219)872-8357), a beautiful inn in the woods with lakes, walking paths, cross-country skiing and ice skating in the winter.

area of the midwest, is within walking distance of the beaches, parks, museums, antique shops, summer theaters and restaurants. It's a short drive from the Indiana Dunes National Park, and a host of new bed and breakfast inns are opening to accommodate visitors to the area.

Lighthouse Place is built as a seaside village. In the summer the courtyard is beautiful with benches and trees, and during winter, roof overhangs protect shoppers from snow or rain as they go from store to store.

STORES: Aileen Outlet, American Tourister, Anko Also, Anne Klein Outlet, B.G. Chicago, Banister Shoe, Bass Shoe, Benetton Italian, Brands Fashion Factory Outlet, Carole Hochman Lingerie, Carter's Childrenswear, Clothes Works, Corning/Revere factory stores, Crystal Works — owned and operated by Nachtmann, Bavaria, West Germany, Dansk Factory Outlet, Fanny Farmer, Fashion Flair/Izod/Ship 'n Shore, Fieldcrest Cannon, 14 plus Pizazz, Gitano, harvé benard, I.B. Diffusion, Jaymar, J.H. Collectibles Factory Outlet, Jindo Furs, Jonathan Logan Factory Outlet, Just Pants Warehouse, Kitchen Collection, Leather Manor, Maidenform Lingerie, Manhattan Factory Outlet, Mushroom Shoes, Oneida Silver Factory Outlet, The Paper Factory, Polo/Ralph Lauren, Prestige Fragrance & Cosmetics, The Ribbon Outlet, Royal Doulton, Sassafras, Skippy's Cards & Gifts, Socks Galore, The Stitchery, Ties Etc., Toy Liquidators, Trendsetters, Van Heusen, Warnaco Outlet Store, Welcome Home.

Nutcracker Inn (219)872-3237, a Victorian bed and breakfast just blocks away from Lighthouse Place. Newly refurbished rooms and good food.

Peggy recommended Dick Christian's Pub for its excellent food, service and ambience and Swingbelly's Restaurant for casual food near the beach.

Plantation Inn (651 E. North, Michigan City, IN 46360; (219)874-2418) has a hospitality room featuring a baby grand piano, small library, microwave, refrigerator with cold drinks available anytime.

Duneland Beach Inn & Hunter Restaurant (3311 Pottawattomie Trail, Michigan City, IN 46360; (219)874-7729).

FABULOUS FINDS

IN

KENTUCKY

It is said that an inspiration for Kentucky's rich culture and special spirit is the beauty of its land. From majestic mountains in the east, to sparkling lakes in the west to deep, lush forests preserved for hiking and camping, Kentucky's beauty offers unlimited nature and recreational opportunities.

Maybe that's why in midtown Manhattan the Kentuckians Society of New York gather twice a year to sing "My Old Kentucky Home," by Stephen Foster. It has been said that you never meet a Kentuckian who isn't "going home." What makes this state so special? Loyalty, rich tradition and historic legend. Kentucky is a land proud of its heritage and confident of its future. The state that spawned bluegrass music has also produced a world-class symphony orchestra.

Kentucky is horse capital of the world and that legendary four-legged creature stands at the center of an industry, a society and in the hearts of the people. Top thoroughbreds are bred, raised, sold and raced. Lexington is the home of the American Saddle Horse Museum, the U.S. Polo Museum and Hall of Fame. You can ride a horse-drawn carriage through the park or see thirty-five breeds of horses perform. Take Exit 120 off I-75.

☞ **FOR MORE INFORMATION**

For more information on travel in Kentucky, Kentucky Department of Travel Development, Kentucky Tourism, Capital Plaza Tower, Frankfort, KY 40601; (800)225-TRIP.

Fabulous Finds in . . .
CARROLLTON
VF OUTLET CENTER

The nice thing about the VF Centers is the sign as you enter the door of the VF store—"Everything in this store is half price."
LOCATION: R.R. 3, Box 110; (502)732-6666.
STORES: The VF Outlet Store will be joined by some old regulars selling shoes, perfumes and cosmetics and apparel for men and women.

Fabulous Finds in . . .
EDDYVILLE
WEST KENTUCKY FACTORY OUTLETS
LOCATION: U.S. 62 at KY 93 in the Barkley Lake area; (502)388-7379 for directions and hours.

DIRECTIONS
I-24 Exit 40, then East on U.S. 62. I-24 Exit 45, then North on KY 93. Western Kentucky Pkwy. Exit 4, then West on U.S. 62.

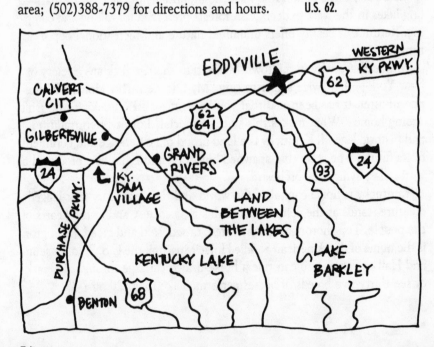

STORES: Kids Port USA, The Wallet Works, Enro/Damon, The Ribbon Outlet, Aileen, Captree, Welcome Home, Bass, Jonathan Logan Outlet, Corning/Revere Factory Store, Banister Shoe, Van Heusen, Prestige Fragrance & Cosmetics, Manhattan, Kitchen Collection, American Tourister, Gitano, Toy Liquidators, Swank, Polly Flinders, Just Pants, Full Size Fashions, Monet/Izod/Ship 'n Shore, London Fog, Paper Factory, Socks Galore and the Sports Outlet.

Fabulous Finds in . . .
GEORGETOWN

CAROLINA POTTERY

Offering bargains from around the world for around your home, Carolina Pottery has everything from silk flowers to wicker baskets, brass, oriental gifts and dinnerware. Carolina Pottery will be opening a new facility here in May 1991. The outlet will be located at I-75, Exit 126, just north of Lexington. Watch for the beautiful horse farms of the Bluegrass region (including the Kentucky Horse Park) and even more beautiful horses. Contact the Georgetown Chamber of Commerce, P.O. Box 224, Georgetown, KY 40324, for area attractions and information. Georgetown is about an hour south of the Cincinnati, OH/Northern Kentucky area, which also offers shopping and lots of attractions. Check those listings for more information.

Fabulous Finds in . . .
NORTHERN KENTUCKY

Northern Kentucky, which includes Florence and Newport, is a historic area poised on the Ohio River. Covington Landing, a restaurant and entertainment facility housed as a riverboat will provide fine dining, as will the entire Riverboat Row. While in the area a stop at Mainstrasse Village, heart of the German community, offers original German restaurants and unique architecture. Contact the Northern Kentucky Chamber of Commerce (50 E. Rivercenter Blvd., Covington, KY 41011; (606)291-5000) for information.

GAP CLEARANCE OUTLET, FLORENCE
Mr. and Mrs. Bertlefe from Dayton, Ohio, referred this store. She says it is their favorite store for the teenagers. "The savings are substantial but the selection can be limited."

LOCATION: I-275 near the Cincinnati/Northern Kentucky International Airport on the Gapway Route.

MILL OUTLET, NEWPORT
LOCATION: Sixth and Washington at Watertower Square. I-75 exit at Fifth St., follow Fifth through Covington to Newport. (606)581-7666.

WANTED
Information about the most interesting things to do in an area already listed in *Fabulous Finds.* Experiences that are memorable. Attractions that you can't forget.

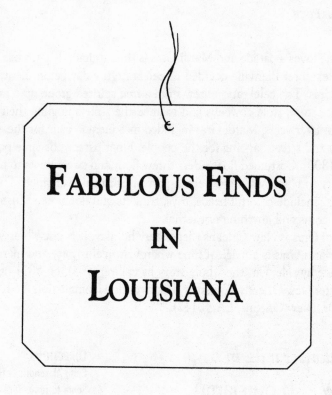

FABULOUS FINDS
IN
LOUISIANA

Start your exploration of Louisiana by ordering a map from the Department of Transportation and Development (P.O. Box 44245, Capitol Station, Baton Rouge, LA 70804), then get set for some other-world experiences. With its bayous and graceful plantation mansions you will be transported into the past. Tour rice mills, sugar factories, the famous Tabasco Sauce factory and an absolutely unforgettable experience in the marshes and swamps even if you never leave I-10.

Plantation Trace information can be ordered from the West Baton Rouge Tourist Center (2855 Frontage Rd., Port Allen, LA 70767). Plantation Trace gives you a glimpse into the past elegance and majesty in times gone by.

Cajun country cuts through the heart of one of America's most unique regions . . . Acadiana. The Cajun culture demands that you "let the good times roll." Food lovers will delight in the Cajun cuisine in the area's many fine restaurants.

And then there is New Orleans—however you pronounce it—which contains enough entertainment and bright lights for everyone. Mississippi River steamboat cruises, the historic French Quarter, horse racing tracks and if you go to New Orleans at the right time of the year—Mardi Gras.

Everyone loves a parade and Mardi Gras is the ultimate. Rumor has it that French explorer Bienville decided to celebrate the day before Lent, thus Mardi Gras. The celebration grew from a free spirited group who raided a hardware store, stole cowbells and roamed the streets jingling their trophies. In later years, Mardi Gras included masquerade balls for the elite of the city and street dancing for the people. Float parades became popular in the 1800s. Costumed float riders threw flour and sweetmeats to parade-watchers and "throws" have been a part of Carnival ever since. Today, "throws" include colorful beads, toys, trinkets and doubloons, custom-minted coins and anything not lethal.

Mardi Gras is New Orleans's legendary holiday; it is jazzy, brassy and sassy. Mardi Gras is a magical time when Carnival royalty and merriment reign side by side. Get the whole story by calling (504)566-5011 or write to Greater New Orleans Tourist and Convention Commission (1520 Sugar Bowl Dr., New Orleans, LA 70112).

Fabulous Finds in . . .
IOWA (Louisiana)

VF FACTORY OUTLET

LOCATION: I-10 to exit 43; (318)582-3568.

STORES: VF Factory Outlet store anchors this

DIRECTIONS

From Alexandria—Hwy. 165 South to Iowa. Turn right on Miller Ave.

From Baton Rouge—I-10 West to Exit No. 43, Iowa.

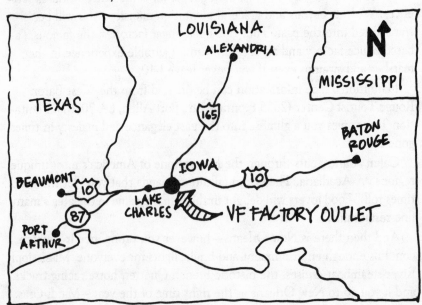

center and they feature products by Lee, Bassett-Walker, Vanity Fair and Heron Cove Casuals. Other stores are Van Heusen Factory Store, Prestige Fragrance & Cosmetics, and Banister Shoe Outlet—featuring Capezio, Pappagallo, Mushrooms, Liz Claiborne, Freeman, French Shriner and Reebok at savings up to 50%.

Fabulous Finds in . . .

SLIDELL

SLIDELL FACTORY STORES

LOCATION: On the northeast side of New Orleans. Take Exit 263 off I-10 in Slidell. Call (504)646-0756 for more information. (See map on following page.)

STORES: WestPoint Pepperell, L'eggs/Hanes, Van Heusen, G.H. Bass, Gitano, Russell Corp., Kitchen Collection, American Tourister, Banister/US Shoe Corp., Buffalo China by Oneida, Famous Footwear, The Paper Factory, Toy Liquidators, Leather Loft, Top of the Line Cosmetics, Just My Size, Socks Galore & More, Welcome Home, Stone Mountain Handbags.

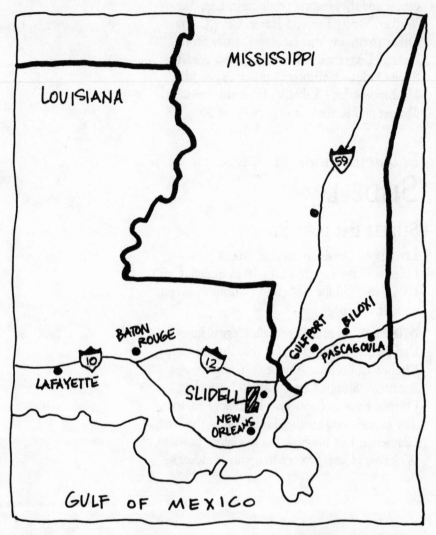

DIRECTIONS
We're easy to find. Just take
Exit 263 off I-10 in Slidell.

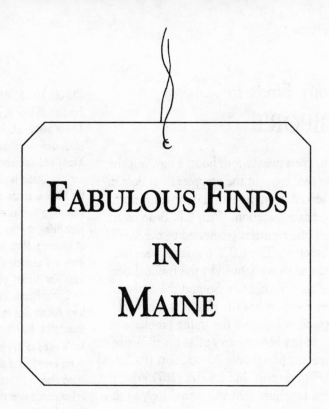

FABULOUS FINDS
IN
MAINE

Maine has an unparalleled coastline with curving coves and beaches, abrupt promontories and secluded islands. Maine has deep glacial lakes that are reflecting pools for towering mountain peaks. Maine has streams and mighty rivers, timeless villages and hometowns. Maine's people are intelligent, creative, capable, independent and neighborly. Maine invites you to visit their timeless villages and towns.

Maine is the state that educated the consumer to factory outlet stores with Dexter, Bass and Timberland shoe outlets along highways. (You will find Dexter Shoes in every nook and cranny of the state.) Tourists came for the seashore, skiing, camping and brought home bounty from the roadside factory outlets.

☞ **FOR MORE INFORMATION**
Useful addresses: Maine Publicity Bureau, 97 Winthrop St., Hallowell, ME 04347; (207)289-2423. Bar Harbor Chamber of Commerce, P.O. Box 158, Bar Harbor, ME 04609.

Fabulous Finds in ...
FREEPORT

L.L. Bean, open twenty-four hours a day, was the attraction that brought the preppies from Boston and also served the nature lovers who came north to fish and take vacation. With L.L. Bean as an attraction, other outlets gravitated to the small town of Freeport. The 6,000 residents were outnumbered and overwhelmed by the traffic. Local businesses moved off Main St. and the outlets took over. Freeport has the charm of a typical New England village and the traffic problems of a big city. It has become an outlet town. Write to the Freeport Merchants Association (P.O. Box 452 FF, Freeport, ME 04032; (207)865-1212) for a brochure that will introduce you to one of the best shopping, sleeping and eating experiences yet. Freeport is unique and special and is just part of Maine's offerings.

LOCATION: I-95, exits 17, 19, 20 and 21 will get you to the Freeport Shopping district.

STORES: In addition to all the arts and crafts shops in the outlet town, the following are awaiting your business:

Accessory Factory. Handbags, scarves, jewelry, watches and accessory items.

Alpine Sheets & Towels. Sheets, down comforters, bedspreads.

Anne Klein Outlet. Accessories—jewelry, handbags and famous fashion.

Banister Shoe Outlet. More than 15,000 pairs of famous brands and you can save up to 50%.

Barbizon Lingerie. Save up to 70% on sleepwear, all first quality.

Bass Shoe. Classic footwear and accessories.

Benetton. Italian sportswear for men, women and children.

PLACES TO EAT AND SLEEP

For fine dining, try Jameson Tavern next to L.L. Bean. Their soups and sandwiches are hearty and delicious. For dinner, the lobster is yummy and the steak is outstanding. If something light is more to your liking, try the salad bar at Delmar's. More than sixty items and as many trips as you want. For dessert, visit Lilly's Ice Cream Palace. Everything from double dips to chocolate cheesecake. No calories.

You'll need to stay overnight to see even half of the outlets in the area. For a cozy evening in Freeport, stay at the Harbor House Inn. The rooms are decorated in English Tudor. Breakfast is served in bed. Fresh flowers complement every room.

The Cabot Lodge will appeal to people traveling with children. It has an indoor pool and game room. For mom and pop there is live entertainment nightly and a scrumptious dining room menu.

For a quiet retreat, try the Adams Bed & Breakfast. Chintz curtains and upholstery, heavy wooden beams and plush carpets lend an air of elegance. Relax in your room in front of the fireplace and sip fine, aged brandy from the crystal decanter you will find on an antique table.

Bogner Outlet Store. Ladies' designer sportswear, golfwear and accessories.

Boston Traders. Sportswear for men and women, big and tall—save 30-70%.

Bow Street Ltd. Home furnishings, accessories, fine linens, dhurrie rugs, down comforters, china and glassware.

Brown Goldsmiths. Original jewelry crafted on premises.

Buttons & Things Factory Outlet. Christmas collectibles, crafts, unique gifts.

Calvin Klein Outlet. Misses, juniors and men clothing.

Cambridge Dry Goods. Ladies' coordinated active wear, sportswear and careerwear.

Carter's Childrenswear. A true manufacturer's outlet featuring layette, infant and toddler.

Casey's Wood Products. Bins and bins of wood turnings, toys and country craft items at factory direct prices.

The Christmas Outlet Store. Ornaments, trees, collectibles and more at 20-50% savings.

Class Perfume & Cosmetics. Better brands and extremely low prices.

Coach Factory Store. Slightly imperfect Coach merchandise for men and women—fine leather bags, totes, briefcases, belts.

Cole-Haan Company Store. Fine footwear, apparel and accessories.

Corning/Revere. Corning Ware, Visions, RevereWare and Pyrex sold at substantial savings.

Countess Mara Outlet. Internationally renowned neckwear, clothing and accessories.

Country Squire Brass. Below retail for lamps and more.

Crystal Factory. Save up to 60% on the finest crystal, Waterford, Baccarat, Gorham, Orrefores and more.

Cuddledown Factory Store. Down filling room,

comforters, pillows, gift items and more—a catalog factory store.

Dansk Factory Outlet. Classic designs in dinnerware, teak, flatware, glassware, cookware, gifts. They ship.

Dexter Shoe Factory Outlet. Men's and women's shoes.

Down Outlet. Outerwear, sportswear, comforters and more.

Earrings & Company. Handmade sterling and gold.

Evan-Picone Factory Store. Save 35-70% on Evan-Picone, Austin-Hill, Eagle, Palm Beach and other recognized brands, dress and casual.

Fanny Farmer Outlet Store. Famous chocolates, fudge, nuts, etc.

Fashion Flair-Izod Company Store. Men's, women's and children's apparel, including LaCoste, Ship 'n Shore and Monet.

Fila Factory Outlet. Italian sportswear, ski, golf, swim and casual wear.

Gant Company Store. Men's sportswear, dress shirts, knits, rugbies, sweaters and slacks.

harvé benard. Designer collection for men and women at dramatic savings.

Jewelry Source. Savings up to 50% off suggested retail.

Johnston & Murphy. Footwear for men and women.

Jones New York. Classic quality business and casual wear up to 70% off suggested retail.

L.L. Bean. Outdoor sporting specialties—open twenty-four hours a day, 365 days a year, and they have an outlet or clearance area.

Laura Ashley. British designer clothing for women and children, home furnishings and accessories.

Leslie Fay Factory Outlet. Famous label dresses, sportswear, separates, designer suits and dresses.

Maidenform Outlet Store. Women's lingerie.

Mainely Bags. Finely crafted leather and fabric bags.

Manhattan Factory Store. Men's and ladies' apparel.

Mikasa Factory Store. Dinnerware, bone china, crystal and cookware.

The Nike Store. Quality athletic footwear and apparel.

Paper Party House. Paper, plastic, balloons and decorations.

The Patagonia Outlet. Clothing for children and adults.

Polo/Ralph Lauren. Men's, women's and boys' apparel, fragrance and home furnishings.

Rawlings Sporting Goods. Complete line of quality sports equipment and clothing, "The mark of a Pro."

Reebok/Rockport/Ellesse/Frye Outlet. Footwear, casual and activewear.

The Ribbon Outlet. Sewing and craft needs.

Samuel Robert Direct/Joan & David. First-quality women's and men's fashions, fabrics, leather and ultrasuede, accessories.

Sisley-Benetton Store. Men's and women's sportswear by Sisley and Benetton Uomo.

The Soap and Candle Outlet. Soap and candles at discounted prices.

Timberland Factory Outlet. Timberland classic footwear, casual apparel and related accessories at savings up to 50%.

Toys Unlimited. Thousands of nationally advertised toys.

The Wallet Works. Factory owned-and-operated offering more than 150 different styles of men's and ladies' leather wallets—save on luggage, handbags, briefcases and gifts.

Fabulous Finds in . . .
KITTERY

Kittery is another outlet town. The Maine Outlet started the shopping center phenomenon and many others have joined in the success of the area. Kittery is a shopping destination or a day trip if you get to the Boston area.

LOCATION: On Coastal Rte. 1; I-95 to Kittery 236 (south) or exit 3 (north).

STORES: The Snappy Turtle, Eurosport — elegant European sportswear, Ripoffs, Sergio Valente, Just My Size, Linens 'n Things, Dress Barn, The Children's Outlet, Fuller Brush, Warnaco, The Book & Music Outlet, Active Sports Outlet, Timberland, The Christmas Place, J.H. Collectibles, Mikasa, Banister, Oneida, Yankee Brass, Red Horse, Mainely Bags, Samuel Robert, Carole Hockman Lingerie.

KITTERY FACTORY STORES

Just a few steps away you will find more stores in the Kittery Factory Stores complex.

STORES: Anne Klein Outlet, The Genuine Article (OshKosh B'Gosh), American Tourister, Liz Claiborne Outlet Store, Hathaway, Van Heusen Factory Store, Shamrock Lingerie, Black & Decker, Bass Shoe, Wallet Works, Carter's Childrenswear.

THE SPRUCE CREEK FACTORY STORES

LOCATION: This same general area.

STORES: Crystal Works, Manhattan Shirts, Prestige Fragrance & Cosmetics, Converse and Jonathan Logan.

87

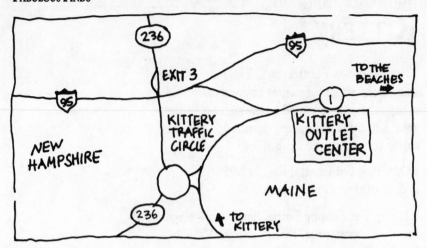

KITTERY OUTLET CENTER

STORES: Royal Doulton Shoppe, Towle Silver Mfg. Co., Mighty Mac, Waterford, Collegetown, LeSportsac Factory Outlet, totes, Alpine Sheets & Towels, Mushrooms, Van Heusen.

OTHER SHOPPING

STORES: In the same area you will find Villroy & Bock, Dunham Shoe, harvé benard, Nettle Creek, Lenox China Shop, Boston Traders, North Country Leathers and the Jewelry Mine. More stores open every week.

DIRECTIONS

From Northern Maine and Canada — I-95 South, Exit Kittery 236 South to Traffic Circle to Coastal Rte. 1 North.

From Massachusetts and New Hampshire — I-95 North to Exit 3, Coastal Rte. 1.

FABULOUS FINDS IN MARYLAND

Maryland offers diverse geography, dynamic cities, recreational opportunities and unique seafood traditions. You won't want to miss the beaches, the mountain lakes, Baltimore Inner Harbor and the Aquarium, Chesapeake Bay and the endless variety that is Maryland.

Visitors love Maryland. Captain John Smith explored Maryland in 1608 and was so enchanted with the Chesapeake Bay that he named an island "Smith." The *National Geographic* wrote in 1932, "Maryland is America-in-miniature." From the deep pools and clear waters of mountain lakes and streams to three thousand square miles of "The White Marlin Capital of the World" in the Chesapeake Bay and Atlantic waters, Maryland is a sportfisherman's paradise ... recreational wonderland—from the mountains in the west to the ocean and bay in the east.

Write to the Director of Tourism (County Office Bldg., 208 N. Commerce St., Centerville, MD 21617) or call (301) 758-0322 for information about Kent Island, the bed 'n breakfasts, restaurants and lodgings. You will find attractions that will fill your time and never let you go.

☞ **FOR MORE INFORMATION**
Write these places: Maryland Department of Economic and Community Development, Office of Tourist Development, 45 Calvert St., Annapolis, MD 21401. National Aquarium in Baltimore,

Pier 3, 501 East Pratt St., Baltimore, MD 21202. Maryland Forest & Park Service, Department of Natural Resources, Tawes State Office Bldg., Annapolis, MD 21401, for a copy of Maryland's State Forests and Parks. For Whitewater Championships, Inc., write P.O. Box 689, McHenry, MD 21541; or call (301)387-4282.

Fabulous Finds in . . .

ANNAPOLIS

BAY BRIDGE MARKET PLACE

LOCATION: 595 Rte. 50 (Revell Hwy.), one mile west of the Chesapeake Bay Bridge (Annapolis side). (301)757-9181.

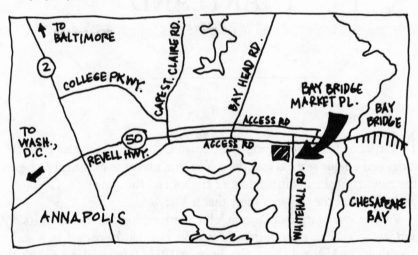

STORES: Aileen, Cape Craft, Cluett Apparel Outlet, Crazy Horse, harvé benard, International Footwear, Linen Warehouse, Mikasa, Old Mill, The Paper Factory, Tahari, Wallet Works, Perfumania, Van Heusen, Ribbon Outlet, Adolfo Sport, Chesapeake, Fudge, Cape Isle Knitters, Davidson's of Bermuda, Miki, Pandora.

DIRECTIONS
Look for Bay Bridge Market Place one mile west of the Bay Bridge on Rte. 50.

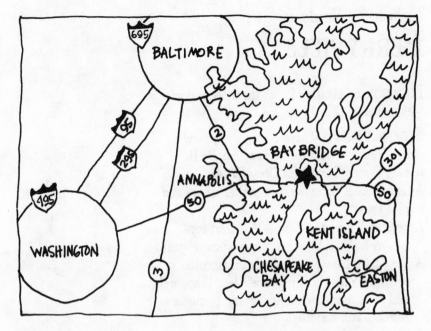

Fabulous Finds in . . .
KENT ISLAND

EASTERN SHORE FACTORY STORES

LOCATION: Five miles east of the Chesapeake Bay Bridge on Rte. 50.

STORES: Aileen, American Tourister, Anne Klein Outlet, Banister Shoe Outlet, Campus Sportswear, Carter's Childrenswear, Chesapeake Carvers, Corning Glass Works, Crystal Works, Fashion Flair, Hamilton Watch & Clock, Kitchen Collection, Leather Loft, Milford Stitching, Petals Silk Flowers, Pfaltzgraff Collector's Center, Prestige Fragrance & Cosmetics, Quoddy Crafted Footwear, Toy Liquidators, Wicker Outlet.

DIRECTIONS
We're conveniently located just 5 miles east of the Chesapeake Bay Bridge on U.S. Rte. 50. We are less than one hour from Baltimore, Washington and Annapolis, on Kent Island.

Fabulous Finds in . . .
PERRYVILLE

LOCATION: 68 Heather Ln. at the intersection of I-95 and Rte. 222.

STORES: **Adolfo II.** Ladies' designer apparel direct from the manufacturers of Adolfo II, Rafael, Donna Toran and Dressy Tessy.

Aileen. Ladies' sportswear in petite, misses and plus sizes.

American Tourister. Save 40-70% on top-quality luggage, business cases and travel gear.

Anne Klein. Direct-from-the-manufacturer savings on first-quality Anne Klein II apparel and accessories including jewelry, perfume, watches and handbags.

Argenti. Exceptional savings on quality dresses, blouses, evening wear, suits and accessories; silk is their specialty in misses, petite and plus sizes.

Barbizon Lingerie. Select from an exciting collection of quality lingerie at affordable prices.

Bass Shoe. Casual footwear and accessories for men and women; shoemakers to America since 1876.

Book Cellar. More than 50,000 hardcover books at paperback prices.

Brass Factory. Factory-direct savings on high-quality solid brass accesssories for home or office.

Cambridge Dry Goods. Save on women's updated traditional sportswear, active wear and career wear.

Cape Isle Knitters. The finest quality, contemporary fashions in 100% cotton sweaters and knits for men and women direct from the manufacturer.

Carole Little. Savings on designer women's apparel for both career and sport.

Corning/Revere Factory Store. Excellent prices on Corning Ware, Pyrex, Corelle, Visions and RevereWare; discontinued products at substantial discounts.

Etienne Aigner. Specializing in women's quality leather footwear, handbags, apparel and accessories at everyday low prices.

Fenn Wright & Manson. Exceptional prices on updated casual and career apparel for men and women.

Fragrance World. 20-60% off suggested retail prices on top-quality selection of world-famous men's and women's fragrances, cosmetics and accessories.

Geoffrey Beene. Fashions for men from an American designer; select from dress, casual and relaxed life-styles.

harvé benard. A wide selection of designer women's apparel and accessories.

He-Ro Group Outlet. Incredible savings on ladies' fashion blouses, sportswear, dresses, leathers, and evening wear.

JH Collectibles. An exciting collection of misses and petite clothing.

Jones NY Sport/Jones NY Factory Store. Featuring Jones New York, Christian Dior sportswear and Jones Sport.

Jordache Outlet. Streetwear, accessories and shoes at yesterday's backstreet savings for men, women and kids.

Just Kids Outlet Store. Quality name brands for kids, direct from the factories — save on Her Majesty, Cole for Kids, Camp Beverly Hills and more.

Kitchen Collection. Exclusive factory outlet for WearEver cookware and Proctor-Silex appliances.

Leather Loft. Save on luxury leather handbags,

luggage, briefcases, jackets and designer accessories.

L'eggs/Hanes/Bali. Slightly imperfects, closeouts and overstocks on brand name hosiery, underwear and lingerie.

Liz Claiborne. Substantial savings on wear-now selections of discontinued first-quality merchandise including dresses and sportswear for misses and petite sizes and Claiborne men's sportswear, dress shirts, neckwear, hosiery and underwear.

Maidenform. Save on first-quality, discontinued and closeout merchandise — bras, panties, camisoles, half slips and lingerie.

Mikasa. Substantial savings, tremendous selection and immediate availability of fine dinnerware, drystal, flatware, housewares and more.

NCS Shoe Outlet. Nickels, Jazz, Via Spiga, Paloma, Studio Paolo and Glacee.

Nike. Specializing in a superb selection of athletic shoes, apparel and accessories.

Peruvian Connection. Designer Alpaca and Peruvian Pima sweaters.

Pierre Cardin. Designer knit coordinate sportswear.

The Ribbon Outlet. Significant savings on more than 2,500 varieties of first-quality ribbon and trim, direct from the factory.

Royal Robbins. A high mountain, a quiet river, a summer breeze, casual clothing with outdoor spirit.

Sassafras. Contemporary life-style products for both kids and adults at prices that fit any budget.

Socks Galore. The world's most delectable assortment of designer socks.

Toys Unlimited. Great savings on thousands of nationally advertised toys.

Van Heusen. Save on first-quality fashion apparel for men and women.

WANTED
New information about factory outlet shopping centers — dead or alive. Tell me if you enjoyed your shopping experiences and why.

Wallet Works. Select from 150 styles of men's and women's leather wallets priced well below retail value.

Welcome Home. Fantastic savings on finely crafted accessories for the entire home.

Wemco Factory Store. A fantastic selection of men's name brand neckwear and classic sportswear at incredible prices.

Fabulous Finds in . . .

QUEENSTOWN

CHESAPEAKE VILLAGE

LOCATION: At the intersection of Rtes. 50 and 301.

STORES: Bass Shoe, Maidenform, Fenn Wright & Manson, Gilligan & O'Malley, Top of the Line Cosmetics, Jindo Fur, Gitano, Barbizon Lingerie, Socks Galore, Nike, Palm Beach, Fanny Farmer, Liz Claiborne, I.B. Diffusion, JH Collectibles.

FABULOUS FINDS IN MASSACHUSETTS

Massachusetts is difficult to condense and define. Its appeal is a result of its innovative people. Throughout history Massachusetts's people have had to rely on skill, imagination and resourcefulness. Over the past two centuries an extraordinary flow of innovations in science, industry, art, medicine, education have originated in Massachusetts. Capturing the essence of the excitement, describing the various geographic features is impossible.

This is the land where America began. In the Bay State, from the Berkshires to Boston and the islands, you'll find the spirit of yesterday, today, and tomorrow. You'll find yesterday in the narrow streets where patriots marched; Concord Bridge, where the "shot heard 'round the world" was fired; and in the historic villages of Plimoth, Deerfield and Sturbridge.

The spirit of Massachusetts is very much alive on Boston's waterfront. Faneuil Hall and Quincy Market are a potpourri of pushcarts, restaurants, specialty shops and street theatre. See the Boston Tea Party reenacted along the wharf. Sense the spirit of inspiration in fine arts, children's and science museums and in world-famous colleges and universities. Listen to the Boston Symphony Orchestra perform at Symphony Hall and under the stars at Tanglewood in the Berkshires. Let the Boston Pops delight you on the Charles River Esplanade.

Share the open spaces from the Mohawk Trail to Cape Cod and the islands. Journey into the past, visit the place where the Pilgrims landed and the American Revolution began. Two miles north of Plimoth Plantation is the town of Plymouth, home of the historic Plymouth Rock and Cranberry World. You can board the authentic seafaring replica of Mayflower II and admire the Pilgrims who sailed to the New World in 1620.

Read through the list of outlet centers; Massachusetts people believe in the outlet concept and support individual stores as well as factory outlet shopping centers. The larger centers are offered here for your pleasure. If you think that your favorite center should be included, fill out a recommendation form in the back of the book, just make sure that there are enough real outlet stores in the center to justify an hour's drive for a stranger to the territory.

☞ **FOR MORE INFORMATION**

Write to Americana Trail, P.O. Box BR-976, New Bedford, MA 02741. Massachusetts: Department of Environmental Mgm't, Division of Forests & Parks, 100 Cambridge St., Boston, MA 02202. Bristol County Development Council, P.O. Box BR-976, New Bedford, MA 02741. Greater Boston Convention & Tourist Bureau, Inc., Prudential Plaza West, P.O. Box 490, Dept. MA., Boston, MA 02199; (617)536-4100. The Spirit of Massachusetts, Division of Tourism, 100 Cambridge St., 13th Flr., Boston, MA 02202. Campers Headquarters Inc., MACO, King Rd. RFD, Dudley, MA 01570, (and send $1 for Campers Headquarters).

Fabulous Finds in . . .
CAPE COD

BAREFOOT OUTLET

LOCATION: In West Yarmouth, on Rte. 28.

STORES: Van Heusen Factory Store, Clothes Works, Kids Port USA, Aileen, Bass Shoe and others.

CAPE COD FACTORY OUTLET MALL

LOCATION: In Sagamore, first exit from the Sagamore Bridge as you enter the cape.

STORES: Van Heusen, Tanner Companies,

Corning, The Leather Loft, Manhattan, Aileen, US Shoe, Bass Shoe, Budget Drapery, Dunham Footwear, The Ribbon Outlet, Gitano, Top of the Line Cosmetics, Crazy Horse, American Tourister, Carter's Childrenswear, Quoddy, Campus Industries, Norwich Togs, Olde Cape Cod Stoneware, the Jewelry Outlet.

FACTORY OUTLET OF WEST YARMOUTH

LOCATION: On Rte. 28, one mile from Hyannis, five miles from Cape Cod Mall.

STORES: Van Heusen, Aileen, Bass Shoe, Health-Tex and others.

VICTORIAN VILLAGE

LOCATION: In South Yarmouth on Rte. 28. I-195 to 495 S. to Rte. 6 (Mid-Cape Hwy.); Exit 8 from Rte. 6 to Rte. 28.

STORES: American Tourister, The Ribbon Outlet, Crazy Horse, Puma, Gitano Factory

DIRECTIONS

From the North—Take 495 South to the rotary circle before the Bourne Bridge, or take Rte. 3 South to the rotary circle before the Sagamore Bridge. At either rotary, take Rte. 6 East (also known as the Mid-Cape Highway). Get off at Exit 8 and bear right to Rte. 28 and South Yarmouth.

From the South—Take I-195 North to 495 South to the rotary circle before the Bourne Bridge. At the rotary, take Rte. 6 East (also known as the Mid-Cape Highway). Get off at Exit 8 and bear right to Rte. 28 and South Yarmouth.

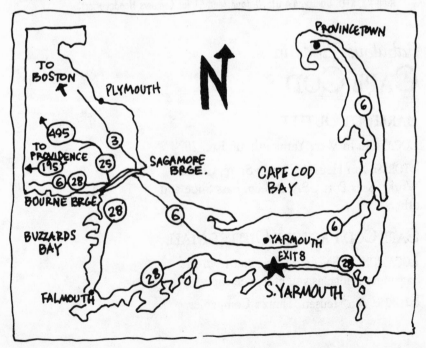

Store, Lawrence David Inc., Potpourri Catalog Outlet.

OTHER SHOPPING

Several other small centers are opening and will offer some new factory outlet stores. Cape Cod attracts money and money attracts retail. Seasonal money attracts factory outlet stores.

Fabulous Finds in . . .
FALL RIVER

Fall River is another outlet town. Stores come and go but the ones that are open when you want to shop are more than enough to make your experience memorable. In the Heart District, some fifty outlet stores can be found in the Quality Factory Outlet Center, Fall River Factory Outlet Center, Tower Mill Outlet Center, Stafford Square Area and the Flint Mills. More information can be obtained from Fall River Factory Outlet District Association (P.O. Box 2877, Fall River, MA 02722; (508)678-6033).

Be prepared to hunt for parking in several different areas. Several centers are within walking distance, so dress comfortably when you get ready to shop the Fall River factory outlet district. Is it worth it? You bet! This is an old garment-making town and if ever there was a deep discount, you will find it in Fall River.

More than 100 years ago Fall River was the largest cotton-producing center in the world. In 1656, a small band of pioneers decided to settle on the site of a former Indian encampment on the banks of the Quequechan stream in Fall River. Not only did the location provide the moist climate needed for cotton weaving, but it provided necessary water power as well. For the rest of the story, write for a *Direct Mail Catalog* (Fall River Knitting Mills, 69 Alden St., Fall River, MA 02723) or go to Fall River and marvel at the industrial ingenuity that produced those white granite mill buildings.

You will find a scattering of discounters and off-pricers in these centers. Discounters and off-pricers are essentially the same kind of operation. An opportunistic merchandise buyer can buy job lots and offer as good a discount as the manufacturer's store, but there is a difference. It pays to know your prices and brand names when you shop the discounter and off-price store. Good quality is sometimes mixed with merchandise that has mediocre fabrics or inferior construction. Buyer beware.

LOCATION: I-195 (E/W) and Rte. 24 (N/S) intersect in Fall River. From I-195 take Exit 8A to Rte. 24, Exit 2. From Rte. 24, Exit 2 to Brayton Ave. The shopping district is off Quequechan, Quarry and Pleasant Streets.

QUALITY OUTLET CENTER

Quality has its own parking lot and a lot of good factory outlet retailers. (508)677-4949.

STORES: Warnaco Outlet Store, Red Horse Factory Outlet (Crazy Horse), Intimate EVE Sleepwear, Corning/Revere Factory Store, Foster Grant Factory Outlet, Van Heusen Factory Outlet, Home Fashions, Candy & Nut Center, 1,000,000 Earrings, Back Alley, Buxton Tie Store, Top of the Line Cosmetics & Fragrance, Classic Fashions by Micki, Table Linen Factory by D. Clarkson Ltd., Handbag Factory Outlet, Fall River Jewelry Factory Outlet, Rolane, Trina Factory Outlet for purse organizers etc., Karen Anne Manufacturing Luggage, G.H. Bass, Devon Factory Outlet, Eric Allen, Dunham Footwear, Ribbon Outlet, Nancee Silk Flowers, Mighty

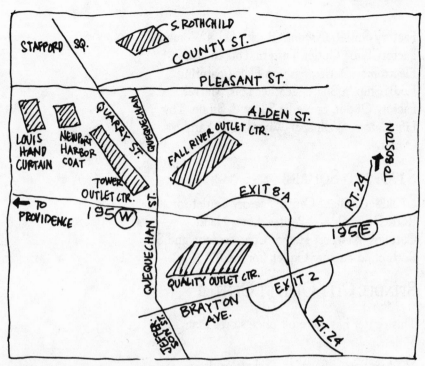

Mac, Swank Factory Outlet, Mainely Bags,
Aileen Factory Outlet, Turquoise Jewelry,
Manhattan Factory Store, Mackintosh of New
England, Crystal Works Factory Outlet,
Vassarette Factory Outlet, Hyde Athletic,
Jonathan Logan, Cranston Fabric & Craft
Outlet.

FALL RIVER OUTLET CENTER

STORES: Adidas Outlet, Branded Shoe Outlet,
Card & Giftwrap Factory Outlet, Curtain
Factory Outlet, Designer Depot, Executive
Neckware Outlet, F.R. Coats, Fall River Factory
Outlet, Garment Center Factory Outlet for R&K
Originals, Golden Branch, Kidstuff Outlet, New
England Sportswear Outlet, Teddy Bear Infants
& Children, The Towel Place, Women's Fashion
Jewelry, Yankee Men's & Women's.

TOWER OUTLET CENTER

STORES: Ashley Scott Factory Outlet, Bay State
Trading Co., Carter's Childrenswear, Converse

Factory Outlet, Discount Books, D.J.'s Woman's
Factory Shoe Outlet, Eastern Tots to Teens,
Electronics Outlet, Fashion Flair (featuring
Izod), Ship 'n Shore, Leather Loft, Marvel
Factory Outlet, Sante Fe Silver & Stone, Toy
Liquidators, Wallpaper Wizard, The Yarn
Outlet.

STAFFORD SQUARE

STORES: Garment Center Factory Outlet for
R&K Originals and Petites, Louis Hand
Curtains, Newport Harbor Coat Factory, and S.
Rothschild Factory Outlet (for men).

SPINDLE CITY OUTLET CENTER

This center has more off-price stores than
outlets.

STORES: Bag & Baggage, Baskets & Brass,
Country Crafts, Darwood Factory Outlet,
Felicia's Gift & Housewares Outlet, Golden
Treasures, Kopper Kettle, The Raincoat Outlet
and other stores with merchandise discounted.

The brochure from the Fall River Factory
Outlet Center Merchants Association will show
other stores and information that you will want.

Fabulous Finds in . . .
LENOX

LENOX HOUSE COUNTRY SHOPS

The specialty shops, factory stores and eateries
are located in picturesque wooden buildings.
Nearby are cultural and recreational activities—
Tanglewood, Jacobs Pillow, Berkshire Theatre
Festival and Shakespeare and Company. You can
experience the pleasures of a day in the country.

LOCATION: In the heart of Berkshire County, two

miles south of Pittsfield near the intersection of US Rtes. 7, 7A and 20. From the Massachusetts Turnpike (Rte. 90), take Exit 2.

STORES: Designers Only Adolfo Women's Apparel, the Outpost at Lenox, Quoddy Factory Outlet, Corning Factory Outlet, Manhattan Factory Outlet, Banister, Bass Shoe, Sheaffer Eaton Outlet, Leather Loft, harvé benard, Top of the Line Cosmetics, Crazy Horse and others.

Fabulous Finds in . . .
NEW BEDFORD

HOWLAND PLACE

LOCATION: 651 Orchard St., New Bedford, MA 02744; (800)327-SHOP. Take I-195 to 140 south. It's a winding path that leads to great shopping here! (See map on following page.)

STORES: Alexander Julian, harvé benard, Hickey Freeman, First Choice (Escada, Laure, Crisca), Oleg Cassini, Royal Doulton, Williwear, Natori, Alessi, I.B. Diffusion, Bourgeat, Fenn Wright & Manson, Crystal Factory, Fanny Farmer, Samuel Robert, Putumayo, Hamilton Watch (and Swatch), Jindo Furs, Alexon, LaMarca (with Carlos Falchi), Vanity Jewelers, Shades of Cape Cod, and Matt Garrett's full-service restaurant.

Fabulous Finds in . . .
NORTH DARTMOUTH

North Dartmouth lies between Fall River and New Bedford.

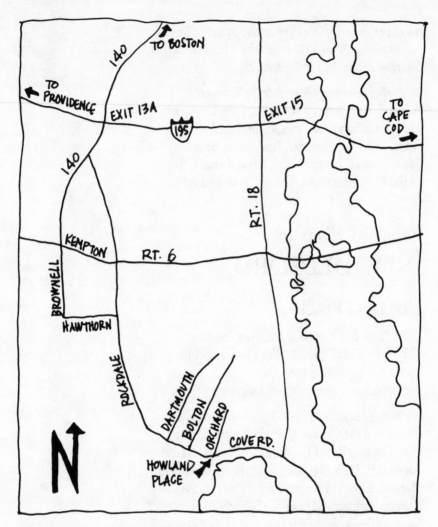

VF FACTORY OUTLET

LOCATION: Take I-195 to Faunce Corner and the Vanity Fair Outlet Center is a half mile north. (617)998-3311. (See map on facing page.)

STORES: **American Tourister Factory Outlet.** Quality American Tourister Luggage, business cases, totes at 40% to 70% off regular prices.

Banister. The official outlet for U.S. Shoe, the world's largest shoe manufacturer, so you can save up to ½ every day on thousands of shoes for men, women, dress, casual and athletic.

DIRECTIONS
From Boston and points north—Take 140 south to end. Cross Kempton St. (Rte. 6) and continue down Brownell. At Hawthorn St. turn left. Take right onto Rockdale Ave. Turn left at third traffic light (Orchard St.).

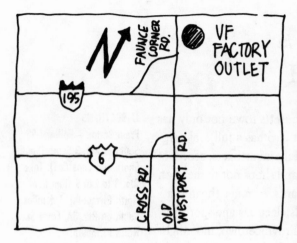

From New York City — Take I-95 North to Providence, RI, then I-195 East to Faunce Corner, No. Dartmouth Exit, left onto Faunce Corner Rd., ½ mile to Factory Outlet on right. From Boston — Take I-93 South to Rte. 24 South, then South on 24 to Rte. 140 South, then Rte. 140 South to I-195 West (New Bedford). Take Faunce Corner Exit, right onto Faunce Corner Rd., ½ mile to Factory outlet on right.

The Clothes Hound. Men's and boys' suits, shirts, sportcoats and accessories; misses, juniors and petite sportswear.

The Jewelry Outlet. America's most popular contemporary fashion jewelry lines, famous brand name watches, clocks, 14K gold jewelry, sterling silver etc.

Jonathan Logan Outlet. Men's, women's and half size rainwear, R&K Originals, Alice Stuart and Villager coordinated sportswear in petite, and half sizes.

Prestige Fragrance & Cosmetics. World-famous prestigious brands of men's and women's fragrances, toiletries, cosmetics and related accessories.

Vanity Fair. Sets the mood for savings with signs that say everything is for sale at half price. They sell activewear, jeans, knit and woven shirts, outerwear, pants, shorts, socks, sweaters, sweatwear, swimwear and underwear . . . and lots of other wardrobe staples.

Van Heusen Factory Store. First-quality Van Heusen, Lady Van Heusen and designer brand apparel.

Fabulous Finds in . . .
PLYMOUTH

This charming Massachusetts town not only has the famous Rock, but it also has a full-scale replica of the Mayflower, Pilgrim artifacts, scores of museums, restorations and shops not to mention famous seafood restaurants, summer theater, a winery and resort motels, deep sea and sport fishing, cruises to historic Provincetown, moonlight excursions around Cape Cod Bay and the exciting Whale Watch Cruises. Write the Plymouth Area Chamber of Commerce (91 Samoset St., Plymouth, MA 02360) for more information.

Visit Plymouth Rock and the Old Fort, the Winery located on Pinewood Road, and the Cranberry World Visitors Center where you can see a working cranberry bog, sample free cranberry drinks, and see interesting displays. For additional information on places to eat and sleep, write to Plimoth Plantation (P.O. Box 1620C, Plymouth, MA 02360); (617)746-1622.

DIRECTIONS

From Boston — Follow I-93 South to Rte. 3 South (South Shore and Cape Cod). Take Rte. 3 to Exit 9 (Kingston/North Plymouth). 1½ miles South on Rte. 3A, Court St., North Plymouth.

From Providence — Take Rte. 44 East all the way to the intersection of Rte. 3A, Court St., Plymouth. Take left onto 3A. Follow 1½ miles North.

From Cape Cod — Follow Rte. 6 West to Rte. 3 North (Boston & Plymouth). Take Rte. 3 to Exit 9 (Kingston/North Plymouth). 1½ miles South on Rte. 3A, Court St., North Plymouth.

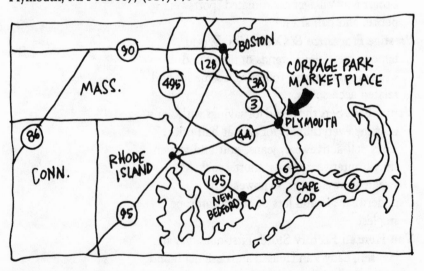

CORDAGE PARK MARKETPLACE

You are going to love this factory outlet center. The buildings once housed the Plymouth Cordage Company, which evolved into the world's largest manufacturer of rope and twine. During the nineteenth century, sailing ships, including the *U.S.S. Constitution*, relied on the superb craftsmanship that characterized Plymouth Cordage products. During its 142 years of continuous production, the Plymouth Cordage Company had a profound effect on the economic and social development of the Plymouth community as the town's largest employer.

LOCATION: On Court Street (Rte. 3A). Call (508) 746-7707 for directions.

STORES: Aileen Factory Outlet, American Tourister Factory Outlet Store, Athletic Outlet, Banister Shoe Outlet, Bass Shoe Outlet, Classic Fashions by Micki, Cape Cod Confections, Cape Isle Knitters, Children's Choice, Clothes Works, Crazy Horse Outlet, Dunham Footwear, Eric Allan, harvé benard, Jindo Furs, Kids Port USA, Kitchen Collection, Leather Loft, Lucia, that's me!, Maidenform Outlet, Mainely Bags, Manhattan Factory Outlet, Mill Store, Prestige Fragrance & Cosmetics, Quoddy Crafted Footwear, Ribbon Outlet, Socks Galore & More, Stephanie Kay Ltd., Towle, Toy Liquidators, Van Heusen Factory Store, Artesan Imports, Bridget's: An Irish Tradition, British Image, Cotton's Country Collection, Country Classics by Dianthus Ltd., numerous gift and specialty stores (including a baseball card shop) and a full-service restaurant.

FABULOUS FINDS

IN

MICHIGAN

Twenty percent of the fresh water in the world fills the five Great Lakes. Four of these freshwater giants border Michigan for more than two thousand miles—the distance between Los Angeles and Chicago. These lakes are even visible from the moon. Surrounded by big water and laced with inland lakes and streams, the two peninsulas of Michigan become one of the glorious recreational discoveries of the globe.

Early road builders, challenged by streams, rivers and lakes, found many ways over the waters. Cross over one of the three international bridges to Michigan through a border as hospitable as a handshake. From Canada, take the Ambassador Bridge to Port Huron and the International Bridge to Sault Ste. Marie. When you visit Michigan, watch for a panorama of bridges.

Seekers of solitude from Hiawatha to Hemingway have found it in Michigan's woods. In some woods, the tall pines all but seal out the sun. The leaves of oak, sumac and birch rustle beneath your feet. Michigan's woods cover half of the total landscape. At 3.8 million acres, Michigan has the largest state forest system in the country.

Hospitality is all around you when you visit Michigan. Lunch on a terrace on the banks of the St. Clair River and watch the big boats wend by. Have a fine dinner at the beautifully restored depot in Ann Arbor and ride the train back to Detroit. Feast on fish in the little fishing town of Bayport or try a pastie, the Upper Peninsula's hearty meat and potato pastry. Savor the famous chicken dinner in Frankenmuth. A warm tradition of welcome is waiting for you in Michigan.

Just for fun, write for a copy of the *Innsider* (P.O. Box 389, Hazel Park, MI 48030) and dream about owning and running a country inn. The ads and offerings are a trip through fantasy land. Michigan Travel Bureau has some interesting publications. They offer a bed and breakfast directory, cabins and cottages directory, campground directory, canoeing directory, charterboat directory, fishing guide, golf directory and a hotel/motel directory.

☞ FOR MORE INFORMATION

For more information or publications, write the Michigan Travel Bureau, Dept. TPS, P.O. Box 30226, Lansing, MI 48909. For additional service, the Michigan Travel Bureau maintains twenty-four-hour toll-free hotlines. Try these for help: (800)543-2937 or (800)722-8191 if you live in Michigan, or (800)292-5404 or (800)248-5708 if you live out of state. For a list of Detroit attractions and a map, contact the Metropolitan Detroit Convention & Visitors Bureau, Suite 1950, 100 Renaissance Ctr., Detroit, MI 48243; (313)259-4333. For Michigan's bed and breakfasts, try the Michigan Travel Bureau (as listed above) or the Michigan Traveler, 422 W. Congress, Detroit, MI 48226; (313)963-8500. Michigan also has regional tourist associations for the Upper Peninsula, West Michigan, East Michigan and Southeast Michigan, and numerous Convention and Visitors Bureaus and Chambers of Commerce.

Fabulous Finds in . . .
BIRCH RUN

MANUFACTURER'S MARKETPLACE

Note: Manufacturer's Marketplace owns several outlet centers throughout the state. General information for all locations can be obtained by calling (800)866-5900.

LOCATION: At exit 136 from I-75.

STORES: Paul Revere Shoppe, Van Heusen Factory Store, Socks Galore, Manhattan Factory Outlets, Aunt Mary's Yarns, Banister Shoe

DIRECTIONS
From Port Huron (81 miles) — Take I-96 West to I-475 to I-75 North to Exit 136.

Outlet, The Wallet Works, Kitchen Collection,
Carter's Childrenswear, totes, Corning Factory
Store, The Paper Factory, Jonathan Logan
Outlet, Old Mill, Gitano, Fashion Flair, Kids Port
USA, Top of the Line Cosmetics, American
Tourister, Pfaltzgraff, Leather Manor, Cluett,
Swank, Cape Craftsman, Aileen, Wisconsin Toy,
OshKosh B'Gosh, Oneida, Fieldcrest Cannon,
Bass Shoe, Kenneth Knits, Pilgrim Glass, Fuller
Brush, Trendsetter Footwear, Salem China, Just
My Size, Sportland USA, Farah Factory Store,
Pewter Creations, King's Row Fireplace & Gifts,
Jeweler's Outlet, Fashion-n-Fun Costume
Jewelry, Sports Wearhouse, Becca Women's
Apparel, Tool Warehouse, Sweatshirt Co,
Fashion Accents Costume Jewelry, Newport
Sportswear, Barbizon Lingerie, Cape Isle
Knitters, Levi Strauss Specials, Ideas, L'eggs/
Hanes/Bali, Multiples Modular Knits, Hathaway,
Salem China, Just My Size and other specialty
shops.

THE VILLAGE SHOPS AT BIRCH RUN

LOCATION: On I-71 across from Manufacturer's
Marketplace.

STORES: Liz Claiborne, Anne Klein, Gilligan
O'Malley, harvé benard, Mikasa, Jindo Furs,
Maidenform, Eagles Eye, Nike, Capezio, Bruce
Alan Bags, Palm Beach, Crystal Works, Prestige
Fragrances & Cosmetics, Fenn Wright &
Manson, Adolfo II, American Tourister, Argenti,
E.J. Plum, Etienne Aigner, Gant Company Store,
He-Ro Group Outlet, J. Crew Factory Store, J.G.
Hook Company Store, Jones New York Factory
Store, Jordache, Just Kids Outlet Store, Kitchen
Place, Linen Mill, Sassafras, Villeroy & Boch,
Wemco, Windsor Shirt Co.

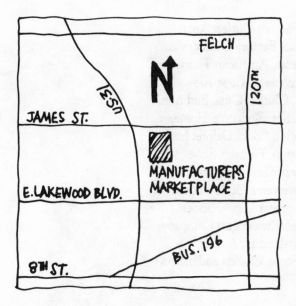

DIRECTIONS

From Grand Rapids (30 minutes) — Take 196 West to Business 196 to U.S. 31 North 1 mile to James St.

From Muskegon (31 miles) — Take U.S. 31 South to James St. (Holland).

From Kalamazoo (55 miles) — Take U.S. 131 North to M89 (M40) West to U.S. 31 North to James St.

From Benton Harbor (54 miles) — From the I-94/U.S. 31 (196) Interchange take U.S. 31 North, through Holland to James St.

From Battle Creek (68 miles) — Take M89 West to M40 West to U.S. 31 North to James St.

Fabulous Finds in . . .

HOLLAND

MANUFACTURER'S MARKETPLACE AT DUTCH VILLAGE

LOCATION: Accessible from I-196, I-94, U.S. 131, M89 and M40. Take any of these to U.S. 31. The center is at the intersection of U.S. 31 and James St.

STORES: Next to Dutch Village: Hush Puppies, Book Warehouse, Kids Port USA, Paper Factory, Famous Designer Outlet, Tanner Factory Store, Knits by K.T., Tiffany Lamp, Dress Barn, Toy Liquidators, Old Mill, Fieldcrest Cannon, Brass Town, Alpine Almonds, Cheri's Jewelry, Marketplace Jewelry, Fanny Farmer, Kilwin's, Mackintosh of New England, Nickels Company

Store, Leather Manor Factory Outlet, Anko
Also, Winona Knits, Bass Factory Outlet, Van
Heusen, Sneakers-n-Cleats, American Tourister,
Manhattan, Hanes Activewear, Cape Isle
Knitters, Wallet Works, Clothes Outs, Barbizon,
Aileen, The Ribbon Outlet, Welcome Home,
Top of the Line Cosmetics, Socks Galore, harvé
benard, Kitchen Collection, Banister Shoes,
Gitano, Carter's Childrenswear, Pfaltzgraff,
Bugle Boy, Action Housewares Outlet, Eddie
Bauer Outlet Store, Jonathan Logan, Socks
Galore, Just About Perfect, Sweatshirt Company,
Famous Footwear, Sportsland USA, Black &
Decker, Farah Factory Store, Oneida and others.

Fabulous Finds in . . .
MONROE

MANUFACTURER'S MARKETPLACE

LOCATION: I-75 to Exit 11 (LaPlaisance Rd.).

STORES: WestPoint Pepperell, Midway Leather,
China Plus, Aunt Mary's Yarn, Sport
Wearhouse, Jordache, Book Warehouse, Stone

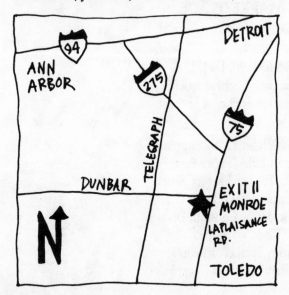

DIRECTIONS

From Windsor/Downtown De-
troit (45 miles) — Take I-75
South to Exit 11.

From Toledo (15 miles) —
Take I-75 North to Exit 11.

From Ann Arbor (43 miles) —
Take I-94 East to I-275 South
to I-75 South, to Exit 11.

From Jackson (84 miles) —
Take I-94 East to I-275 South
to I-75 South, to Exit 11.

Mountain Handbag, Multiples Modular Knits,
Evan-Picone, Fragrance World, Banister Shoe,
McGregor, Henson-Kickernick, Socks Galore,
Wemco, Welcome Home, Barbizon Lingerie,
Cape Isle Knitters, Just My Size, Hanes
Activewear, Dress Barn, Old Mill, Specials by
Levi, Johnstons Fashions for Children, Farah
Factory Store, Tool Warehouse, Swank, Knits by
K.T., Captree, Aileen, Corning/Revere, Factory
Store, harvé benard, Salem China, Sportsland
USA, Sneakers-n-Cleats, Royal Robbins,
Maidenform, Fanny Farmer, The Ribbon Outlet,
Gold-n-Treasures, The Jewelry Wave, Tiffany
Lamps, Brass Factory, Kilwin's, Top of the Line
Cosmetics, Leather Manor, Manhattan, Paper
Factory, Gitano, Bass Factory Outlet, Socks
Galore, Nilani, Carter's Childrenswear, Ideas,
Van Heusen, Famous Footwear, Wallet Works,
American Tourister, L'eggs/Hanes/Bali, Kitchen
Collection, Sweatshirt Co., Toy Liquidators.

Fabulous Finds in . . .
ROCKFORD
ROCKFORD FACTORY OUTLET MALL
LOCATION: 235 Main St., right at the
manufacturing plant. (See map on following
page.)
STORES: Little Red Shoe House, Clothes Hound
(another way of saying Palm Beach), Winona
Knitting Mills, Clothes Works and other little
shops.

Fabulous Finds in . . .
TRAVERSE CITY
The Sleeping Bear Dunes National Lakeshore,
Gold Coast Golf Course, Interlochen Center for

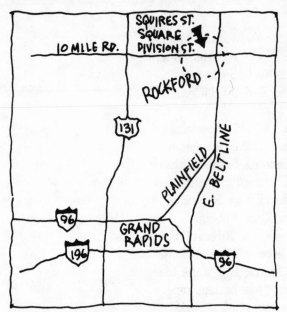

DIRECTIONS
Rockford is twenty minutes north of Grand Rapids with access from new U.S. 131 at 10 Mile Rd., just west of the city limits.

the Arts and the National Cherry Festival are there also for your pleasure.

THE MANUFACTURER'S MARKETPLACE

LOCATION: Grand Traverse County, on the U.S. 31/M37 junction near Wyatt Rd., three miles west of downtown Traverse City. (See map on facing page.)

STORES: Jordache, Levi Strauss Specials, Corning, Great Outdoors, Hush Puppies, Kitchen Collection, Gitano, Bass Shoe, L'eggs/Hanes/Bali, Eddie Bauer, Barbizon, Polly Flinders, Leather Manor, Fragrance World, Banister Shoe, Carter's, Bugle Boy, Book Warehouse, Westport Ltd., Welcome Home, Stone Mountain, Swank, Famous Brands Housewares, Russell Mills, Socks Galore, Great Outdoor Clothing, with more to come.

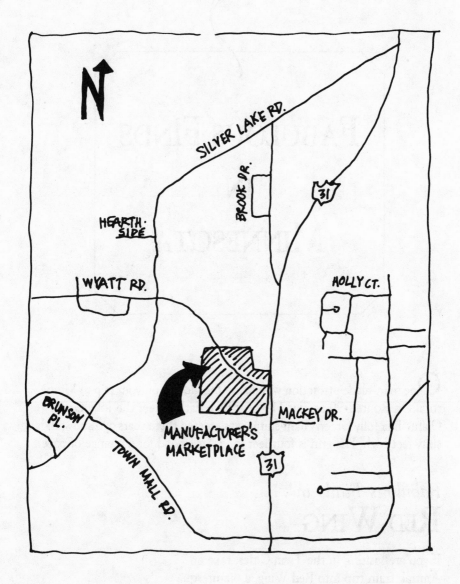

FABULOUS FINDS IN MINNESOTA

One man-made attraction will please the kiddies on your trip to Minnesota. On Route I-90 at Exit 119 near Blue Earth, meet the Jolly Green Giant. The Jolly Green Giant statue was erected there years ago and stands sixty feet high. His grin is four feet long. He's good for a change of pace.

Fabulous Finds in . . .
RED WING

If you are visiting in the Twin Cities, take an Amtrak train trip into Red Wing, a picturesque river town tucked between Barn Bluff and Sorin's Bluff along the wide Mississippi. In the 1700s, early French explorers sighted the bluffs that now protect the city. In the 1880s, Chief Red Wing and the Dakota Indians greeted the first white settlers who came to live beside the Mississippi.

When you travel to Red Wing, the bays, channels and sloughs of the river leave a lasting impression on you. Life in Red Wing revolves around the natural beauty of the area. The river gives romance to this gracious town where historic preservation plays a major role. The river offers boating, fishing and water skiing, while sportsmen enjoy hunting wildlife in the nearby bluffs with a camera or a gun. The bluffs provide downhill and cross-country skiing and snowmobiling in winter as well as hiking and hang gliding in the warm weather. Does this sound like fun?

The St. James Hotel, built in 1875, and the Pottery Place have been splendidly restored to offer luxurious sleeping overlooking the river. The Pottery Place factory outlet center was the home of Red Wing Potteries until 1967 and part of the original equipment is still in place. Exposed brick and old wood floors add an authentic ambience.

RED WING POTTERY SALES

LOCATION: 1995 W. Main St.; (612)338-3562. (See map on following page.)

STORES: Banister Shoe, Little Red Shoe House, Clothes Works, Wallet Works, Van Heusen, The Woolen Mill, Winona Glove Company, Munsingwear, Bass, Aileen, Prestige Fragrance & Cosmetics, Cape Isle Knits, Corning/Revere, A Small World, Vassarette Factory Store, Benetton Factory Outlet, Old Main Street Antiques, Pottery Place Restaurant, The Big Old Cone Shoppe.

WANTED
Your gems. The true shopping aficionado will always know about a few great little stores in the middle of nowhere that have wonderful buys. Researching for these little "gems," as we did for *SOS*, is expensive but you can make the difference if you think of *Fabulous Finds* when you shop.

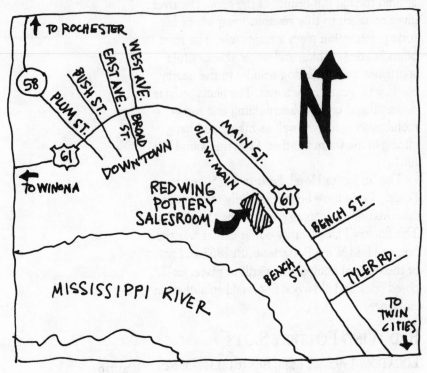

TO ROCHESTER

58

BUSH ST.

EAST AVE.

WEST AVE.

PLUM ST.

BROAD ST.

61

DOWNTOWN

TO WINONA

MAIN ST.

OLD W. MAIN

61

RED WING POTTERY SALESROOM

BENCH ST.

BENCH ST.

TYLER RD.

TO TWIN CITIES

MISSISSIPPI RIVER

N

DIRECTIONS
One hour from the Twin Cities
or Rochester, and minutes
from downtown Red Wing.

FABULOUS FINDS
IN
MISSOURI

From country ham to corn cob pipes, from autos to aerospace components—"made in Missouri" means it's made right. And when it comes to crafts—something handmade by a skillful artisan—whether woven, thrown, carved or sewn—it is a treasure to be enjoyed.

The Oregon and Santa Fe trails, which originated in Independence, sent many a hopeful pioneer on the hard journey west. There were no outlets on those trails you can bet! Everything was handcrafted, and a strong Missouri tradition for crafts began. The Ozarks—through which many craft shops and fairs are spread—are especially noted for crafts.

Missouri has a surefire recipe for vacation fun—"All you do is add water." In Missouri, adding water doesn't make mud, especially when the water is from Missouri's 902,000 acres of water, split between rivers and lakes. Missouri has plenty of water for boating, skiing, swimming, fishing or just plain relaxing. The Lake of the Ozarks, for example—created when the Bagnell Dam was built across the Osage River—accounts for more than 65,000 acres of water and boasts numerous developed attractions. Natural lakes, surrounded by thousands of acres of public land, can be enjoyed for hunting, camping, hiking and other outdoor fun.

Missouri's rivers have always been highways—liquid thoroughfares for

Indians, explorers and settlers. It's no coincidence that many of their great cities and historic communities are river towns. And Hannibal—one of the state's most famous river towns—houses Mark Twain's boyhood home, a must-see visit for anyone traveling northeastern Missouri.

Fabulous Finds in . . .
BRANSON

Branson is very close to a variety of water facilities. During the past few years, Branson has become known for fine country music entertainment and family attractions.

FACTORY MERCHANTS

LOCATION: On Hwy. 76.

STORES: Carter's, Aileen, Kitchen Collection, Fashion Flair, Paul Revere Shoppe, Oneida, Polly Flinders, Van Heusen, Bass, The Wallet Works, Campus, Banister Shoe, Manhattan, Prestige Fragrance & Cosmetics, Jaymar, harvé benard, Socks Galore, Ribbon Outlet, Jonathan Logan, Corning, Cape Isle, Dunn Woodcrafters, Toys Unlimited, Rawlings, The Leather Factory, Sans Souci, Gitano, totes, Fieldcrest Cannon, Welcome Home, Famous Footwear, Bruce Alan Bags, Little Red Shoe House, OshKosh B'Gosh, Book Warehouse, Mushroom Shoes, Tanner Factory Store, Pfaltzgraff, London Fog Factory Store, Evan-Picone Factory Store, American Tourister and others.

Fabulous Finds in . . .
LEBANON

VF FACTORY OUTLET

LOCATION: 2020 Industrial Dr., I-44, exit 129/ Hwy. 5 south; (417)588-4142.

THINGS TO SEE AND DO
When you visit St. Louis, be sure to ride the Gateway Arch Tram to the observation room at the top; (314)982-1410. And try the Anheuser-Busch Brewery tour through the brewhouse, bottling and packaging plant and the Clydesdale stables; (314)577-2626. See St. Louis Union Station, beautifully restored as a retail complex; (314)421-6655. St. Louis Zoological Park is home to more than 2,500 animals; (314)781-0900. Thirty minutes from St. Louis, ski Hidden Valley; (314)938-5373. Eight miles from Eureka (in the St. Louis area), visit the Black Madonna Shrine and Grotto; (314)938-5361. Poco Loco Western Town in High Ridge (close to Eureka) is an 1870s western town with historic furnishings; (314)376-4561. If you are traveling west, stop at the Stone Hill Winery at the intersection of U.S. 19 and 100 in Hermann. Tours and wines are available; (314)486-2221. The Onondaga Cave is not too far from the winery; make a side trip to see the largest cave in Missouri. It is just off Rte. 44; (314)245-6200.

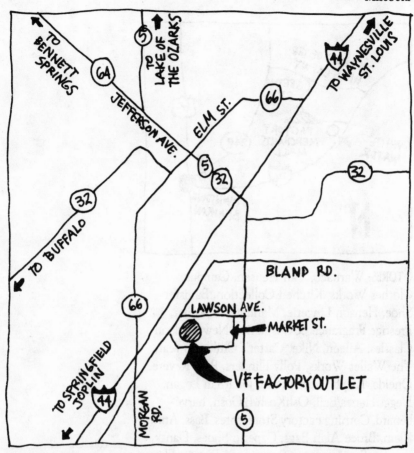

STORES: VF Factory Outlet, Banister Shoe, Jonathan Logan, The Paper Factory, Prestige Fragrance & Cosmetics, Evan-Picone, totes, Van Heusen, Corner Stores, Your Toy Center, Reading Bag.

DIRECTIONS
From St. Louis — Take I-44 West to Exit 129/Hwy. 5 South. Turn right onto Lawson Ave. to Market St. Turn left to VF Factory Outlet.
From Springfield — Take I-44 East to Exit 129/Hwy. 5 South. Turn right onto Lawson Ave. to Market St. Turn left to VF Factory Outlet.

Fabulous Finds in ...
OSAGE BEACH

While at Osage Beach enjoy the Lake of the Ozarks and its fine water sports.

FACTORY MERCHANTS MALL AT OSAGE VILLAGE

LOCATION: On Hwy. 54 in a quaint shopping center.

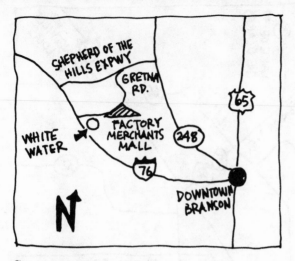

STORES: Warnaco, Van Heusen, Campus, Clothes Works, Kitchen Collection, Banister Shoe, Henson Lingerie, Manhattan, Jaymar, Prestige Fragrance & Cosmetics, New England Classics, Aileen, Nike, Carter's Childrenswear, The Wallet Works, Polly Flinders, Paul Revere, Oneida, Ralph Lauren/Polo, Jonathan Logan, L'eggs/Hanes/Bali, OshKosh B'Gosh, harvé benard, Corning Factory Store, totes, Bass, Anne Klein, Bruce Alan Bags, Capezio Shoes, Dansk, London Fog, Leggoons Sportswear, Factory Shoe Outlet, Hanes Activewear, The Ribbon Outlet, Gant Company, Evan-Picone, Izod Company Store, J.G. Hook Company Store and Toys Unlimited.

Fabulous Finds in . . .

WENTZVILLE

BELZ FACTORY OUTLET MALL

At Belz Factory Outlet Mall you buy directly from manufacturers through their outlet stores, cutting out high markups and middlemen.

LOCATION: At the intersection of I-70 and Rte. 40.

STORES: **Amy Stoudt.** Large-size work, day-into-evening and weekend wear.

Bag & Baggage. Famous-name luggage, business cases, handbags and small leather goods.

Banister Shoe Outlet. Capezio, Pappagallo, Mushroom, Liz Claiborne, Freeman, French Shriner, Reebok and other name brands at up to 50% savings.

Bookland Outlet. More than 100,000 books at discounts up to 90%.

Burlington Coat Factory Warehouse. Woman's, children's, and men's wear; London Fog raincoats for men and women; also, dresses, sportswear, handbags, children's wear, men's clothing, shoes, linens and bath accessories at savings of 25%-70%.

Burlington Shoe. Men's, women's and children's dress and casual styles and a large selection of athletic shoes for women and men at savings of 20-60%.

Crown Jewels. Fashion jewelry at 50% off.

Dress Barn. Famous updated women's fashion labels at 20-50% off.

Famous Footwear. Brands like Reebok, Nike, Adidas, Jacqueline, Mushrooms, Candies, Nunn Bush, French Shriner.

Fieldcrest Cannon/Beacon Linens. Featuring selected closeouts, discontinued and slight imperfections on towels, sheets, pillowcases, bedspreads, comforters, blankets, bath rugs/sets and kitchen accessories.

Gitano's. Savings of up to 50% on casual and active sportswear lines.

Gold Connection. 14K gold jewelry, custom design, repair, fine estate jewelry and coins.

Jewelie's. Costume earrings, necklaces, bracelets, gift items, watches, perfumes, clocks, key chains and more.

Kitchen Collection. Factory outlet for WearEver cookware and Proctor-Silex appliances: dinnerware, stemware, flatware, table linens, giftware, cookware and more.

L'eggs/Hanes/Bali. Save 20-50% and more on slightly imperfects, closeouts and overstocks on hosiery, underwear, lingerie, socks, activewear and more.

Mikasa Factory Store. Dinnerware, stemware, flatware, table linens, giftware, cookware, etc.

Music Vision. 45s, LPs, cassettes, compact discs, recording tapes, record care products, carrying cases and posters.

Old Mill Ladies' Sportswear. Exclusive factory outlet for women's apparel at 25-70% savings.

Old Time Pottery. Wicker baskets, silk flowers and arrangements, crafts, lamps, pictures, pottery, dinnerware, crystal, cookware, bakeware.

Plumm's. First-quality styles for work, day-into-evening and weekend wear at 20-50% off.

Reading Footwear. Save 25% and more on Weejuns, Bucs, Sunjuns and other footwear and accessories.

Regal. Cookware and kitchen appliances—stainless steel, cast aluminum and drawn aluminum range-top cookware, microwave ovenware and accessories, food processors, electric knives, juicers, coffeemakers and corn poppers, vacuum cleaners and air cleaners.

The Ribbon Outlet. More than 2,500 varieties of first-quality ribbon and trims—cut your own "by the yard," precut or entire spools in bulk; also, handcrafted gift items, selected craft supplies, novelty and seasonal items.

Top of the Line Cosmetics. Designer and brand name cosmetics and fragrances at 25-75% off; also, gift sets, makeup brushes, skin care, travel bags and designer fragrances for men and women.

Toy Liquidators. Thousands of brand name toys at less than manufacturer's original wholesale prices.

FABULOUS FINDS
IN
NEW HAMPSHIRE

No matter when you go or how long you stay, New Hampshire is filled with new discoveries and fond memories. The seasons change but there is always something to do and see. The scenery is spectacular regardless of the time of year that you visit this state.

In the spring, budding trees and blossoming wildflowers lift the spirit. Streams rushing with snow-melt invite you to fish, canoe or kayak. Or you can visit one of the many sugar shacks where sap is transformed into pure maple syrup.

Summer means a visit to the White Mountains. Mt. Washington rises 6,288 feet above sea level and is the highest mountain north of the Carolinas and east of the Rockies. Legend has it that the Indians never ascended Mt. Washington because they believed this mountain to be the private dwelling place of their gods. Thousands of tourists visit the top to enjoy the awe-inspiring grandeur and vista.

The countryside explodes with color in the fall. Autumn foliage at its peak, and "Golden Pond's" tranquility—broken only by the call of the loon—will renew your spirits and help you get in touch with yourself.

Winter means skiing in the White Mountains alongside World Cup racers. Roam the picturesque mountains, refreshing rivers and streams any time of year. Visit the coast or the music festivals. New Hampshire is a state of mind that always feels right. Treat yourself to a bed 'n breakfast when you visit here.

Fabulous Finds in . . .
CONWAY/
NORTH CONWAY

Rte. 16 is "outlet highway." Browse up one side of the town and down the other. North Conway is the jumping-off point and revitalization center for mountain lovers as it is the gateway to the Mt. Washington Valley area.

CONWAY CROSSING OUTLET CENTER

LOCATION: On Rte. 16. (See map on facing page.)

STORES: Crystal Works, Leather Loft, Jonathan Logan, American Tourister, Prestige Fragrance & Cosmetics.

L.L. BEAN SHOPPING CENTER

STORES: L.L. Bean Outlet Store, harvé benard, Anne Klein, Oneida Silver, Cole-Haan, J.G. Hook, Ellen Tracy, Evan-Picone Outlet, Gant and Joan & David Shoes.

LIZ CLAIBORNE CENTER

STORES: Calvin Klein and Liz Claiborne.

MT. WASHINGTON FACTORY OUTLET CENTER

STORES: Timberland Factory Outlet, Van Heusen, Revere Shoppe, Aileen, Londontown,

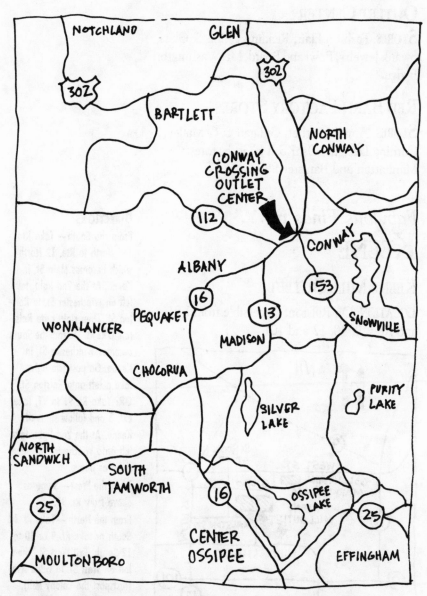

Le Sportsac, Cape Isle Knitters and Chuck Roast.

MOUNTAINVIEW OUTLET CENTER
STORES: Campus, Wallet Works, Barbizon and others.

DIRECTIONS
From Fryeburg (ME) and points east — Rte. 302 into Conway Village (NH) at junction of Rte. 16 & 153.

NORTH CONWAY FACTORY OUTLET CENTER

STORES: Fashion Flair, Reading China & Glass, Swank Jewelry, Bowl and Board, Mt. Washington Fudge.

RED BARN FACTORY STORES

STORES: Amity Leather, Gilligan & O'Malley, Corning Designs, OshKosh B'Gosh, totes, Manhattan and Banister Shoe.

Fabulous Finds in . . .

KEENE

KEENE MILL OUTLET

LOCATION: On Ralston. Accessible from I-91 and Rtes. 9, 10, 12 and 101.

STORES: Aileen, Shoe Bazaar, Kids Clothing Studio, harvé benard, Steilmann European Selection, Gitano, AJ's Jean Outlet, The Athletic Outlook, Macgregor Sporting Goods,

DIRECTIONS

From the South—Take Rte. 140 North to Rte. 12 North which becomes Main St. in Keene. At the 2nd light, take left on Winchester St. to Ralston St. Then right onto Ralston. **OR:** Rt. 10 from the South becomes Winchester St. in Keene. Go past two lights, take a left onto Ralston St. **OR:** Take Rt. 91 to VT, take Exit 3 and follow signs to Keene. At the 2nd light, take left onto Winchester St., then same as above.

From the West—Same as above from Rt. 91.

From the North—Take Rt. 12 South or take Rt. 9 or 10 to 12 South. Exit West St., then left on West St. to Gilbo Ave. (just past the Colony Mill). Turn right.

From the East—Take Rt. 101 West. Turn right at the 2nd group of lights in Keene (Main St.). At the next light, turn left onto Winchester St. Take a right onto Ralston St.

Eric Allan, Westport Ltd., Dunham Quoddy, The Ribbon Outlet, Donn Kenny, Mighty Mac, Crazy Horse, Toy Liquidators, Bass, Book Warehouse, Van Heusen.

PANDORA OUTLET CENTER

Pandora Industries, Inc. was established more than fifty-five years ago. One of the largest sweater and sportswear manufacturers in the United States, Pandora's vertical manufacturing facilities, located in Manchester, New Hampshire, produce garments for the junior, missy, large size and children's customer. In addition, Pandora designs and manufactures a line of uniquely styled afghan-throws for home use. Pandora's sweaters and coordinated sportswear are

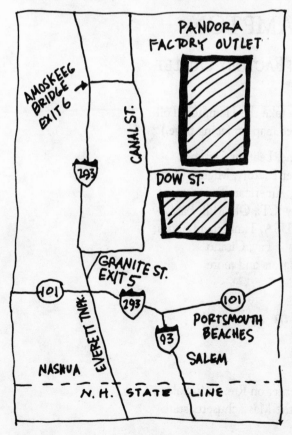

DIRECTIONS
From the North — Take Rte. 293 South to Exit 6. Cross Amoskeag Bridge to Canal St. From the South — Everett Tpk. or 93 North to 293 North to Exit 5. Right on Granite St. Left on Canal St.

styled for today's knowledgeable consumer. Pandora's New England craftsmen ensure quality by selecting only the finest yarns and fabrics. They are proud to sew the Pandora label in every garment they manufacture. Pandora sells direct from its factory to the customer at half off the nationally advertised prices.

LOCATION: I-293 to exit 6 (south) or exit 5 (north) to Canal and Dow Streets; (603)668-4802.

STORES: Pandora Industries, Burlington Coats, Carter's Childrenswear, Kayser Roth Hosiery and others.

Fabulous Finds in . . .
NORTH HAMPTON

NORTH HAMPTON FACTORY OUTLET CENTER

LOCATION: On Rte. 1 — take the Hampton Toll Gate exit from I-95. (See map on facing page.)

STORES: Welcome Home, Leather Outpost, Cape Isle Knitters, Paper Factory, Mighty Mac, Damon, Nilani, Aileen, American Tourister, Ribbon Outlet, Knits by K.T., Old Mill, Bass Shoe Outlet, Kids Port USA, Timberland Shoes, Van Heusen Shirts, Leslie Fay, Gitano, Manhattan, Toy Liquidators and more.

Fabulous Finds in . . .
SALEM

There is a small strip center on Rte. 28 in Salem, just one mile north of the Massachusetts state line.

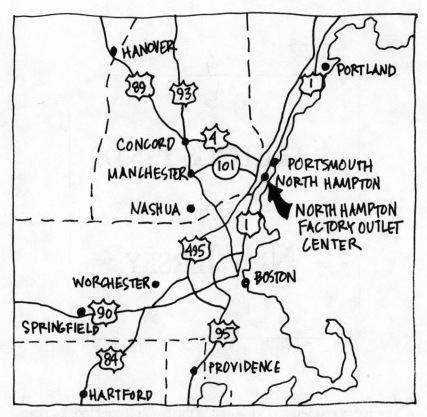

STORES: Van Heusen, Prestige Fragrance & Cosmetics, Bass, Dunham, Tooty's Good Shoes, Towels & More Factory Outlet, Aileen, Converse Factory Store, DAMART and others.

DIRECTIONS
We are located on Rte. 1, near Portsmouth.

FABULOUS FINDS
IN
NEW JERSEY

New Jersey eats out and while you're there, you should too. You can enjoy some of the best food ever if you plan your way through the state. One of the best ways to do that (aside from word-of-mouth referrals) is to write to Sheila and Steve Barbe at RRC Publications (Mountainside, NJ 07092) and ask for their free publication *New Jersey Eats Out*.

New Jersey brochures say, "So much to see, so much to do." From the Skylands Region to the Southern Shore Region below Atlantic City, New Jersey is a hustling, bustling state. Atlantic City is a world of its own and the Cape May shoreline is nature at its best.

New Jersey is only seventy miles wide and 166 miles long and is very convenient to visit. In New Jersey, the only limitation is time. You just can't see it all in one vacation. From the hustle of the boardwalk or to a deserted beach or canoeing down historic waterways, you can choose the attractions and entertainment that suit your mood.

The Garden State has always been a place of special historical, cultural and social significance. There are celebrations and festivals, folk art and colonial crafts, ballet and opera, outdoor concerts and innovative theatre for adults and children.

There is the fun and excitement of harness racing. Sophisticated nightlife. The quiet charm of an authentic pre-Revolutionary War village and more. New Jersey—diverse and exciting.

Fabulous Finds in . . .
FLEMINGTON

Numerous off-price shops and wonderful food services make this trip a full day's shopping.

LIBERTY VILLAGE

A quaint reproduction of French Revolution architecture houses more than eighty factory outlets and small, unique off-price stores. This facility has an exciting variety of current designer fashions and clothing for the whole family.

LOCATION: If you need directions, call (201)782-8550.

STORES: **Adidas Outlet.** Sportswear and accessories.

Aileen Factory Outlet. Sportswear factory direct—save to 70%.

Anne Klein Outlet. Direct factory outlet.

Bagmakers Factory Store. Handbags, casual luggage, etc.

Butcher Block Factory Outlet. Tables, carts, chairs, etc.

Calvin Klein Outlet. Jeans, skirts, sweaters and shirts.

Cambridge Dry Goods Outlet Store. Sportswear and career wear.

Capezio Shoes. Factory direct includes Bandolino and Calvin Klein.

Carter's Little Gallery. Children's clothing.

Corning Factory Outlet. Corning Ware, Pyrex, Corelle, Microwave.

Crystal Works. Stemware, bowls, vases—factory direct.

PLACES TO EAT AND SLEEP
Write to Bed & Breakfast of New Jersey Inc. (Suite 132, 103 Godwin Ave., Midland Park, NJ 07432) or call (201)444-7409 for information on where to stay if you want something different from the hotels and motels. Get to know the state by staying in accommodations that provide personal service.

Damon Factory Outlet. Damon, Bill Blass and Courcheval apparel.

Delta Hosiery Outlet. Hosiery for the family.

Eire Factory Outlet. Waterford crystal, Aynsley china at savings.

Executive Neckwear. Neckwear at factory prices.

Fenn Wright & Manson. Sportswear Systems, Intro, Workshop, etc.

First Choice. European designer sportswear at big savings.

Flemington Fur Co.'s Coat World. This is the store that put Flemington on the map along with Flemington Glass.

The Gem Vault. Gold jewelry, gems and mountings.

Hamilton Clock Factory Outlet. Fine watches and clocks.

harvé benard Outlet. Designer's collection — save up to 61%.

Joan & David Shoes. First quality — savings to 50%.

L'eggs/Hanes/Bali Factory Outlet. Closeouts and overstocks.

Manhattan Factory Outlet. Men's and women's apparel.

Perfumes Plus. Fragrances and cosmetics.

Petals Silk Flowers Factory Outlet. Silk and dried flowers.

The Ribbon Outlet. More than 3,000 varieties of ribbons and crafts.

Royal Doulton Shoppe. Fine English dinnerware.

Skyr. Cotton and wool sweaters, turtlenecks, sleepwear and more.

Sweaters Plus Outlet. Cottons, rag wools, hand knits and more.

Van Heusen Factory Outlet Store. Save up to 50%.

Village Jewelry Outlet. Gold, silver, pearls, etc.

Villeroy & Boch. Fine china and bakeware.

WANTED
Interesting and unique lodgings, not chains — they are easy to find. Think of *Fabulous Finds* as the connecting link to thousands of other travelers and think what you would like to recommend to them.

Fabulous Finds in . . .
SECAUCUS

Two shopping centers are developed in the center of the Meadowlands area. It will take more than a day to shop the blocks of stores in this area. Since it is so close to New York City, some unique shops started their outlet career right here.

There are hotels nearby, so you can sleep over and shop the next day. If you are traveling by car, the traffic is a hassle but a car is the only way to get around this large area.

LOCATION: Take the New Jersey Turnpike to Rte. 3 to the Meadowlands Parkway exit. Traffic moves fast, so read your map before you start *and* watch for signs.

HARMON COVE OUTLET CENTER

For information, call (201)348-4780.

STORES: Emerson Radio Outlet, Gourmet Kitchen Bazaar, Van Heusen Factory Outlet Store, The Company Outlet Store, Sportswear Systems, Intimate Eve, Jacques Cohen, International Gold Products, Bally Shoes and Leatherwear, Tahari, Dali B, The Children's Outlet, Brandstand Shoe, Jonathan Logan Outlet, Executive Neckwear, Maison Emanuelle, The Gold Outlet, Perfumes Plus, Damon Creations, Barbizon Lingerie Factory Outlet, East Hampton Clothing Co., Calvin Klein Outlet, Cambridge Dry Goods, The Kitchen Place, Accessories Plus, Bed 'n Bath, Fashion Flair, Secaucus Handbag Outlet, Designer Luggage Depot, Nilani Outlet, Urban Clothing Co., Campus, Gitano Factory Store, Williwear, Hosiery Mill Outlet, The Best Outlet Store, World Toys Distribution.

OTHER STORES

Some food and many outlet neighbors, including:
Mikasa, Member's Only Outlet Store, NBO
Warehouse Store, Kleter's Jewelry, Just Coats-
Central Park Outlet, Gucci, The Fur and Coat
Company, Marty's Warehouse Shoe Outlet, Liz
Claiborne Outlet Store, Natori Outlet, The En-
terprising Woman, Formfit Famous Maker Out-
let, Jindo Furs, Burlington Coat Factory Ware-
house, Carole Hochman Lingerie, Aris Isotoner
Gloves, Schrader Sport, Sasson Factory Outlet,
Biderman Industries designer clothing, Adrianna
Papell silks, Bag City, European Designer Outlet,
Suzelle-Stephanie Outlet Store, Barbara's Outlet, harvé benard, George Barry Furs, Preganetti's
Maternity Outlet, Church's English Shoes Outlet Store, Syms Corporation, Ellen Tracy Inc.,
and a constant turnover of shops that offer everything from the ridiculous to the sublime. Some
prices are fantastic and some are only slightly
discounted.

NY NY

LOCATION: 55 Hartz Way and Secaucus Rd.

STORES: This new center has the collection of
designers, some of which are named above.
Others included in this easy-to-find center are
Argenti, Icelandic Outlet, Names for Dames,
Puma, Bern Conrad, Kenar, Andrea Carrano,
Jindo Furs, Solange and they are worth your time
to shop.

FABULOUS FINDS
IN
NEW YORK

Capturing the diversity of New York state or New York City just to give you a taste for the attractions, the things to see and think about is more than one book can justly manage. Call (800)225-5697 from the lower fourty-eight, or if you are calling from Canada (518)474-4116 and use a touch-tone phone to get the exact information you want.

The map that comes as a result of pushing the right number gives you an overview of the various sections of the state. The Niagara Frontier means spectacular beauty, roaring thunder and frothy mists from the 167-foot-high falls and a gorge that is seventy miles long. The power of the Niagara River was first used to run a sawmill in 1750. Buffalo was a frontier outpost until 1825 when the Erie Canal turned it into one of the world's great inland ports.

The Finger Lakes are eleven long lakes set amid hillsides lined with vineyards. When newborn America moved away from the coastal area, the hills and plains of this fertile region became the breadbasket for the fast-growing eastern cities. The Finger Lakes headquarters New York's wine industry with more than forty wineries, many offering tours.

Central-Leatherstocking is in the heart of New York state, stretching into the foothills of the Adirondacks. Leatherstocking was used to describe the leather leggings the settlers wore to protect themselves against scratchy underbrush.

Thousand Islands-Seaway region is where two countries meet—green upstate New York, and blue Lake Ontario and the St. Lawrence River. This area was originally part of the Mohawk Indian nation. It was explored and settled by French, and later, the British colonists. Water in the rivers drain the western Adirondacks and are famous for their fishing, as canoe routes and for white-water rafting. Frederick Remington left Ogdensburg for the West and produced an unmatched collection of paintings and sculptures depicting the western frontier. F.W. Woolworth's original home was Watertown, which has had major expansion at Fort Drum.

The Adirondacks covers more than six million acres, five chains of mountains, lakes and river valleys. These mountains are made of rocks more than a billion years old, its peaks and valleys were scoured and scraped by glaciers of three ice ages, its two thousand lakes left behind when the ice retreated. It is a region that is ideal for the whole family to enjoy in all seasons and all ways.

Saratoga Springs is a center for education and entertainment. It is famous for its spas, its thoroughbred race course, and its Performing Arts Center, which is summer home to the New York City Ballet, the Philadelphia Orchestra and the New York City Opera Company. Saratoga's strategic location where the Mohawk meets the Hudson has made it both physically and historically the crossroads of New York State.

The Catskills are mountains and resorts, three thousand square miles, next to the biggest metropolis on the Atlantic seaboard. The Catskills are world famous as nightspots and recreation. Some of the biggest names in show business got their start in the famous resort hotels and nightclubs.

The Hudson Valley is grand scenery. Henry Hudson searched this valley for the Northwest Passage to the Orient. Artists established the Hudson River School of art. The Valley has earned a reputation as an antique collector's paradise. You can just follow the river from town to town. And you can find a very special factory outlet center in this area. That listing will follow this overview of New York state splendors.

Long Island is the largest island on the Atlantic seabord and yet it has room to be alone with nature. Long Island is a gift from the Ice Age. When they melted ten thousand years ago, they left behind a sand and boulder-strewn island surrounded by hundreds of miles of spectacular beaches, bluffs, barrier islands, wetlands and natural harbors. The waves of the Atlantic Ocean and Long Island Sound shaped the island's shore but the Indian Settlers, Colonial and American immigrants, farmers, tourists and commuters have shaped its landscape.

From Niagara Falls to Long Island, New York has your vacation. From Lake Ontario to the Atlantic Ocean you'll never be bored. Look at the map, choose any region and you will find natural and man-made wonders.

New York City is a man-made wonder that is known worldwide. Surely, everything known to man is available in New York City.

Where can you find more diversity of dining pleasures or art museums or cityscapes? The plays, theater, sightseeing is more than the uninitiated can undertake without serious planning.

☞ **FOR MORE INFORMATION**
Start with the New York Convention and Visitors Bureau, Inc., (212)397-8222 or (212)397-8200 and be prepared to sort through tons of materials, brochures and maps. Start early and narrow down the information so you can make sense of a state and city that are world class. Infinite pleasures, infinite possibilities.

Fabulous Finds in ...
BELLPORT ON LONG ISLAND

You can find this outlet center on Rte. 27 Sunrise Hwy. and the regular outlet tenants are all present and accounted for. Nike, Maidenform, L'eggs/Hanes/Bali, Argenti, Capezio, Crazy Horse, Wisconsin Toy, Royal Doulton, Jones New York, Van Heusen, Bass Shoe, Cape Isle Knitters, I.B. Diffusion, American Tourister, Welcome Home, Barbizon Lingerie, Fanny Farmer, Evan-Picone, Leather Loft and more stores coming.

Fabulous Finds in ...
CENTRAL VALLEY

WOODBURY COMMON

Woodbury Common is an exciting shopping village with extraordinary values for the whole family. For information, call (914)928-7467.

LOCATION: At the junction of Rte.17 and the New York State Thruway (87), Harriman exit 16.

STORES: Aileen, Van Heusen, Royal Doulton, Boston Trader, Petals Silk Flowers, Just Coats, Liz Claiborne, Leslie Fay, Anne Klein, Manhattan, Damon, Banister Shoe, Tahari, Gitano, Delta Hosiery, First Choice, harvé benard, Wallet Works, Crystal Works, Corning, Joan & David Shoes, Hamilton Clock and Watch Shop, Ribbon Outlet, Carter's Childrenswear, Adolfo, Dansk, Jindo Furs, Calvin Klein, American Tourister, Skyr, Gucci, Carole Little, Prestige Fragrance & Cosmetics, Warnaco/Divine Yard, and many other off-price stores.

Fabulous Finds in . . .

FISHKILL

FISHKILL OUTLET VILLAGE

LOCATION: At the intersection of I-84 and US 9.

STORES: Bass Shoe Factory Outlet. Factory direct prices on first-quality men's, women's and children's Bass shoes and accessories including Weejuns, Bucs, Sunjun, Sandals, boots and casual styles.

Olga Warner's. Saves shoppers 30% or more on famous-maker designer and better intimate apparel. Assortment includes first-quality bras, panties, day wear, shape wear and sleepwear from Olgas, Warners, Vanentino, Ungaro and Blanche.

Prestige Fragrance & Cosmetics. Offers world-famous brands of men's and women's fragrances, toiletries, cosmetics and accessories.

Van Heusen Factory Store. Offers 20-50% savings on extensive selection of dress shirts, accessories and sportswear for men and women.

Welcome Home, Banister Shoe, Westport Ltd., Corning Revere, Leather Loft, Hathaway, Cape Isle Knitters, Geoffrey Beene are new stores coming into the Village.

Fabulous Finds in ...
LAKE GEORGE

This recreational area is full of factory outlet clusters. Each belongs to a different owner and you will find it easy to shop if you ignore the brand names out front and just cruise one side of the street then cross over and go back along the other side. Traffic is fierce, so be careful. Alphabetically by project name you can shop the following on Rte. 9:

ADIRONDACK FACTORY OUTLET CENTER

STORES: Manhattan Factory Outlet, Swank, Van Heusen, Aileen, Barbizon Factory Outlet, Warnaco Sportswear, Corning, Champion Sportswear—and if you dig around or take kids, you will buy something, Polly Flinders and a couple of other stores.

FRENCH MOUNTAIN COMMONS

STORES: Scandia Trading (Skyr), Mighty Mac—you can see how they started this company in their profile, Fieldcrest Cannon, Little Red Shoe House and a few other stores.

LAKE GEORGE PLAZA OUTLET

STORES: harvé benard, Fenn Wright & Manson, Dansk, Polo, London Fog, Gilligan & O'Malley and others. Coming soon: Anne Klein, American Tourister, Bass Shoe and others.

LOG JAM FACTORY STORES

This is a fun place to shop and you will remember the environment as well as the stores.

STORES: Leather Loft, Maidenform, Ribbon Outlet, Banister Shoe, Prestige Fragrance & Cosmetics, totes, Carter's Childrenswear and others.

Fabulous Finds in . . .
MALTA

SARATOGA VILLAGE

LOCATION: At exit 12 off Rte. 87.

STORES: Tahari, Ribbon Outlet, Flemington Fur, Adidas Outlet, Cape Isle Knitters, Joan & David Shoes, Jones New York, Adrienne Vittadini, Sweaters Plus, Ellen Tracy, JH Collectibles, Sportswear Systems, Fanny Farmer, Gitano, Banister Shoe, Prestige Fragrance & Cosmetics, Van Heusen, Carter's Childrenswear, Manhattan, Fashion Flair, harvé benard, Dexter Shoes, Royal Doulton, Red Horse (Crazy Horse brands), Aileen, Wallet Works and more.

Fabulous Finds in . . .
MONTICELLO

APOLLO PLAZA MANUFACTURER'S OUTLET CENTER

Get ready to shop until you are either out of your charge card limits or out of energy. If you are a

PLACES TO SLEEP AND EAT
Brickman Hotel, Concord Hotel, Hotel Gibber, Grossingers, Pines Hotel, Vegetarian Hotel — and there are many more famous watering holes in the Catskills.

Restaurants are plentiful: Bernie's Holiday, Dodge Inn, El Monaco, House of Lyons, La Stella & Patsy's, The Lantern, Willie's, Monticello Raceway. The area code is (914)555-1212 if you want to check with information.

senior citizen, ask for your discount; some of the shops give 10 percent.

LOCATION: Take the Quickway exit 106 from Rte. 17. If you need directions, call (914)794-2010.

STORES: Aileen. Sportswear and activewear, with savings up to 70%.

Banister Shoe. "The 40-brand outlet."

Barbizon Factory Outlet Store. Up to 60% savings on intimate apparel.

Bass Factory Outlet. With original Bass Weejuns, Bucs and saddle shoes.

Beacon Linens. An outlet of Fieldcrest Cannon, factory direct.

Big Ben Jewelry. Savings of 40-60% on gold.

Campus Factory Outlet. First-quality men's and boy's apparel.

Clothes Works. Famous-maker sportswear.

Cluett Apparel Outlet. Arrow, Lady Arrow, Donmoor, Gold Toe.

Corning Factory Store. The biggest selection you will find of Pyrex, Visions, and Corning.

The East Hampton Clothing Co. Sportswear for misses and juniors.

Jonathan Logan. Famous-label dresses, sportswear, raincoats, etc.

Kids Port USA. Including Health-Tex labels.

Little Red Shoe House. World Wide Wolverine.

Londontown Factory Outlet Store. Famous labels, great prices.

Manhattan Factory Outlet. Sportswear for men and women.

Top of the Line Cosmetics Warehouse Outlet. With more than 50 nationally advertised brands; savings of 30-60%.

Van Heusen Factory Store.

Wallet Works. Handbags, luggage, planners, briefcases and more.

Warnaco Outlet Stores. Save 50% on leading
labels.

Fabulous Finds in . . .
NIAGARA FALLS
FACTORY OUTLET MALL

This is one of the largest outlet centers in the
state so allow plenty of time.

LOCATION: At 1900 Military Rd. near Rte. 62.
Call (716)886-0211 if you get lost.

STORES: Kids Port USA, Fanny Farmer, Aileen,
Mikasa, harvé benard, Shapes Activewear,
Kitchen Place, Calvin Klein, Benetton, Danskin,
Jaeger Outlet, Oneida, Ruff Hewn, Paper
Factory, Top of the Line Cosmetics, Caron Yarn,
Pfaltzgraff, Cape Crafts, Swank, Banister Shoe,
Van Heusen, Bass Shoe, OshKosh B'Gosh, Royal
Doulton, Polo/Ralph Lauren, Corning, Old Mill
and many others.

RAINBOW OUTLET CENTRE

LOCATION: Downtown, a half block from Niagara
Falls and close to the bridge to Canada.

STORES: Jindo Furs, Leather Loft, Prestige
Fragrance & Cosmetics, Polo/Ralph Lauren, JH
Collectibles, Designer Luggage Depot, Knits by
K.T., Joan Vass and others.

Fabulous Finds in . . .
UTICA
CHARLESTOWN FACTORY OUTLET CENTER

One of the very first outlet centers in the country
and still offering bargains. Try off-track betting

and make a little extra shopping money.

LOCATION: Located 3 ½ miles from the New
York Thruway—take exit 31 to Turner Street.

STORES: Leslie Fay Factory Outlet, Old Mill,
Carter's Childrenswear, Kids Port USA, Campus
Factory Outlet, Palm Beach, Londontown
Factory Outlet, Manhattan Factory Outlet,
Designer Factory Outlet, Van Heusen,
Munsingwear/Vassarette Factory Outlet, Bass
Shoe, Little Red Shoe House, Quoddy Crafted
Footwear.

FABULOUS FINDS IN NORTH CAROLINA

Four hundred years ago, a colony of English men and women created a new civilization on this continent. The culture and heritage in North Carolina was shaped by the people who came to America in 1584. In 1587, Virginia Dare was born, the first English child to be born in America. The 117-person colony disappeared without trace sometime between 1587 and 1591. This was known as Sir Walter Raleigh's lost colony. For more information, call (919)441-8144 or write, North Carolina Travel & Tourism Division, Dept. of Commerce, Raleigh, NC 27611.

At Edenton, ladies protested unfair taxation policy in one of the nation's earliest public demonstrations by women.

North Carolina was the last state to secede during the Civil War, yet its soldiers suffered more casualties than any other Southern state. North Carolina's proud history is studded with significant achievements that have occurred in special places and involved special people.

Three Presidents were born there. Man's first powered aircraft flight took place in 1903 at Kitty Hawk. Cape Hatteras became the first national seashore in 1937. The nation's first gold and silver mines were established in North Carolina.

In the fall, Outer Banks is spectacular. Near Nags Head the cold south-

146

bound Labrador Current collides with the warm northbound Gulf Stream and the ocean boils. Natives claim this is the best surf fishing in the nation. Ordinary fishermen become world-class anglers when a "blitz" occurs. Schools of bluefish chase schools of smaller fish and sometimes end up on the beach waiting for the next wave to carry them back into the ocean. The beaches in this area give new meaning to catching fish.

The attractions in North Carolina range from spectacular scenery to wonderful arts and crafts and the best way to acquaint yourself with these bountiful attractions is to call (800)438-4404 out-of-state; (800)334-1051 in-state. And remember that North Carolina is the furniture outlet state. You can order a list of seventy-five furniture outlets by sending $3 to Iris Ellis, 9109 San Jose Blvd., Jacksonville, FL 32257.

Fabulous Finds in . . .
ASHEVILLE

Asheville is home to the Southern Highland Handicraft Guild and the High Country Art & Craft Guild. Stay at some of the great old bed and breakfast inns while you enjoy the uplands of North Carolina. Don't miss Biltmore House at Christmastime, or Blowing Rock where light objects float upward on the wind currents. Blue Ridge Parkway is a trip into nature, and you can visit the Folk Art Center east of Asheville. Enjoy snow skiing, river rafting, mountain climbing, communing with nature, or watching one of the many falls.

RIVER RIDGE MARKET PLACE FACTORY OUTLET & OFF-PRICE CENTER

Factory outlets are mixed with off-pricers.

STORES: There is something for everyone from Carter's Childrenswear to Londontown outerwear, Banner House, Van Heusen, Aileen, and other stores.

Fabulous Finds in . . .
BLOWING ROCK

SHOPPES ON THE PARKWAY

STORES: Aileen, Cape Isle Knitters, Kilwin's Ice
Cream & Chocolate, Absorba French-designed
children's wear, Bass Shoe, Anne Klein, Banister
Shoe, Royal Doulton, Aileen, Designer's Only/
Adolfo II, Euro Collection, Evan-Picone Factory
Store, Gilligan & O'Malley Factory Store, harvé
benard, Jo-Duvall's Jewelry, Multiples Modular
Wear, The Necklace Factory, London Fog, Van
Heusen, Hanes Activewear, L'eggs/Hanes/Bali,
Socks Galore, Ribbon Outlet, Gilligan &
O'Malley, Corning, Toy Liquidators, Kitchen
Collection, Prestige Fragrance & Cosmetics and
other stores.

Fabulous Finds in . . .
BURLINGTON

The city of Burlington is located in north-central
North Carolina in the heart of America's furniture and textile manufacturing country. Contact
the Greensboro Area Convention & Visitors Bureau (220 S. Eugene St., P.O. Box 1588, Greensboro, NC 27402; (800)344-2282) for information about area attractions.

BURLINGTON OUTLET MALL

LOCATION: Alongside I-85 at Exit 143.

STORES: Waccamaw, Bur-Mart, Banister Shoe
and Rolane. At this exit you can also shop
Carter's, American Tourister, Finish Line and Liz
Claiborne.

148

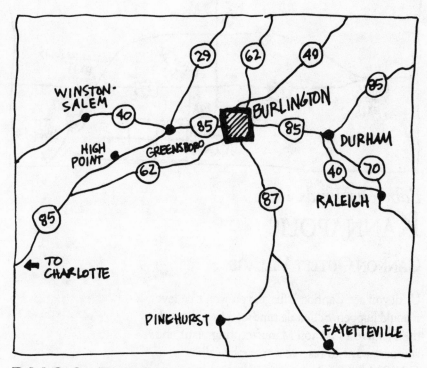

B.M.O.C. (BURLINGTON MANUFACTURERS OUTLET CENTER)

This is a blockbuster with seventy-five stores. Cherry pick the retailers to get true factory outlet savings.

LOCATION: Just one intersection to the east (145) of the Burlington Outlet Mall (above).

STORES: Carter's Childrenswear, Prestige Cosmetic & Fragrances, Campus Factory Outlet, Eagles Eye, Hanes Mill Outlet, Jonathan Logan, Ship 'n Shore, Southland Shirt, Talbot, Van Heusen Factory Outlet, Way Station, Allen-Edmonds, Bass Shoe, Corning, Mikasa, Hyalyn Ceramics, Kitchen Collection, Manhattan Factory Outlet, Midshipman Sportswear, Old Mill Ladies' Factory Outlet, Quail Hollow Factory Outlet, Quality Mills and many off-price stores.

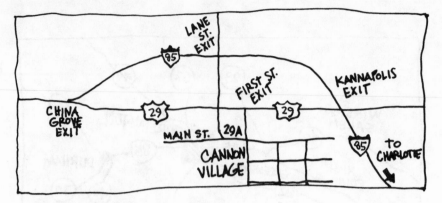

Fabulous Finds in . . .

KANNAPOLIS

CANNON OUTLET VILLAGE

Until you see Cannon Village, you won't believe it could happen. Schedule time for a tour through the Fieldcrest Cannon Manufacturing plant and you may want to reserve a space by calling (704)938-3200. Then prepare to shop in an enchanting environment. A street of shops was moved in order to build the Cannon Outlet Village.

LOCATION: 15 miles northeast of Charlotte off I-85.

STORES: **Aileen.** Casual sportswear in petite, missy and plus sizes.

Banister Shoe Outlet. 40 major brands from US Shoe — women's and men's dress, casual and athletic shoes — save 50%.

Bass Factory Outlet. Famous Bass shoes at factory direct prices.

Cannon Bed & Bath Outlet. An outlet of Fieldcrest Cannon — savings of 40-60% on irregular and discontinued styles.

Clothing Warehouse. Da'nelle Store — men's, ladies' and children's clothing at wholesale prices.

Creighton Shirtmakers. Featuring men's

pinpoint oxford shirts and related traditional separates for men and women.

Fostoria. Featuring lead crystal, giftware and candles.

Granite Knitwear. Men's, women's and children's activewear, sweatshirts, jogging suits.

Hamilton Luggage. Better-quality handbags, luggage, business cases.

Jonathan Logan. 30-70% off regular retail prices on some of America's most famous labels.

Kitchen Collection. Featuring WearEver cookware, Proctor-Silex and Anchor Hocking.

L'eggs/Hanes/Bali. Factory outlet prices on brand name slightly imperfects, closeouts and overstocks.

London Fog Factory Store. High-quality rainwear, jackets, outerwear, leathers, slacks, sportswear, umbrellas, hats and scarves at fantastic savings.

Manhattan Factory Store. Sportswear for men and women.

Paper Factory. A complete store for all occasions.

Ribbon Outlet. More than 2,500 varieties of ribbons and trims.

Toy Liquidators. Thousands of nationally advertised toys at savings up to 75%.

Van Heusen. Dress shirts and sportswear, including Lady Van Heusen.

Waccamaw. Featuring home decor at low prices—silk flowers, crafts, brass, lamps, wicker, wood.

Wallet Works by Amity. Ladies' and men's wallets, key cases, travel gifts, briefcases, luggage and handbags—save up to 70%.

Fabulous Finds in . . .
LUMBERTON

This project is revamping and upgrading so it will provide a nice stop.

LOCATION: On I-95 just about twenty miles north of the South Carolina border.

STORES: Van Heusen, Carter's Childrenswear, Campus, Bass Shoe, Converse, London Fog, Newport Sportswear, and other stores as they open.

Fabulous Finds in . . .
NAGS HEAD

SOUNDINGS FACTORY STORES

Nags Head has some of the best sports fishing on the east coast, a Shakespearean festival during

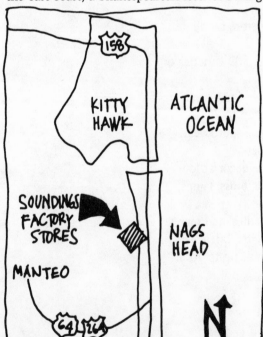

DIRECTIONS
On U.S. 158 at U.S. 264, Mile Post 16½ on the By-Pass.

152

the summer, and forty miles of beach.

STORES: Aileen, Bass Factory Store, Benetton, Corning/Revere Factory Store, Island Gear, L'eggs/Hanes/Bali, London Fog, Manhattan, Island Shirts, Old Mill, Rack Room Shoes, Secaucus Handbags, Socks Galore & More, Tie One On, Van Heusen Factory Store, The Wallet Works, Westport Ltd., and more stores opening soon.

Fabulous Finds in . . .
SMITHFIELD

CAROLINA POTTERY OUTLET CENTER

LOCATION: When traveling I-95, watch for the crossroads of US-70 and 70-A.

STORES: Carolina Pottery, Aileen, Banister Shoe, Leather Loft, Prestige Fragrance & Cosmetics, Royal Doulton, Manhattan Factory Store, Ann's Jewelry Outlet, Westport Ltd., Towle Silver, Bon Worth, harvé benard, Levi Specials, Kids Port USA, Toy Liquidators, Van Heusen, Gitano, Jonathan Logan, Bass Shoe, Ribbon Outlet, Book Warehouse, American Tourister, Le Creuset, Campus Factory Outlet Store, The Paper Factory, Carolina Linen, Capezio, Regal Ware, L'eggs/Hanes/Bali, Benetton, Old Mill, Wallet Works and other stores.

Fabulous Finds in . . .
WILMINGTON

OUTLET MALL

LOCATION: On South College Rd.

STORES: Rolane Factory Outlet, Fieldcrest Cannon, Van Heusen, Newport Sportswear and several other outlet stores.

WANTED
Great restaurants—big or small, but not chains. When you eat in one chain, you've got the menu locked into your brain. Travelers are "strangers in town" and they need some objective guidance to good food and good service ... the kind that makes you want to tip!

153

FABULOUS FINDS
IN
OHIO

Living well could describe the Buckeye State. To learn about the thousands of Ohio attractions, festivals, and events, contact the Ohio Office of Travel and Tourism (P.O. Box 1001, Columbus, OH 43216-1001; (800)BUCKEYE).

Amusement and theme parks, a great state fair, county fairs, educational activities for families and kids of all ages, zoos, aquatic exhibits and shows featuring animals and fish in natural environments, and rail and boat rides on restored historic canals and roadbeds. Professional major league sports teams, universities and colleges, the arts, humanities, research centers, medical centers of national prominence—culture, history, fine dining. Ohio has a lot to offer. Write to the Ohio Travel Association (120 N. 5th St., Newark, OH 43055) for starters.

Long before recorded history, the Mound Builders left their imprint on this state. Their earthworks are visible today. The Wyandotte Indians used the Olentangy Caverns with the maze of beautiful winding passages and underground rooms as a haven from their enemies, the Delaware Indians. One of the cavern rooms contains "Council Rock" used by the Wyandottes for tribal ceremonies. It is believed that the Wyandottes used the Council Room for making arrows and other stone implements as recently as 1810.

You can tour the Caverns from April through October.

The first white men who came to Ohio were probably hunters. Shortly after the Revolutionary War, an influx of pioneers poured into this rich land. Settlers fleeing from religious persecution came to Ohio in 1805 and founded a town about four miles from Lebanon. These Shakers named their settlement Union Village. They favored a simple, austere life-style, and their tools, clothing, furniture and cooking utensils reflect that simplicity. They prospered there for more than one hundred years.

Lebanon is home to the Golden Lamb Restaurant. Ohio's oldest restaurant and inn dates back to 1803 and has hosted ten presidents and other prominent people. This nationally known inn offers four floors of antiques in a museum setting. Warren County also has an ancient Indian fort that is more than twenty-four hundred years old. This rich and rolling land has been populated from earliest times.

Fabulous Finds in . . .

AURORA

Flea Market & Farmer's Market every Wednesday and Sunday. Something is always happening in this outlet center that is just a part of the overall fantasy land at Aurora Farms. Aurora Farms became part entertainment center in 1929 and is still a unique expression of imagination.

AURORA FARMS FACTORY OUTLET

Some of the best outlet shopping in Ohio.

LOCATION: On Rte. 43, four miles north of the Ohio Turnpike exit 13, at 549 S. Chillicothe Rd.; (216)562-2000. (See map on following page.)

STORES: Corning, Salem China, Aileen, Van Heusen, Wallet Works, Ribbon Outlet, Carter's Childrenswear, Manhattan Factory Store, Paper Outlet, Prestige Fragrance & Cosmetics, Bass Shoe, American Tourister, Banister Shoe, Jonathan Logan, Warnaco, Fashion Flair and other stores.

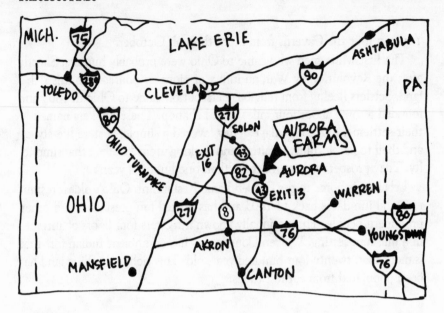

Fabulous Finds in . . .

CINCINNATI

If you are shopping Cincinnati, you may also want to go across the Ohio River and shop in northern Kentucky. Check Kentucky for Mill Outlet, the great old Palm Beach mill store; and the Gap Clearance Outlet.

SHAPELY OUTLET

This is a small center but it has some very good stores. Cincinnati is the hometown of some of these manufacturers. (See map on facing page.)

LOCATION: 2430 E. Kemper Rd., close to I-275. If you get lost and the map doesn't help, call (513)771-9828.

STORES: Shapely Outlet Store, Fashion Factory Outlet, Old Mill, Polly Flinders, Jewelie's, Cotton Mill Factory Outlet, Newport Menswear, Head Sportswear Factory Outlet and a restaurant.

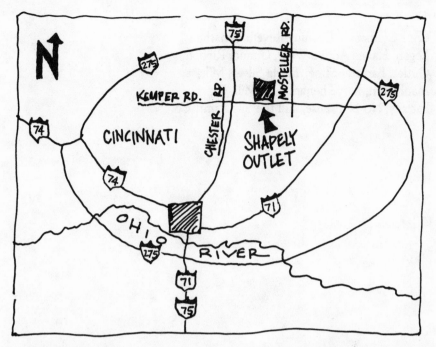

Fabulous Finds in . . .
SANDUSKY

You'll have a good time in this area. Things to see and do include: Cedar Point Amusement Park, Deer Park, Blue Hole, Thomas Edison's Birthplace, Milan's Historical Museum, African Lion Safari, Seneca Caverns, Pelee Island, Kelley's Island, Catawba Island and Put In Bay Island Wineries.

LAKE ERIE MANUFACTURER'S OUTLET SHOPPING CENTER

LOCATION: At exit 7 (US 250) and I-80, I-90 main entrance to Cedar Point and to the islands. This is Ohio's vacationland and an outlet center adds to the fun.

STORES: Kitchen Collection, American Tourister, Bass Shoe, Van Heusen, Prestige Fragrance & Cosmetics, Wallet Works, Fanny Farmer, Aileen, Wisconsin Toy, Leather Manor,

DIRECTIONS

From the South — I-75 North, I-275 East to Mosteller Rd. exit, left to Kemper, right to Shapely Outlet Center.

From the North — I-75 South, I-275 East to Mosteller Rd. exit, left to Kemper, right to Shapely Outlet Center.

From the East — I-71 to I-275 West to Mosteller Rd. exit, left to Kemper, right to Shapely Outlet Center.

From the West — I-275 East to Mosteller Rd. exit, left to Kemper, right to Shapely Outlet Center.

Cape Craftsman, Corning/Revere, Jonathan
Logan, Hanes Active Wear, Gitano, Ribbon
Outlet, Banister Shoe, Towle Silver, Mikasa,
Manhattan, harvé benard, Old Mill, Paper
Factory, No-Nonsense, and the Sweatshirt Co.

FABULOUS FINDS IN OREGON

Unique circumstances have converted Oregon's four hundred miles of open coastline into one of the world's most spectacular parks. When commercialism threatened many beaches in the 1960s, the Oregon Legislature passed an extraordinary bill that forever preserved the beaches for "free and uninterrupted use" by the public. While hikers explore the forested headlands, beachcombers hunt for shells and agates.

You can also tour a cheese factory or watch skilled craftsmen form myrtlewood into a variety of objects. Festivals and events are happening somewhere along the coast every month of the year. Lodging choices include award-winning luxury resorts, moderately priced motels lining both the beach and US 101, and rustic beachside cabins.

Butter clams, mussels, octopus, Dungeness crab, Oregon shrimp, petrale sole, ling and black cod, salmon, tuna, snapper, squid and halibut are native to the Oregon Coast. Contact the Oregon Coast Association (P.O. Box 670, Newport, OR 97365, (503)336-5103) if you are going to be touring in this fascinating and diverse part of the state.

If you have any time left, visit the Wildlife Safari in Winston off I-5. Stay in your car and drive through the park to see lions, tigers, cheetahs, zebras and other exotic animals.

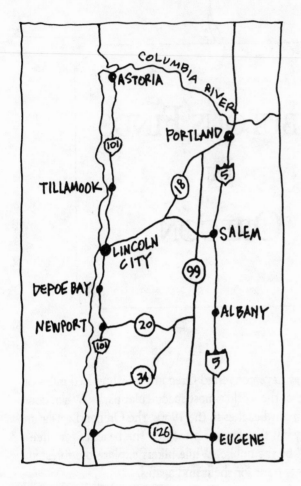

Fabulous Finds in . . .

LINCOLN CITY

Lincoln City has charm, roadside stands with fresh food, art galleries, and shops stocked with unique arts and crafts. Lincoln City is one of Oregon's leading tourist destinations and has a wide range of recreational activities, magnificent scenery and uncrowded beaches. Contact the Lincoln City Chamber of Commerce (P.O. Box 787, Lincoln City, OR 97367; (800)452-2151, in-state, or (503)994-8378, outside Oregon).

QUALITY FACTORY VILLAGE

Chateau Benoit with fabulous food, Snack City and Sweet Delights will keep the energy level high enough to enjoy the shopping.

LOCATION: Corner of Hwy. 101 and East Devils Lake Rd.

STORES: Mikasa, American Tourister, Ribbon Outlet, Corning/Revere, Westport Fashions, Aileen, Welcome Home, Wicker Factory, Banister Shoe, Van Heusen, Cape Isle Knitters, Gitano, totes, Fragrance World, Leather Loft, Kitchen Collection, Oneida, Toy Liquidators, Old Mill, London Fog, Amity Leather, harvé bernard, Polly Flinders, Adolfo II, Campus, Duffel, Eddie Bauer, Full Size Fashions, Hanes Activewear, John Henry & Friends, L'eggs/Hanes/Bali, London Fog, Maidenform, McKenzie Outfitters, OshKosh B'Gosh, Sierra Shirts, Accessorize, Wemco, Capezio Factory Direct, Converse, Book Warehouse, The Paper Factory, Pfaltzgraff, Royal Doulton and more stores coming soon.

Fabulous Finds in . . .

TROUTDALE

COLUMBIA CROSSING FACTORY STORES

LOCATION: Off I-84, 17 miles east of Portland.

STORES: Leather Loft, Banister Shoe, Corning, Oneida, Van Heusen, Cape Isle Knitters, American Tourister, Toy Liquidators, Kitchen Collection, Leather Loft, Welcome Home, Hawaiian Cotton, Paper Factory, Ribbon Outlet, Wicker Factory, Diamonds Direct, New York Express, Book Warehouse, Socks Galore and more.

FABULOUS FINDS IN PENNSYLVANIA

The state of Pennsylvania says: "For millions of years, Mother Nature has been grooming Pennsylvania. She's provided lush green forests filled with game, clear rushing streams teeming with fish, mountains ripe for scaling and skiing. She's paved trails for hiking and biking and opened up beautiful blue lakes for sailing and snorkeling."

An interesting phenomenon occurred in Pennsylvania . . . opportunity for bargain-minded shoppers when the factories offered their overstocks and year-end merchandise direct to the public at 50-75 percent below retail prices. This coming together of *demand and supply at the right price* set the factory outlet industry in motion. Factory outlet shopping is a consumer driven change in retail. This change began in the sixties, was reported by my *Save on Shopping Directory* in the early seventies, and started to become somewhat organized in the early eighties. Shoppers made their preference known and business accommodated that changing demand. Reading, Pennsylvania, is a monument to the power of people at the grass roots level.

When women went into the workplace, they changed their habits again. They began shopping on the weekend or on vacation and they especially liked to shop in tourist destinations where dad and the kids had other things to do. This gave the family buyer time to shop . . . and since day-trippers or vacationers usually take along a little extra money (and it is illegal to take that money back home), impulse shopping reigned in the factory outlet centers. Women finally allowed themselves to buy things they wanted (as opposed to needed) when they earned the money that paid for the merchandise.

The retail opportunity in Reading, the thrifty habits of the local shoppers, then the opportunistic shoppers who followed, and changing times and work habits came together in the Reading, Pennsylvania area, and an *explosive* change occurred. Women drove the economy in Reading and ultimately *in every community listed in this book.*

This is a salute to the women who knew what they wanted and supported it with their dollars or rejected unsatisfactory concepts that didn't meet their needs and wants. People can change the world and women did just that. Women will always be partners in the Fabulous Finds Publishing venture. They are invited to share their comments about stores, savings, service, factory outlet centers, surrounding attractions, places to eat and sleep and other things to do to make their experience more fulfilling.

Pennsylvania's natural attractions and historical background will have to take a backseat to the women in the Reading area who made this factory outlet retail concept happen.

Fabulous Finds in . . .
LANCASTER

Route 30 is the magic highway to factory outlet shopping centers. The two centers listed have the biggest collection of good factory outlet stores so they offer the most convenient shopping. There is additional shopping opportunity but space and organization in this directory would be difficult to achieve when outlet stores are scattered. Watch for billboards and share any information that you feel is pertinent to shopping in the Lancaster area.

QUALITY OUTLET CENTER

LOCATION: At the corner of Rte. 30 and 896. This center is located six miles east of Lancaster and the traffic can be a nightmare so be patient,

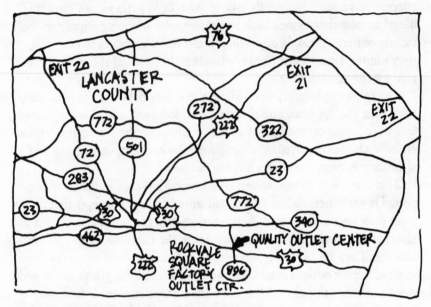

cruise the area, then turn around and go back.
Everything happens in just a couple of miles. If
you need information, call (717)299-1949.

STORES: Mikasa, Royal Doulton, Fanny Farmer,
totes, Manhattan, Delta Hosiery, Fieldcrest
Cannon, Jewelry Outlet, Franciscan Store,
Villeroy & Boch, Gold Exchange, Nike, Zen's
Gifts, a brass and snack shop and restaurant.

ROCKVALE SQUARE
FACTORY OUTLET VILLAGE

This large complex sits back from the highway.
Read the roster of stores and you will see that it
is worth the effort to get into this factory outlet
shopping center.

LOCATION: Almost directly across Rte. 30 from
the Quality Outlet Center (above).

STORES: Corning, Jonathan Logan, Eagle's Eye
Sportswear, L'eggs/Hanes/Bali Factory Outlet,
Toy Liquidators, Fashion Flair, Kitchen
Collection, Banister Shoe, American Tourister,
Little Red Shoe House, London Fog, Leather

Loft, Ribbon Outlet, Crazy Horse, The Lenox
Shop, Petals silk flowers and arrangements,
Nettle Creek, Wallet Works, Pfaltzgraff, harvé
benard, Pewtarex, The Knittery, Evan-Picone,
Susquehanna Glass, VIP Outlet, Names for
Dames (Adolfo), Hamilton Watch & Clock
Shoppe, Reading China & Glass, Barbizon
Lingerie, Book Warehouse, Mushrooms Factory
Store, The Footfactory, Bag & Baggage luggage
and handbag outlet, Cambridge Dry Goods,
Dansk Factory Outlet, Windsor Shirt Co., Farah
Factory Store, Bugle Boy, Factory Linens,
Famous Brands Housewares Outlet, Oneida
Factory Store, Warnaco Outlet Store, Van
Heusen, Aunt Mary's Yarns, Aileen Factory
Outlet, Prestige Fragrance & Cosmetics,
Brassworks, Paper Factory, Executive Neckwear,
Sweaters & Ski & Sportswear, Skyr, Socks
Galore, Wicker Unlimited, Just Coats,
Maidenform, Sports Wearhouse, Reed & Barton,
Bruce Alan Bags, Cape Isle Knitters, Champion
Activewear, Bass Shoe Factory Store and several
other stores that are discounting prices on brand
name goods.

Fabulous Finds in . . .

MORGANTOWN

(Reading area)

MOM, MANUFACTURER'S OUTLET CENTER

Built directly onto MOM is a 200-room Wilson
World hotel. The center has a food court with
national tenants such as Arby's, Bagelworks and
China Court.

LOCATION: In the Reading area, at exit 22 off the
Pennsylvania Turnpike in Morgantown.

STORES: Executive Neckwear, Genesco Factory, Gold Plus, Aileen, All-in-One Linen, Argo Children's Wear, Bag & Baggage, Cluett Apparel, Heathrow Chocolates, Johnston & Murphy Factory Outlet, Judy Bond Blouses, Kidstuff, L'eggs/Hanes/Bali Factory Outlet, Little Red Shoe House, Londontown Factory Outlet, Manhattan, Munsingwear, Old Mill Sportswear, Sweater Mill, Toy Liquidators, Van Heusen, Izod-Ship 'n Shore-Monet, Damon, Delta Hosiery, Jenny Ann Outlet, Madron Tool Co., Posy Peddler, Shirt Factory Outlet, Val Mode, Van Heusen, VIP Outlet Center.

Fabulous Finds in . . .

PHILADELPHIA

Get ready for a blockbuster. This is not a factory outlet in the strictest sense, but it is a retail experience that people love. A letter that came to the Fabulous Finds offices commented, "In Bucks County is a fabulous new outlet called Franklin Mills." She said that she preferred not to be named. We honor requests like hers because we want to bring you referrals from customers. We prefer to name names, but we don't use addresses.

FRANKLIN MILLS

LOCATION: Just off I-95 at Woodhaven Rd.

STORES: Briefcase Unlimited, Delta Hosiery, Designer Luggage, Hamilton Luggage, Helen's Handbags, Leather Gallery, Secaucus Handbags, Shades of Cape Cod, Sears Outlet, J.C. Penney Outlet, Carfour Food Store, Port of the World, Designs Inc., East Hampton Clothing, Kids Barn, Merry Go Round, National Locker Room, Sweats FX, United Outlet Center, Bed Bath & Beyond, Cargo, Fantes, Lechter's, Linens 'n Things, This End Up, Best of Times, Bijou Catrin, Dazzles,

Gold Market, Melart Jewelry, Jewelry
Warehouse, Solid Gold, Bugle Boy, Casual Male,
Big & Tall, Chess King Garage, Contemporary
Man, Executive Neckwear, Formal Celebration,
Gooch Outlet, S&K Menswear, Van Heusen
Outlet, Wallach's, Windsor Shirt Outlet,
Prestige Fragrance & Cosmetics, Ribbons,
Athlete's Foot, Bally, Banister Shoe, Children's
Bootery, Famous Footwear, Lady Footlocker
Outlet, Marty's Shoes, Parade of Shoes, Puma,
Rack Room, SneaKee Feet, Amy Stoudt, Chicos,
Clothes Out, Cornerhouse, Dress Barn Outlet,
Eagle Clothes, Fashion Corner Plus, Fashion
Factory, Filene's Basement, Intimate Eve,
Pandora, Parallel Outlet, Petite, Plumm's, Rave
and Westport.

Fabulous Finds in . . .
READING

Welcome to Reading, Berks County . . . and
Pennsylvania Dutch land. This is the land of festivals. Berks County offers many colorful festivals
and folk exhibitions throughout the year where
you'll see craftsmen practicing old-world trades
like tin-smithing, hex painting, candle making
and quilting. Of course, there's always the food —
the famous Pennsylvania Dutch treats like funnel
cake, shoofly pie or schnitz and knepp to name
a few.

In Pennsylvania Dutch country, you are in the
heart of three centuries of American history, an
area familiar to the pioneers and early leaders of
this nation. Today's Pennsylvania Dutch are de-
scended from German immigrants who settled
these rich fields and rolling woodlands in the late
1600s. They were called the Pennsylvania "Deut-
sch," a term the English later changed to
"Dutch." There are two fairly distinct groups.

PLACES TO EAT AND SLEEP:
Bucks Country Vineyard (tast-
ing and sales of the award-
winning wines of Bucks County
vineyards — wine- and
cheese-tasting arranged for
bus groups).
Shoppers Restaurant (cafe-
teria-style service. Choice of
local and international food.
Moderately priced breakfast
and lunches. Ice cream foun-
tain.)
Sweet Street Desserts (for
some of the treats indigenous
to the area. In the Reading
China Building. Call (215)378-
0408 for directions.

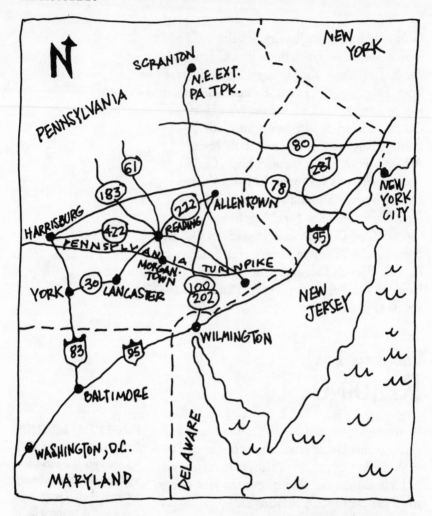

The Amish, Mennonites and Dunkards followed a rather strict and austere way of life. The other, larger group was known as the Fancy Dutch due to their less rigid attitudes and their love of the fancy such as color, art, music, fellowship and good food.

Here you'll see magnificent historic buildings, outstanding tourist attractions, arts and crafts, inns providing excellent lodgings. You'll enjoy the fabulous foods that have brought gourmets from around the world to Pennsylvania Dutch Country.

Berks County is known as the "factory outlet capital of the world." It was so named in 1972 by

Colebrookdale Inn. Features French and Nouvelle Cuisine with emphasis on quality and freshness. Homemade desserts and candies. Elegant Victorian restoration. Call (215)367-2353 for directions.

The Flowering Pot, twelve miles north of Reading, at Rich Maiden Golf Course, has a delightful atmosphere and they say it's worth the drive; (215)926-1606.

the Associated Press when they counted the factory outlet listings in the *SOS Directory*. Reading, Pennsylvania, is an outlet town with several factory outlet shopping areas and they are all fun. Plan to spend a couple of days, wear comfortable shoes, and shop all 300 outlets.

READING CHINA AND GLASS

World-class china and glass store with products from around the world. This store is as big as some factory outlet centers and could easily take a day to shop. In most cases, this store buys its inventory directly from the manufacturer in very large quantities and that qualifies Reading China for major discounts. Bargain hunters have a field day here. Brands include Royal Worcester, Haviland, Lenox, Rosenthal, Fitz & Floyd, Royal Doulton, Noritake, Wedgwood, Mikasa, Franciscan, Johnson Brothers, Riedel, Waterford Kosta Boda, Orrefors, Revere, Farberware, Lodge, Calphalon, Anchor Hocking, Colony, Libbey and Lladro . . . just to name a few.

They sell glassware of all kinds—figurines chosen from a vast international selection, more than 500 china patterns, barware to make your socials a showy occasion, a major collection of conventional and microwave cookware, fine cutlery, potato peelers, spatulas, basting tools, cutting blocks, bread and cheese slicers, pasta tongs, collanders and hundreds of other tools and accessories to make the cook look professional. You will also find silk flowers and unique dried flowers and a large assortment of wicker, china and glass containers.

LOCATION: Reading China headquarters are in West Reading at the VF Factory Outlet Complex, Eighth and Reading; (215)378-0413. Reading China and Glass has other locations that you will want to note: Hershey and Lancaster, Pennsylvania; and Boaz, Alabama.

Glockenspiel between Allentown and Reading offers excellent cuisine, leisurely dining and unique shopping; (215)683-5480.

Joe's Restaurant in Reading has creative specialties with wild mushrooms discovered and collected in Berks County; (215)929-6794.

The Peanut Bar is Reading's most unique restaurant and tavern. Free peanuts, throw the shells on the floor. Something to tell the folks about when you get back home; (215)376-7373.

Bed and breakfast information of southeast Pennsylvania; (215)845-3526. Service arranges accommodations & matches guests with host homes for short stays.

READING OUTLET CENTER

A complex of old mill buildings. Plenty of parking in off-street lots. A trip through the old mills, full of some of the best brands in the country is a memorable experience with more than 60 money-saving stores under one roof. Savings as high as 75% of recognized retail prices.

LOCATION: In the 800 block of N. Ninth St.; (215)373-5495.

STORES: **Acme Boot Co.** Featuring Acme, Dingo and Dan Post.

Aileen Factory Outlet. Juniors, misses and larger women's sportswear — first-quality merchandise at 50% off suggested prices.

All-In-One Line. Wamsutta, Martex, Fieldcrest Cannon, Burlington, Springmaid — factory direct savings on everything for bedroom, bath, living room and kitchen.

Allen Edmonds, Nobody's Perfect, Shoe Outlet. Save 35-50% on fine shoes for men — they also carry hard-to-fit sizes.

Argo Direct Factory Outlet. Famous-label sportswear for men, women and children, featuring Coyote, Runner-up, Tulip Top, Spalding, MacGregor and Head sport — save 40-60%.

Bag and Baggage. Famous brand name luggage, business cases, backpacks and handbags at 20-50% savings.

Beauty Scenter. Fragrances and cosmetics outlet, featuring Ralph Lauren, Nina Ricci, Norell, Revlon, Halston, Houbigant with savings to 70%.

Big R Sporting Goods Factory Outlet. Sporting goods and activewear by Rawlings, Fred Perry, Rawlings Golf and Etonic — savings up to 75% off retail.

Branded Shoe Outlet. Bostonian, Clarks of England and other famous-brand men's and

THINGS TO SEE AND DO:
When you visit Reading area, save time for the wonderful restaurants. The Amish Farm & House is a must. Learn about the way of life with the Amish people. Enjoy operating the farm with its variety of farm animals.

The Amish Village will provide you with a guided tour of an Amish home, blacksmith shop, one room Amish school, operating smoke house and more; (717)888-9999.

Hersheypark is a theme park in the middle of candyland. Family fun with roller coasters, Canyon River Rapids, live entertainment. Good restaurants in the area; (717)888-9999.

The Folk Life Museum Center has five buildings of exhibits, demonstrations and special activities; (904)888-9999.

Be sure to see the Pennsylvania Dutch Folk Culture Center — Lenhartsville, Pennsylvania. One room School House, Log House, Folklife Museum and gift shop; (215)562-4803.

The Old Candle Barn offers a view of candle making and a large selection of candles and rings. They also have other handmade gift items and would love to give you a special deal on their seconds; (717)888-9999.

women's shoes — plus hosiery for the entire family.

Carry-Alls. Handbags, luggage, umbrellas, attachés, backpacks, duffels — save up to 50% and more.

Carter's Factory Outlet. Featuring Carter's layette, playwear, sleepwear and underwear — save 40-60% more.

Children's Bootery/Jumping Jacks. Savings of 30-60% on Jumping Jacks, Little Capezio, Moxees and other footwear.

Clothes Works. Wide selection of first-quality famous-maker sportswear, featuring Jack Winter, at 20-60% below nationally advertised prices.

Corning Designs Factory Outlet. Outstanding values in Pyrex, Corningware, Corelle and Corning design products.

Delta Hosiery. Featuring pantyhose, stockings, knee socks, panties, bras, slips, leotards, tights and men's underwear.

Designers Intimate Outlet Room/Dior. Factory owned and operated, featuring lingerie and loungewear by Christian Dior, Carole Hockman, Sara Beth, Mollie Parnis and Gottex swimwear for men and women.

Designer's Outlet. Savings up to 50% on Jones New York, Christian Dior, Gloria Vanderbilt, Norma Kamali, John Meyer, Saville Suits.

Eagle's Eye Company Store. Manufacturers of superior-quality and classic-designed ladies' and children's sportswear — savings of 30-50%.

Fisher-Price Toys. More than 200 Fisher-Price toys — selected Playskool toys, a stuffed animal line and much more.

The Fur Factory Outlet. Factory outlet for five manufacturing furriers featuring savings of 30-50% on nationally distributed furs from rabbit to mink.

Housewares Plus. Rubbermaid products,

Contact the Berks County Pennsylvania Dutch Travel Association at (215)375-4085 for more information.

171

stoneware, copper and glassware—extensive selection of housewares for the kitchen and dining areas.

Jaeger. British-made fine-quality ladies' sportswear at greatly reduced prices.

Jonathan Logan Outlet. Manufacturer's outlet for Villager, Act III, R&K Kollections in petites, missy and half sizes. Misty Harbor raincoats, Etienne Aigner shoes, handbags and accessories up to 70% off.

Kid's Creations. A manufacturer's outlet for high-quality European children's clothing, featuring many items of 100% cotton—size infants through pre-teen.

Kids Port USA. Children's playwear—infants', toddlers', boys' and girls' sizes 4-14.

LF Factory Outlet. Division of Leslie Fay; famous label dresses and sportswear—50% and more off nationally advertised prices.

Lancaster Lingerie Outlet. Lingerie direct from nearby factory at discounts of up to 75%—famous brands of foundations, and hosiery.

L'eggs/Hanes/Bali Factory Outlet. Save 20-50% and more on suggested retail prices on slightly imperfects, closeouts and overstocks—choose from hosiery, underwear, lingerie, socks and active wear and much more.

Londontown Factory Outlet Store. London Fog's own outlet store—rainwear, outerwear and jackets for men, women and children—save 50%.

Manhattan Factory Outlet. Factory-owned-and-operated store—men's and ladies' apparel at 25-60% below suggested retail prices—also, a large and tall department for men.

Manufacturer's Outlet. Featuring OshKosh B'Gosh, leading manufacturer of bib overalls—children's, women and men's sportswear.

Munsingwear Factory Outlet. Internationally known manufacturer of men's and boys' sportswear and underwear—also, Vassarette lingerie and foundations—50% off suggested retail.

Newport Sportswear Company Store. Action activewear, woven and knit shirts, sweaters, pants and outerwear—manufacturer owned and operated.

Old Mill Ladies Sportswear Factory Outlet. Manufacturer owned and operated—25-70% off current retail on first-quality, coordinated sportswear, dresses and suits.

P&D Fashion Accessories. High-fashion costume jewelry, belts and accessories—14K gold chains, bracelets and necklaces at 40-60% off.

Pantry Housewares Outlet. Factory direct savings on Rubbermaid, WearEver, Microwave, Hamilton Beach, Washington Frye.

Polo/Ralph Lauren Factory Store. Men's, women's and children's apparel, home furnishings, and fashion accessories—savings of 25-75% off suggested retail.

Queen Casuals. Misses and large size sportswear—25-75% off regular retail prices.

Quoddy Crafted Footwear. Full range of styles of shoes for the family, emphasising the casual—all leather.

Season's Best. Manufacturers of better-quality contemporary women's sportswear—35-70% off retail.

Ship 'n Shore. Direct manufacturer's outlet for Ship 'n Shore, Monet Jewelry and Izod for men, women and children—savings up to 60% and more.

totes Direct Factory Outlet. Featuring totes rainwear, including umbrellas, footwear, luggage, coats, hats and other accessories at savings up to 75%.

V.I.P. Yarn and Craft Center. Yarn, stitchery, needlepoint, macrame, latch hooking,

needles, books, accessories — as well as Little
Lord Stuart children's sportswear.

Van Heusen Factory Store. Save 30-60% every
day on Van Heusen, Lady Van Heusen and
designer shirts and sportswear, outerwear and
accessories.

Windsor Shirt Company Factory Outlet. Men's
and ladies' dress and sports shirts — extensive
big, tall and accessory departments.

Winona Knitting Mills Factory Outlets. Knit
sweaters, including Raggwool, Shetland and
acrylics, accessories, sportswear, outerwear —
save up to 50%.

THE BIG MILL

LOCATION: At the corner of Eighth and Oley.

STORES: Delta Hosiery Mills, Intimate Eve,
Gitano Warehouse, Top of the Line Cosmetics,
Chaus, Adolfo Collectibles, Deerskin Shoe,
Petticoat Corner, Custom Sportswear, Crown
Jewels and others.

Other small factory outlet centers in Reading
that may interest you if you have enough time:

FOUR SQUARE OUTLET CENTER

STORES: Sweater Outlet, and others.

HEISTERS LANE OUTLET CENTER

STORES: Londontown Factory Outlet Store,
Munsingwear/Vassarette Factory Outlet, Mikasa
Factory Store, and others.

Fabulous Finds in . . .

ROBESONIA

(Reading area)

LOCATION: Robesonia is about an hour west of
Reading on Rte. 422 and has a small outlet center

WANTED
Information about the most
interesting things to do in an
area already listed in *Fabulous Finds.* Experiences that
are memorable. Attractions
that you can't forget.

with some interesting stores. Fifteen stores filled with aisle after aisle of direct-from-factory merchandise with items priced far below regular retail.

STORES: **The Bag Outlet.** All kinds of handbags and carry-on luggage.

Canoe Manufacturing. Children's wear, sizes newborn to 18, featuring Wilson Fleece activewear, Wilson summer tops and bottoms, and more.

Gloray Knitting Mills. The most spectacular brands sold in this country.

The Knit Pikker. A small, local factory outlet store. Save 30-75% off retail on a variety of knit accessories and socks for the entire family from infants to adults.

Ocello Inc. Ladies' and children's fashion thermals, fashionable knit tops and an outstanding collection of daywear and lingerie.

The Paper Outlet. Big selection of paper party products for birthdays, showers, weddings, anniversaries and any happy occasion.

Talbot. "Traveler" bouclé knits with matching shirts and slacks—big savings on Dutchmaid underwear and lingerie.

V.I.P. Yarn and Craft Center. Yarns, kits and accessories.

Fabulous Finds in . . .
SOMERSET

As you approach Georgian Place on the Pennsylvania Turnpike, you will spot a classic twenty-two-room Georgian Mansion, built in 1919 by a local coal baron. The mansion is the focal point and entrance to Georgian Place. This historic home houses a very special Inn and information center and sets the theme for the architectural style of the center. For a lodging and dining guide, call (814)445-6431 or write to the Somerset County Chamber of Commerce (829 N. Center Ave., Somerset, PA 15501). Camper information will be included.

LOCATION: Somerset Place is about 45 miles east of Pittsburgh in the heart of the Laurel Highlands.

STORES: Adolfo II.

Aileen.

American Tourister. Bags and luggage.

Banister.

Bass Shoe.

Book Warehouse. Books, books, books.

Cape Isle. If you want a sweater, you will find one here.

Corning/Revere.

Crystal Works. Gifts and decoration items.

Fieldcrest Cannon. The *SOS Directory* owners voted this as best bed and bath outlet store in their letters.

Fragrance World. For world-renowned fragrances and cosmetics.

Hanes. Nationally advertised underclothing.

harvé benard.

Jones New York.

Kitchen Collection. An amazing store if you love to cook or eat.

Leather Loft. Bags and purses, all leather items.

Mackintosh of New England. An old-line company for outerwear.

Manhattan.

Nichols Factory Store.

Oneida Silverware. If you still eat at home, eat elegantly with affordable tableware.

Socks Galore.

Stone Mountain Handbags. Tempting leather and great designs.

Van Heusen.

Welcome Home. A country craftsy store.

Westport Ltd. Women's wear of all kinds.
Wisconsin Toy.

This is a partial list of stores; more will be coming as this directory goes to print. You will find a restaurant, snack shops; and if you are staying in the area, resorts are nearby.

Fabulous Finds in . . .
WAYNESBORO

WAYNESBORO FACTORY OUTLET BARN

This is one of the first outlet centers, and the synergism between the frugal shoppers and the manufacturers who needed clearance made this a landmark in its time. It also seems to be an incubator for intimidated manufacturer's outlets. Over the years, several heavy hitters have opened their first store here and learned how to be retailers, how to make presentations . . . then they became national chains. See what you think.

LOCATION: At Walnut and Third Streets; (717)762-7123.

STORES: Bag & Baggage, Candle Crafter, Kids In Bloom, Corning Factory Store, Delta Hosiery, Dress Outlet, Norton McNaughton Outlet, Manhattan Factory Outlet, Mister Ed's Candy Outlet, New Horizon Sportswear & Sweats, The Little Red Shoe House, Sheet & Towel Outlet, Sirkels of New York, Van Heusen Factory Store, Fashion Flair, Freeman Shoe Outlet, The Mill Outlet — with brands like Pierre Cardin, Evan-Picone, Eagle, Austin Hill, United Shoe Outlet — selling Revelation and other brands including Kangaroos.

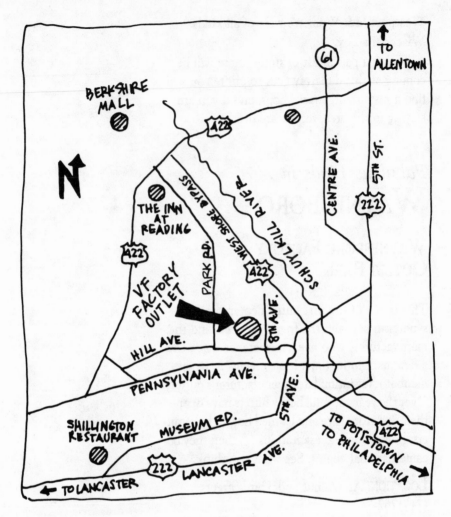

Fabulous Finds in . . .

WYOMISSING

(Reading area)

VANITY FAIR OUTLET

The home of the famous VF Factory and many outstanding factory outlets. Many first-time shoppers are simply amazed — not only by the incredible savings they find here but also by the quality and diversity of merchandise available.

LOCATION: In Wyomissing, an extension of Reading.

STORES: **Adidas.** Athletic leisure and footwear.

American Tourister. Big and small bags, totes, garment bags.

Black & Decker. Hardware items, small appliances, power tools and accessories, most of the items sold by Black & Decker.

Bollman Hats. Dress, western and sport hats for men and women.

Candy Crafters. Luden's Factory Outlet — 5th Avenue Bars, Mellomints, Sugar Jellies, hard candies, famous cough drops, seasonal hollow and solid chocolate novelties — a chocoholics version of heaven.

Carter's Childrenswear. A longtime favorite of American mothers.

Clothes Hound. Evan-Picone, Palm Beach, Pierre Cardin, Gant, Haspel, and Eagle's Eye — sweaters, tops, and sportswear, plus Freeman Shoes.

The Electronics Outlet. Home and car stereo equipment, telephones, radar detectors, CBs, accessories.

Famous Brands Jewelry Outlet. Fantastic selection of brand name costume jewelry plus 14K gold, sterling, gold-filled and vermeil.

The 40 Brand Outlet. More than 75,000 pairs of men's and women's dress, casual, athletic and golf shoes — save up to 50%.

Jonathan Logan Outlet. Featuring Etienne Aigner and Misty Harbor, Villager, Act III, R&K, Amy Adams.

Nanny's Shoppe. Handcrafted gifts — Calico specialties, folk art, primitives, slates, apple people dolls, and more.

North Face. Functional outdoor clothing, skiwear, rugged sportswear, Gore-tex fabric clothing.

Oneida Factory Store. Oneida stainless flatware, silverplate, holloware.

Oxford Brands. Merona and Fresh Start dresses and sportswear.

Prestige Fragrance & Cosmetics. Cosmetics, fragrances and sun products for men and women.

Skyr. Beautiful sweaters, tops and sportswear.

totes. Rain outerwear and totes.

Van Heusen. Men's and women's shirts and tops, ties and accessories.

Your Toy Center. Toys and games — Fisher-Price, Mattel, Coleco, Playskool, Milton Bradley, Matchbox and others.

Fabulous Finds in . . .
YORK

York and Lancaster are both on Rte. 30; you may want to shop both when you are in the area.

Take time for interesting historical background on York. "York was the first capital of the United States. After a treaty signed by the Penns and the Indians in 1736, the Proprietors took title to certain lands west of the Susquehanna River. One of the early settlers of the region, Baltzer Spangler in 1740 obtained permission from Thomas Penn to lay out a town where the Monacacy Indian Path crossed the Codorus Creek.

"During the bitter winter of 1777-1778, the American Revolution was at 'low ebb.' As British troops marched on Philadelphia in the autumn of 1777, members of the Continental Congress fled westward in search of a safer meeting place. Once safely across the expanse of the Susquehanna River, the delegates found lodging in the log homes and 'publick houses' of York. From September 30, 1777 to June 27, 1778, the Conti-

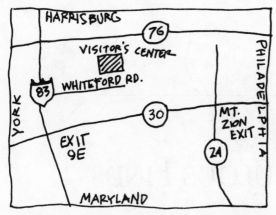

nental Congress governed the fortunes of the struggling colonies from the courthouse in York, Pennsylvania. Proud of its colorful and dramatic heritage, York preserves the past and provides for the future in its historic district, the largest in Pennsylvania outside Philadelphia."

THE VILLAGE AT MEADOWBROOK

Here factory outlet shopping is an experience that you will remember. The presentation of the center and the quality of the stores along with the dining has been planned by a master hand. (Dinner reservations are suggested at the Meadowbrook Restaurant; (717)757-3500). It would be interesting to add your comments about your experience to this listing in future editions.

LOCATION: Mt. Zion Rd. at Rte. 30; (717)755-0899.

STORES: Doespun Factory Outlet, Izod, harvé benard, Jonathan Logan, Prestige Fragrance & Cosmetics, Nilani, Slumbertogs, Crazy Horse, Pfaltzgraff Store, Christmas Tree Hill, Van Heusen Factory Outlet Store, Hamilton Watch & Clock Shoppe, Delta Hosiery, The Pewtarex Store, Ribbon Outlet, Petals Factory Store, Leather Loft, Banister, Manhattan Factory Store, Toys Unlimited, The Knittery, Bass Shoe Outlet.

FABULOUS FINDS IN SOUTH CAROLINA

By far South Carolina's greatest tourist attraction is Myrtle Beach and the Grand Strand. The five miles of gently sloping beaches are the widest you'll ever see. Every March thousands of tourists come to these beaches to celebrate Can-Am Week—a perfect time of year to hunt for shells, fish, swim, sunbathe, or just stroll along some of the prettiest beaches on the Atlantic coast.

Of interest to the shopper is South Carolina's textile heritage. South Carolina is a land of water, although this doesn't immediately present itself to someone unfamiliar with the natural splendor of the state. Miles of ocean, acres of lakes in all parts of the state, tidal marshes, savannas and inland rivers and streams spelled early economic success for the northern textile mills that moved to the Carolinas. Spurred by cheap labor, abundant materials provided by the long growing seasons of the plants needed for natural fibers, and a more hospitable climate, the textile industry enjoyed much success. As a result, North and South Carolina were among the first states to benefit from factory outlet shopping, a natural spin-off of textile and apparel manufacturing.

If you travel I-95, billboards will demand that you stop to see Pedro. Pedro is 104 feet high, has four miles of wiring and weighs 77 tons. Near him are restaurants, a miniature indoor golf course, a nine-hole golf course and gift shops. This is marketing. If you are interested, watch for the town of Dillon, just as you enter South Carolina on the northern boundary.

South Carolina offers many attractions — including several important Revolutionary War battlegrounds.

☞ **FOR MORE INFORMATION**
Contact the South Carolina Division of Tourism (P.O. Box 71, Columbia, SC 29202; (803)734-0235) for details and literature about all the state has to offer — in addition to some great shopping!

Fabulous Finds in . . .
FORT MILL

OUTLET MARKETPLACE

LOCATION: At the intersection of I-77 and Carowinds Blvd. at the entrance to Carowinds Theme Park.

STORES: Carolina Pottery, Aileen, Wallet Works, Gitano, Campus Factory Outlet, Van Heusen, Wamsutta Mill Store, Prestige Fragrance & Cosmetics, Bass Shoe, The Ribbon Outlet, Diamond & Jewelry Outlet, Eva Factory Outlet, and an assortment of discounters and off-price stores.

Fabulous Finds in . . .
HILTON HEAD

This semitropical island off the coast of South Carolina is that rarest of finds: a resort where you can set your own pace, where relaxation and excitement are available in whatever combination you choose. Hilton Head Island has been a destination for nature lovers and sightseers for years, and you'll love the shopping.

For vacation information for Hilton Head Is-

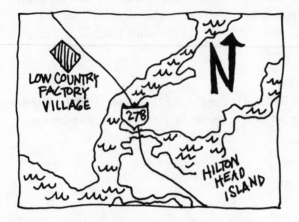

land, here are contacts that may be useful: Hilton Head Island Chamber of Commerce (P.O. Box 5647, Hilton Head Island, SC 29938). Marketing Department, The Sea Pines (P.O. Box 7000, Hilton Head, SC 29938). Island Dining & Entertainment Guide — (803)681-2219.

Low Country Factory Village

Since this center is a pass-by with absolutely nothing to do in the vicinity, it will be interesting to hear your comments.

Location: In Bluffton on Hwy. 278, 2.2 miles from the bridge to Hilton Head.

Stores: Bass Shoe, Van Heusen, Danskin, American Tourister, Ribbon Outlet, Damon/ Enro, Nilani, Prestige Fragrance & Cosmetics, Kitchen Collection, Gitano, Welcome Home, London Fog, Book Warehouse, Dan Rivers, Levi Strauss & Co, Mainely Bags, Reebok, J. Crew, Capezio, Micki Designer Separates, Toy Liquidators, Olga Lingerie and others.

Shoppes on the Parkway

Location: On 278 between Palmetto Dunes and Shipyard.

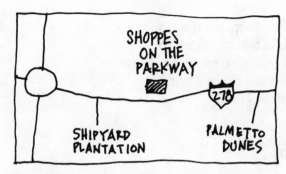

STORES: Aileen, Clothes Works, Dansk Factory Outlet, First Choice, Gilligan & O'Malley Factory Store, Hilton Head Shirt Co., Island Wear/Swimsuit Source, Kids Port USA, Anne Klein Outlet, Leather Loft, Jonathan Logan Outlet, Old Mill, Palmetto Linen Outlet, Player's World of Golf, Prestige Fragrance & Cosmetics, Paul Revere Shoppe, Rocky Mountain Chocolate Factory, S&K Famous Brand Menswear, Silkworm, Shoe Strings #3, Socks Galore & More, totes Direct Factory Outlet, Trendsetter Footwear, Van Heusen Factory Store and the Wicker Warehouse.

PINELAND MALL

LOCATION: On Hwy. 278 (William Hilton Parkway) at Mathews Dr.

STORES: Barbizon Lingerie, Bass Factory Outlet, Bruce Alan Bags, Converse footwear and clothing, Cape Isle Knitters, Adolfo II, Fieldcrest Cannon, Pfaltzgraff, Player's World, Royal Doulton Direct, Socks Galore, Towle 1690 House, Van Heusen Factory Store, ACA Joe, Hilton Head Shirt Co., Socks Galore, Heritage Jewelers, Swank, California Kids, I.B. Diffusion, Designers Extras, several restaurants and other stores.

OTHER SHOPPING

Mrs. Harry Stulz found another store in Hilton Head that she recommends. "In Hilton Head we found the Shoe String Shoe Shop, and it was a dream come true. If you love beautiful shoes, not cheap — but they were cheap for expensive merchandise — try it." She also says that she found "lots of good places in Hilton Head."

Fabulous Finds in . . .
MYRTLE BEACH

One of the favorite spots for Great Lake states and northeast visitors during the winter. Called the Grand Strand, there are many reasons to plan a Christmas vacation at this five-mile stretch of public beaches. Sun, swimming, shopping, golfing and restaurants.

It is an area with more than forty-five championship golf courses and more fine restaurants than you can sample in a month . . . then add factory outlets to that. Contact the Myrtle Beach Area Chamber of Commerce (1301 N. Kings Hwy., P.O. Box 2115, Myrtle Beach, SC 29578-2115; (803)626-7444), or Charleston Trident Convention & Visitors Bureau (P.O. Box 975, Charleston, SC 29402) for tourist information for the South Carolina coast.

DIRECTIONS
We're on Hwy 501 at the Waterway in Myrtle Beach.

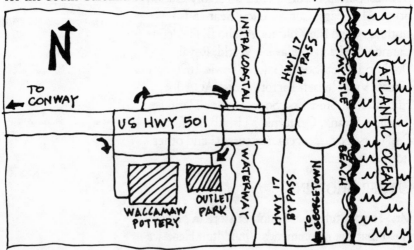

WACCAMAW POTTERY

Discover a new world of shopping fun and savings . . . there's so much for so little. More than 200,000 items are warehoused at discount prices in this off-price giant. Dinnerware, glassware, housewares, wicker, dried and silk flowers, flower arrangements, giftware and much more, all discounted as much as 80% off regular retail price. Brand names include Mikasa china, Libbey glassware, Rubbermaid & Ecko housewares, Corning, Anchor Hocking and others. Waccamaw Pottery buys in large quantities direct from the factory and countries all over the world, passing the savings on to their customers. You'll love to browse through Waccamaw Pottery and enjoy the thrill of finding true bargains. (Waccamaw Pottery also has a store in Spartanburg, South Carolina.)

OTHER SHOPPING

Neighbor stores are mind-boggling.

STORES: Newport Sportswear, Jumping Jacks's, Clothes Works, Captree, Old Mill, Kids Port USA, Casual Male, Barbizon, Burlington Bag & Baggage, Burlington Brands, Creighton Shirtmakers, totes, Jaymar Ruby, Jonathan Logan, The Wallet Works, Way Station, Top of the Line Cosmetics, Londontown, Formfit Roger, Legsense, OPO, Bon Worth, Brand Name Fashion Outlet, Toy Outlet, 14K unlimited, Barewood Furniture, Freeman Shoe, Goldcrafters, Good Shop Lollipop, Quail Hollow, American Tourister, Aileen, Leather Loft, Sports Wearhouse, Fashion Flair/Izod/Ship 'n Shore, Gitano, Manhattan Outlet, Shapes Activewear, The Ribbon Outlet, Van Heusen, Designer Outlet by Rodier, Young Generation, Cosmetic Factory Outlet, Beacon Linen, Designer Yarns and many more.

THINGS TO SEE AND DO

Brookgreen Gardens, eighteen miles south of Myrtle Beach is a world apart. Development began when the property was purchased by Archer and Anna Huntington in 1930. Their original plan was to build a winter home here, but inspired by the overwhelming natural beauty of the site, they decided instead to create a sanctuary for living and growing things. Brookgreen Gardens exists to exhibit and preserve American sculpture and the plants and animals of the region in a dynamic outdoor museum.

Before the war between the states, when rice plantations dotted the South Carolina lowlands, Pawleys Island became a summer refuge for the prosperous rice planters of the area. The well-to-do chose this out-of-the-way paradise to avoid the much feared malaria of that time. The seabreezes helped sweep away the malaria-carrying mosquitos and cool the steamy, southern nights down to a comfortable temperature for sleeping.

Also south of Myrtle Beach there are fifteen delightfully different shops and a restaurant within the tranquil grounds of the Hammock Shop Plantation Stores.

Fabulous Finds in . . .
SANTEE

Lake Marion is one of the most famous meccas for freshwater fishing in the U.S. Fishermen go there for freshwater striper, largemouth bass, and several varieties of catfish. The deer season lasts from August 15 to the last day in December and just about every bird hunted in North America lures wing shooters from all over.

Sixteen golf courses are in the region and a state sponsored golf course convention center and marina is coming soon.

The magnificent city of Charleston is only an hour away. Rainbow row, charming courtyard inns such as the Indigo Inn, The Ansonborough Inn along with great restaurants including the fabulous Gatsby's or the Ferantes will transport visitors to the time of Rhett Butler.

SANTEE VILLAGE FACTORY STORES

The stores in Santee Village are some of the best factory outlets in the U.S. and Europe. If you are driving by or visiting Lake Marion, make time to have fun shopping the factory outlets. Santee Village is a traditional layover for tourists traveling north and south with 1,500 motel and hotel rooms. Millions of people frequent the recreational facilities including golf, fishing and hiking.

LOCATION: At the intersection of I-95 and Rte. 6—Exit 98, the center for all tourism on the northeast corridor.

STORES: Manhattan, Fashion Flair, Kids Port USA, Aileen, The Ribbon Outlet, Wisconsin Toy, Oneida, Kitchen Collection, Royal Doulton, American Tourister, Bass/Van Heusen,

DIRECTIONS
Take I-95 to Exit 98 (Hwy. 6) to Santee, Carolina.

RevereWare, Gitano, Jonathan Logan, Banister Shoe, US Shoe, Campus Sportswear, Swank, Cape Craftsmen, Welcome Home, Corning Factory Store and Westport Ltd.

Fabulous Finds in . . .
SPARTANBURG

OUTLET PARK AT WACCAMAW

LOCATION: At intersection of I-26 and New Cut Rd. about one mile north of I-85.

STORES: Rolane's, Bass Shoe, Newport Sportswear, Captree, Aileen, Jonathan Logan, Waccamaw Pottery, Specials by Levi Strauss, Prestige Fragrance & Cosmetics, Top of the Line Cosmetics, Fieldcrest Cannon, Fashion Flair, Kids Port USA, Van Heusen and many discounters and off-price stores. Some food kiosks — comments, please.

WANTED
New information about factory outlet shopping centers — dead or alive. Tell me if you enjoyed your shopping experiences and why.

FABULOUS FINDS
IN
TENNESSEE

T ennessee has a variety of attractions ranging from Graceland, Dolly-wood, The Hermitage (Andrew Jackson's home) and Ober Gatlinburg. For a wealth of information, contact the Tennessee Department of Tourist Development (P.O. Box 23170, Nashville, TN 37202; (615)741-7994).

Nashville and Opryland are tourist attractions that just keep on keeping on. With all the shows, rides, shops and restaurants, you can't see it all in one day. The shows alone are well worth a trip. The costumes, talent and music are extraordinary. You can cruise on the General Jackson, a grand old showboat, or see the legendary Grand Ole Opry and stay at the Opryland Hotel. Call (800)USA-OPRY, or write to Opryland USA (2802 Opryland Dr., Nashville, TN 37214).

☞ **FOR MORE INFORMATION**
Write or call: Chucalissa Museum, Memphis State University, 1987 Indian Village Dr., Memphis, TN 38109; (901)785-3160. Nashville hotels and motels: Chamber of Commerce, 161 Fourth Ave. N., Nashville, TN 37219; (615)259-3900. Upper East Tennessee Tourism Council, P.O. Box 375-A, Jonesborough, TN 37659; (615)753-5961. Chattanooga Area Convention & Visitors Bureau, Civic Forum, 1001 Market St., Chattanooga, TN 37402; (615)756-2121, for outstanding dining experiences. Tenessee Tourist Development, P.O. Box 23170, Nashville, TN 37202; (615)741-2158, for accommodations. Tennessee bed and breakfast in home and

country inns: (615)741-2158. Your Vacation Guide, Oakley Enterprises, P.O. Box 1296, Gatlinburg, TN 37738; (615)453-1044.

Fabulous Finds in . . .
CHATTANOOGA

Scenery, history, nature or nostalgia, Chattanooga has a lot in store. Chattanooga is the scenic center of the South—it's within a day's drive of half the nation's population. If you are traveling in the autumn, take advantage of the unsurpassed beauty of the more than 300 kinds of trees. Color begins in September and lasts until December.

For more information, write to Chattanooga Area Convention & Visitors Bureau (Civic Forum, 1001 Market St., Chattanooga, TN 37402; (615)756-2121).

WAREHOUSE ROW

Great old mill buildings have been converted into a factory outlet center. The ambience of the converted mill buildings combined with the brilliant architectural concept will give you a memorable day's shopping. The Freight Depot across

PLACES TO EAT
Try Cafe' Français, Taiwan Express, Cozzoli's Pizza.

DIRECTIONS
Take the Market St. Exit off I-24 North to 11th St.

191

the street has a nice lunchroom and other boutique shops.

LOCATION: Just off I-24 on N. Market St. If you need hours or help, call (615)265-1000.

STORES: **Adrienne Vittadini.** Sweaters.

Albert Nipon.

Argenti. Famous for their women's silks and knits.

Bass Shoe.

Coach. Leather goods and accessories.

Designer's Extras. Soft-looking women's apparel.

Ellen Tracy. Upscale women's wear.

Guess? Men's and women's fashions.

harvé benard. Men's and women's apparel.

Helen's Handbags.

I.B. Diffusion. For the soft look you'll love.

J. Crew. Men's and women's apparel, the same as the catalog.

Jewelry by the Village Goldsmith.

Joan & David Shoe.

Johnston & Murphy's. Shoes.

Natori. Fashions and lingerie that men love to buy.

Nautica's. Outdoor fashions.

Oleg Cassini. Fashions for women and men.

Perry Ellis Portfolio. Fashions for men and women.

Perry Ellis Shoes. And accessories.

Polo/Ralph Lauren. Fashions and a home furniture and accessories shop.

Springmaid-Wamsutta. Linen and domestics.

Vakko Suede and Leather. Fashions and accessories—this is a famous name that you can trust.

Westport Ltd. Women's apparel.

THINGS TO SEE AND DO

Try white water rafting on the Ocoee River. The average gradient of over fifty feet per mile provides a roller coaster ride full of big waves, giant holes and steep drops.

Rock City Gardens at the top of Lookout Mountain will give you an experience that you won't forget. You can see seven states from Lover's Leap.

Chattanooga Choo Choo Complex has the county's biggest restaurant, a group of 1890 shops and nostalgia.

If you have ever driven on I-75 you must have seen the signs, "See Ruby Falls" painted on signs, barns ... everywhere. See Ruby Falls when you visit Lookout Mountain.

Sail the Lost Sea in Sweetwater, Tennessee, in a glass bottom boat. The Lost City features early Tennessee cabins, working craftsmen and a train ride.

Fabulous Finds in . . .
CROSSVILLE
THE VF FACTORY OUTLET
LOCATION: On I-40 at the Crossville exit. Call
(615)484-7165 if you need assistance.
STORES: VF Factory Outlet Store, Banister Shoe,
Prestige Fragrance & Cosmetics, Van Heusen
Factory Store.

Fabulous Finds in . . .
MEMPHIS
Cotton and the Mississippi River made Memphis
a great commercial city. During the late 1800s
flatboats by the hundreds brought loads of the
"white gold" to the crowded markets on Front
Street. Paddle wheelers lined the waterfront
docks along the Mississippi waiting to take on
vast cargos of cotton destined for the textile mills
in Europe. Today, if it is a normal year, more than
three million bales of cotton are produced from
the rich fields of the mid-south region surrounding Memphis. Leaving the waterfront is the famous Beale Street, where W.C. Handy first wrote
the blues and Blues Alley, a nightclub that keeps
the blues tradition of Memphis alive with nightly
performances by outstanding blues artists.
   In the Mississippi River, just a few hundred

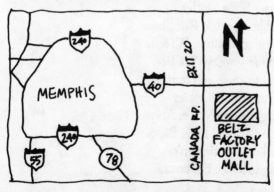

yards from downtown Memphis, lies an island which, according to legend, formed around a Yankee ironclad grounded during the Civil War. The low, frequently flooded island has long been a Memphis landmark with the unflattering name of Mud Island. Dredging raised the island above the floodplain and today the ghost of the ancient ironclad is present at the multi-million dollar Mud Island complex. Mud Island describes itself as a themed river family entertainment complex. Its most spectacular attraction is the River Walk, an authentic replica of the river itself depicting the 1,000 miles of the Lower Mississippi. Built to scale, with one step equalling one mile, it extends for five city blocks (2,000 feet). This ingenious miniature Mississippi faithfully reproduces the exact river channels, the twisting, floodplains and tributaries of the river. The flowing water rises and falls as the real river's flow changes. For more information on Mud Island, contact Mud Island Marketing, 125 N. Main, Memphis, TN 38103; (901)528-3595.

BELZ FACTORY OUTLET MALL

Here you buy directly from manufacturers through their outlet stores, cutting out high markups and middlemen. (See map page 193.)

LOCATION: 3536 Canada Rd. in Lakeland. Exit Canada Rd. from I-40.

STORES: Bass Shoe, Banister Shoe Outlet, Genesco Factory To You Shoes, Little Red Shoe House, Bag & Baggage Outlet, Custom Watch & Jewelry, Jewelie's Costume Jewelry, Wallet Works, Binswanger Glass furniture and mirrors, Corning Factory Store, Furniture Factories Showroom, Linens 'n Things, Regal Ware, Anna Maria Accents, Bargain Box, Casual Male Big & Tall, Cotton & Wool Locker, Gentlemen's Wear-House, Gitano, Handmacher Fashions,

Judy Bond Blouses, Kids Port USA, L'eggs/
Hanes/Bali, Maidenform, Manhattan Factory
Outlet, Munsingwear, Sock it to Me, Van
Heusen, Hibbett's Outlet Sports, Old Time
Pottery, Publisher's Book Outlet, The Ribbon
Outlet, Toy Liquidator, snack shops.

Fabulous Finds in . . .

MURFREESBORO

Antique Center of the South. Browse through
antique malls and many shops located throughout the county. For details on lodging, dining,
shopping and other things to see and do, write
P.O. Box 64, Murfreesboro, TN 37130 or call
(615)893-6565. You won't want to miss Opryland USA, Country Music Hall of Fame, Country
Music Wax Museum, Twitty City, Music Row
and the Hermitage in Nashville, less than an
hour's drive away.

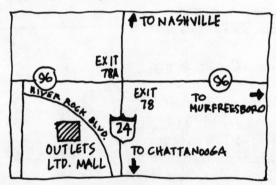

DIRECTIONS
Murfreesboro, TN — I-24, Exit
78 (westbound), or Exit 78A
(eastbound), 20 minutes
southeast of Nashville.

OUTLETS LIMITED MALL

LOCATION: Take exit 78 off I-24 at the
intersection of US 96; call (615)895-4966 if you
make a wrong turn.

STORES: **Acme Boot Outlet.** Boots for men,
women and children at great savings, plus
western wear.
Bargain Box. Movie Star and Standmark-

Stardust sleepwear, loungewear, panties, slips, camisoles and more.

Bass Shoe. Factory direct prices on Bass shoes.

Book Island. Books and paperbooks, 10-75% off; specializing in best-sellers, children's books and the Civil War.

Bruce Alan Bags. Leather goods, including luggage, backpacks, briefcases, attachés, handbags, wallets, umbrellas, and belts.

DonnKenny. First-quality clothing for career and leisure in petite, missy and full-figure sizes.

Dress Barn. Famous labels at 20-50% off.

Famous Footwear. Shoes at everyday savings of 10-50% — if you consider your time to be worth more than a 10% discount, then tell them so.

Genesco Factory to You Shoes. Nationally advertised men's and ladies' shoes at savings of 35-50% off.

Gentlemen's Wear House. For excellent values in tailored clothing for men and women including suits, sportcoats, slacks, skirts and jackets at 35-50% off.

Gitano Warehouse Clearance Center. Savings direct from the manufacturer.

The Gold Rush. 14K gold and sterling silver chains, charms and earrings at 20-40% off.

Haspel Factory Outlet. Save 35-70% on brand name tailored clothing and sportswear for men and women, including Evan-Picone, Gant, Austin Hill and Haspel brands.

Jewelie's. One of America's premier fashion jewelry manufacturers, offering costume jewelry at 50-90% off retail prices — *all right!*

L'eggs/Hanes/Bali. Save up to 50% on slight imperfect, closeout and overstock brand name hosiery, underwear, lingerie, socks, activewear and much more.

Little Red Shoe House. Brand name dress,

casual and athletic footwear for your entire family.

London Fog. Men's, women's and children's rainwear, outerwear, jackets, wool coats, leathers and slacks.

Old Mill. The latest ladies' fashions at savings of 25-70%.

The Paper Chase. Office supplies and unique novelty gifts, party supplies at great discount prices.

Prestige Fragrance & Cosmetics. 20-60% off cosmetics.

Socks Galore & More. A sock lover's dream— more than 60,000 pairs of socks for the entire family, at prices 25-80% off retail.

Van Heusen Factory Store. With savings of 30-60% on first-quality, current season men's and women's apparel.

Welcome Home. Decorative Victorian home furnishings and gift items at discount prices.

Fabulous Finds in . . .
PIGEON FORGE

Everybody knows about the smoky cool blue of Gatlinburg . . . right? Gateway to the Great Smoky Mountains, Gatlinburg has grown from a quaint mountain village in eastern Tennessee into a major resort area. It's unofficially the craft capital of the state. Nestled into the pearly blue mists of the Smokies, Gatlinburg honors the past with authentic Appalachian craft communities and celebrates today with almost every tourist attraction imaginable.

Located just seven miles northwest of Gatlinburg is Pigeon Forge. Pigeon Forge was once a small community with an iron forge and a grist mill. The mill is still open and is a popular attraction, as is Silver Dollar City, and about a

THINGS TO SEE AND DO
Pigeon Forge is action packed. There is nothing like it anywhere! Six miles of family attractions . . . log flumes, water slides, miniature golf, name entertainment, a giant wave pool, motor racing carts, bumper boats, live shows, thrill rides . . . if it is family fun you will find it in Pigeon Forge. Take time to enjoy the mountains. Write to the Gatlinburg Chamber of Commerce, Gatlinburg, Tennessee 37738 or call (800)251-9868 or if you are from TN, call (615)436-4178.

dozen other museums, boats, slides and live country music.

Not only does Pigeon Forge offer the beauty of the mountains and entertainment but it has some pretty irresistible shopping as well.

For more information, write to the Pigeon Forge Department of Tourism (P.O. Box 1390 G, Pigeon Forge, TN 37863; (800)251-9100 outside Tennessee, (615)/453-8574 in-state), or Gatlinburg Chamber of Commerce (Gatlinburg, TN 37738; (800)251-9868 outside Tennessee, (615)436-4178 in-state).

BELZ FACTORY OUTLET MALL

LOCATION: 1000 Teaster Ln.; (615)453-7316.

STORES: **Amy Stoudt.** Fashions for the large size

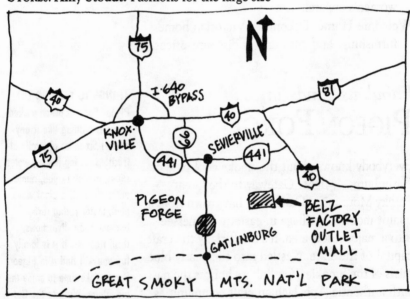

woman at 20-50% off—styles for work, day-into-evening.

Bag & Baggage. Business cases, handbags, luggage and small leather goods.

Bass Shoe Factory Outlet. Weejuns, Bucs, Sunjuns sandals and other footwear and accessories.

Bon Worth. Petite, missy and women's sizes.

Burlington Brands. Men's and women's apparel at 50-75% off.

Carole Hochman Lingerie Factory Outlet Store. Intimate apparel — savings of 30-60% on Christian Dior, Sara Beth, Lily of France, etc.

Casual Male Big & Tall. Caters to "the hard-to-fit man"; brands include Girbaud, Bugle Boy, Williwear, Jordache, Harbor Bay, Mark Elliot and Introspect.

Converse Factory Outlet. 40-70% off athletic footwear and activewear clothing, plus spectacular savings on all children's shoes.

Creations by Carole. Original sculptures, hand-cast in durable "bonded oak," handcrafted candles, and handmade trolls.

Crown Jewels. Fashion jewelry — most items 50% off.

Damon Shirt Outlet. Men's first-quality merchandise direct from the manufacturer at 30-60% savings.

Danskin. Leotards, tights, unitards, leg warmers, panty hose, for dance and activewear; savings of 50% or more.

Devon. Missy, large sizes and petite sportswear at 30-70% savings.

Diamond Factory & Eelskin Outlet. Genuine imported eelskin handbags, accessories and shoes up to 50% off; plus, turquoise and silver Indian jewelry.

DonnKenny. Related separates for career and sportswear, dresses and sleepwear; at least 50% off.

Dress Barn. Famous labels at 20-50% off updated fashions.

Famous Footwear. Brand name shoes for the entire family.

Fuller Brush Factory Outlet. Save 25-50%.

Gitano. Casual and active sportswear lines — tops, pants, skirts, dresses, fashion jeans,

PLACES TO EAT

Eat right in the Belz Factory Outlet Mall — take your choice from Geno's Italian Eatery, New Deli, Smoky Mountain Express, Subway or snack at the Pigeon Forge Fudge Company, The Great American Cookie Company or Yogurt De'Lites.

199

swimwear, outerwear, shoes, underwear and accessories.

Gitano/Kids. Gitano fashions for kids at tremendous savings.

Islandgear. Save up to 60% on Islandwear and other nationally recognized brands of swimwear for men and women.

Jonathan Logan Outlet. First-quality, current famous-label women's apparel at 40-70% off — Villager sportswear, Misty Harbor rainwear, RoseMarie Reid and Bill Blass beachwear.

Judy Bond Outlet. First-quality blouses, skirts, pants, split skirts, sweaters, shorts.

Kids Port USA. Kidswear for boys and girls from newborn to size 14 — savings of 25-70%.

Kitchen Place. A complete kitchen store.

Knits by K.T. Current season, first-quality ladies' sweaters and knit tops by Kenneth Too and other famous makers.

Leather Loft. Luxury leather for less — handbags, luggage, briefcases, wallets, belts, executive gifts and designer accessories, all at 40-60% off.

Palm Beach Factory Store. Save 35-70% on quality clothing — labels include Palm Beach, Gant, Evan-Picone, Eagle and Austin Hill.

The Paper Factory. A complete line of party goods and decorations, home and office supplies, greeting cards, books, games and puzzles; savings up to 50%.

Pinehurst Lingerie Factory Store. Fine intimate apparel at 40-60% off suggested retail.

Prestige Fragrance & Cosmetics. 25-75% off on prestigious brands of men's and women's fragrances, toiletries and cosmetics.

Regal Ware. Cookware and kitchen appliances — stainless steel, cast aluminum and drawn aluminum range-top cookware, microwave ovenware, food processors, coffeemakers, etc.

The Ribbon Outlet. Cut your own "by the yard," pre-cut, or entire spools in bulk—handcrafted gift items, selected craft supplies, novelty and seasonal items.

Royal Doulton. Dinnerware, crystal, giftware, nurseyware and figurines at 20-60% off.

Ruff Hewn. Men's and ladies' sportswear offering rugged comfort for every occasion—save 25-50%.

Sans Souci Lingerie. Popular priced daywear and sleepwear lingerie, up to 50% off.

Socks Galore & More. More than 60,000 pairs of socks; save 25-80%.

Sweats Etc. Lightweight jersey pants, shorts and tees; fleece tops and bottoms for men, women and children.

Toy Liquidators. Thousands of brand name toys at less than manufacturer's original wholesale prices.

Trendsetter Footwear. Brand name footwear at 25% off manufacturer's suggested retail prices.

Van Heusen Factory Store. Save 25-60% on current, in-season merchandise for men and women—dress and sport shirts, blouses, activewear, outerwear, sportswear, pants, skirts, sweaters and accessories.

Young Generations Factory Outlet. Products of this quality manufacturer—Ruth of Carolina and Picture Me fashion dresses and sportswear.

Also, the Knife Factory, WestPoint Pepperell Mill Store, Specials Exclusively by Levi Strauss, Rack Room Shoes, Bugle Boy, No-Nonsense and the Boot Factory.

FACTORY MERCHANTS ETC.

LOCATION: 821 N. Parkway on US 441.

STORES: Banner House, Corning Designs, Warnaco, totes, Van Heusen, Campus, Paul Revere Shoppe, Captree, Manhattan, Formfit,

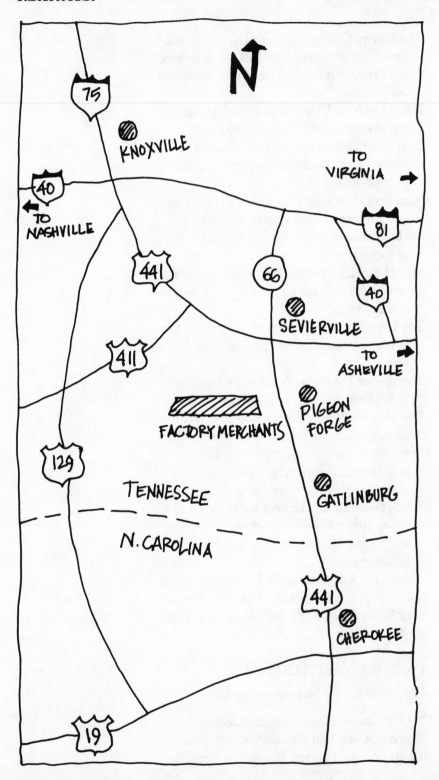

Mikasa, Aileen, Socks Galore & More, Fieldcrest
Cannon, Jaymar, JH Collectibles, London Fog,
Top of the Line Cosmetics, Pfaltzgraff, American
Tourister, Nike, Oneida Silver, Kitchen
Collection, Black & Decker, Skyr Sportswear,
Bass Shoe, Banister/Mushroom Shoe, Carter's
Childrenswear, Aunt Mary's Yarns, Polly
Flinders, Fashion Flair, OshKosh B'Gosh,
Gorham, Wallet Works by Amity, Petals, Sergio
Valente, Capezio, General Housewares, L'eggs/
Hanes/Bali, Lenox Outlet, Rawlings Sporting
Goods, Sergio Tacchini, Book Warehouse, Evan-
Picone, Bike Athletic, Tanner Outlet and others.

FACTORY STORES

LOCATION: Just off the Parkway behind the
"track." Look for the Green Roof and prepare to
shop some wonderful outlets.

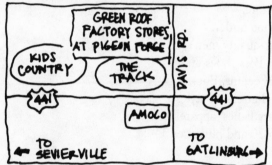

DIRECTIONS
Look for the Green Roof just
off the Parkway, behind "The
Track."

STORES: Liz Claiborne Outlet Store, Anne Klein
Outlet, Calvin Klein Outlet, harvé benard, J.G.
Hook, Reebok, Dansk, Barbizon, Bruce Alan
Bags, Manhattan Factory Stores, Stone
Mountain Craftsmen's Guild, Fenn Wright &
Manson, Samsonite, Farberware, Wembley Ties,
Leslie Fay, Henson Kickernick, Swank, Gilligan
& O'Malley, S&K, Linen's Plus and more to
come.

Fabulous Finds in . . .
TRI-CITIES

Tri-Cities is a gateway to the Great Smoky Mountains and is a popular area during fall foliage.

CAROLINA POTTERY OUTLET CENTER

Highly visible from the interstate, this center is situated among three markets: Kingsport, Johnson City and Bristol, Virginia/Tennessee.

LOCATION: Adjacent to I-81 and Hwy. 126. The center is located six miles north of Tri-Cities Airport.

STORES: **Aileen.** Women's sportswear in misses and plus sizes . . . and more.

Banister. The 40 brand shoe outlet.

Bass Factory Outlet. First-quality men's, women's and children's Bass shoes and accessories, including Weejuns, Bucs, Sunjuns, sandals and other casual styles.

Bon Worth. Contemporary ladies' apparel featuring misses sizes 6-20 and plus sizes 34-46.

Book Warehouse. Thousands of books, 50-90% off publishers' retail—also, computer software, gift items and special purchases, all discounted.

Bugle Boy. Savings of 30-70% on men's, women's and children's contemporary sportswear.

Captree. Ladies' clothing, factory direct.

Carolina Pottery. Everything from silk flowers to wicker baskets, brass and oriental gifts to dinnerware—famous names at prices that will surprise you.

Corning/Revere. Corningware, Pyrex, Corelle, RevereWare, and Visions.

Factory Linens. Bed and bath fashions.

Gitano Warehouse Clearance Center. First-quality active and casual sportswear priced at $19.95.

KB Lynn Factory Store. Ladies' knit dresses, sportswear, accessories, jewelry and eelskin at savings of up to 60%.

Old Mill. Save 25-70% on first-quality ladies' fashions, sizes 4-18 and petites 4-16.

The Paper Factory. Party goods, gift wrap, greeting cards and more—savings up to 50% every day.

Prestige Fragrance & Cosmetics. 25-60% off world-famous brands.

Rack Room Shoes. Famous brand shoes—first quality, great selection of styles, sizes and colors.

The Ribbon Outlet. Specialty retail chain carrying more than 3,000 varieties of ribbons and trims; also, craft and floral supplies, silk and dried flowers, gifts and accessories.

Swank. Quality leather goods, accessories and travel items.

Van Heusen. The factory-to-you store where the sale never ends.

Westport Ltd. Labels for the career woman, including Princeton Club, Atrium and Melano Design Group—dresses, suits, sportswear and separates.

Fabulous Finds in ...

UNION CITY

VF FACTORY OUTLET CENTER

VF Factory Outlets feature first-quality, brand name merchandise sold direct from the manufacturer to the consumer. This was voted one of the "ten best outlet shopping malls" by *Consumer's Digest* in 1985.

LOCATION: 601 Sherwood Dr. Call (901)885-6465 if you need help.

STORES: Banister. The 40 brand shoe outlet—Capezio, Pappagallo, Mushrooms, Liz Claiborne, Freeman, French Shriner, Reebok and 32 other brands, at 50% savings.

Prestige Fragrance & Cosmetics. Prestigious brands of men's and women's fragrances, toiletries, cosmetics and related accessories at 25-60% off.

VG Factory Outlet. Where everything is half off.

Van Heusen Factory Store. Save 25-60% on first-quality in-season fashion apparel.

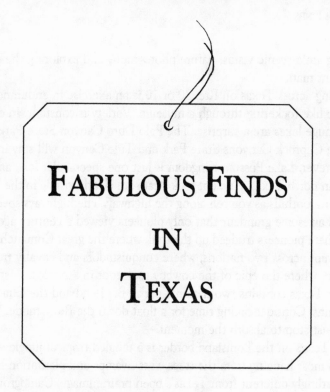

FABULOUS FINDS
IN
TEXAS

There's an old quote about Texas: "Other states were carved or born; Texas grew from hide and horn."

The real West is waiting for you where it all began in the Ft. Worth/Dallas area. More than a century ago, millions of Texas longhorns were driven to the Kansas railheads, three hundred dust-chewing miles away for the cowboys herding them along the legendary Chisholm Trail.

Fort Worth was the last chance for rest and revelry on the way north and the first on the way home. Dozens of saloons and dance halls cropped up to accommodate the saddle-weary cowhands. Today, you can walk the same wood-covered sidewalks and brick streets that cowboys and cattle barons once walked. In the historic Stockyards, you can sense the past all around you. It's located at North Main and Exchange Ave. and has lots of western wear stores, restaurants, saloons and a beautiful river walk area.

The name Texas is from "tejas," an Indian word meaning friendly. That ancient language is heard no more, but the spirit of "tejas" lives on in today's Texas—America's Friendship state.

The great outdoors is ever present on the Texas Panhandle-Plains. Lifestyles and recreational styles are keyed to abundant open-air activities—

camping amid scenic vistas, nature photography and exploring the paths of ancient man.

Driving across Texas on Rte. 20 or 10 is an exercise in endurance but it is also like rocketing through a museum. Variety is constant. In dusty Texas, huge lakes are a surprise. The Palo Duro Canyon State Park is inviting; Caprock Canyons State Park and Tule Canyon will stay in your mind forever. Lake Possum Kingdom is just one spectacular lake among dozens in north Texas. Ancient rock strata are clearly visible in the Rocky Mountain foothills as you roll along the highway. The highways speed you through awesome grandeur that only pioneers viewed a century ago. Explore where pioneers trudged up the trail, where the great Comanche War Trail swept across two nations, where conquistadors and cavalry troopers marched, where the epic of the cowboy took root in American history.

West Texas contains two national parks, Big Bend and the Guadalupe Mountains. Consider taking time for a float down the Rio Grande. Visit a fort or just stop to absorb the moment.

East Texas on the Louisiana border is a tangled tropical jungle with Spanish moss hanging from the trees, vast swamps and plantation homes. It is startlingly different from Texas's open prairie image. Campgrounds, more state parks, fishing, exploring the watery byways in a canoe are just part of east Texas.

Traveling north to south, the terrain changes dramatically; Texas is a land to relish right down to the port cities of Houston and Corpus Christi. The Texas gulf coast stretches from the moss-covered bayous of Louisiana to the sun-parched shore of Mexico. Texas is home to bird sanctuaries that attract the grey sandhill crane and whoopers. Padre Island is a retiree's paradise. Texas is a world apart from the Alamo to the wind-swept prairies in the north. Take time to visit Texas and "Live the Legend."

☞ **FOR MORE INFORMATION**

Texas travel information: Bed & Breakfast Texas Style, Inc., 4224 W. Red Bird Ln., Dallas, TX 75237; (214)298-5433. Guide to Historic Texas Hotels and Country Inns, O'Reilly Advertising, Suite C, 3600 Commerce, Dallas, TX 75226; (214)828-0100. Texas Travel & Information Division, 11th & Brazos Sts., Austin, TX 78701.

Fabulous Finds in . . .
HEMPSTEAD

VF FACTORY OUTLET CENTER

You'll enjoy shopping in the VF centers . . . the price is always right.

LOCATION: 805 Factory Outlet Dr. Call (409)826-8277 for directions.

STORES: VF Factory Outlet Store and other factory outlet stores that sell cosmetics, shoes, apparel for men and women.

Fabulous Finds in . . .
KINGSVILLE

VF FACTORY OUTLET SHOPPING CENTER

LOCATION: 1601 US Hwy. 77; (512)592-4380.

STORES: VF Outlet Store and factory outlets for fragrances and cosmetics, men's and women's apparel and other direct manufacturing stores.

Fabulous Finds in . . .
LIVINGSTON

VF FACTORY OUTLET CENTER

LOCATION: 440 US 59 Loop S.; (409)327-7881.

STORES: Vanity Fair Outlet Store and other factory outlet stores selling cosmetics, shoes and apparel for men and women.

Fabulous Finds in ...
MINERAL WELLS
VF FACTORY OUTLET CENTER
LOCATION: 4500 Hwy. 180 East; (817)325-3318.

STORES: Vanity Fair Outlet Store and the other stores in this center offer deep discounts on shoes, apparel and cosmetics.

Fabulous Finds in ...
NEW BRAUNFELS
THE MILL STORE PLAZA

Some of the shopping is different from the east coast outlet centers. Just check the stores.

DIRECTIONS
From I-35, take Exit 187 or 189 New Braunfels, TX.

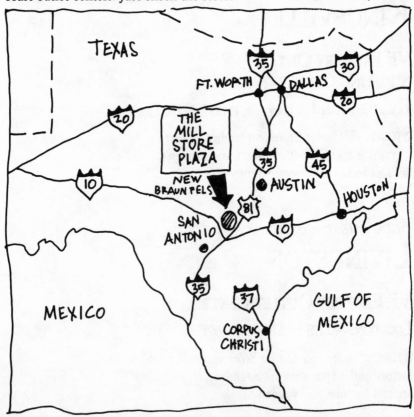

LOCATION: Adjacent to I-35 at the New Braunfels exit 189.

STORES: Pfaltzgraff, Cape Craft, Leather Loft, Aileen, Manhattan, Russell, Famous Footwear, Carter's Childrenswear, Henson Lingerie, Corning, Maidenform, Royal Doulton, Prestige Fragrance & Cosmetics, Van Heusen, Bass Shoe, Kitchen Collection, Gitano, Amity Leather, The Ribbon Outlet, Oneida Silver, Paper Factory, Banister Shoe, American Tourister, harvé benard, Paul Revere Shoppe, Palm Beach Co., Jindo Furs, Full Size Fashions, Lenox, WestPoint Pepperell, Toys Unlimited, Johnston's Fashions for Children, snack shops, a bakery and lots of fun.

Fabulous Finds in ...
SULPHUR SPRINGS

VF FACTORY OUTLET

LOCATION: The VF outlet offers you a choice of exits to reach it. Exit Hwy. 24 off I-30 or exit Hwy. 154 North off I-80; (214)885-0015 if the map fails to get you to the shopping center. (See map on following page.)

STORES: VF Factory Outlet Store, Banister Shoe, Prestige Fragrance & Cosmetics, Van Heusen, Kitchen Collection, Reading Hand Bag, The Paper Factory, Your Toy Center, Fieldcrest Cannon and Bon Worth.

WANTED
Your gems. The true shopping aficionado will always know about a few great little stores in the middle of nowhere that have wonderful buys. Researching for these little "gems," as we did for *SOS*, is expensive but you can make the difference if you think of *Fabulous Finds* when you shop.

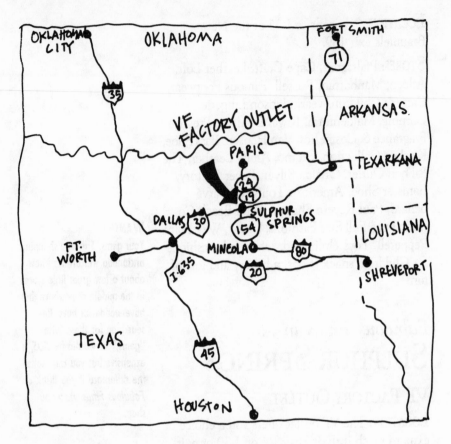

DIRECTIONS

From Dallas/Fort Worth —
I-30 East.

From Houston — I-45 North to
I-635 North. I-30 East.

From Texarkana — I-30 West.

From Shreveport — I-20 West
to I-80 to Mineola. Then Hwy.
154 North direct to VF Factory
Outlet.

From Oklahoma City — I-35
East to I-635 South. Then I-30
East.

From Fort Smith — Hwy. 71
South to I-30 West.

Traveling East on I-30: Broadway Exit. Take first left across
I-30. Right on Service Rd. Left
on Radio Rd. to VF Factory
Outlet.

Traveling West on I-30:
Broadway Exit. Right on In-
dustrial to Radio Rd. to VF
Factory Outlet.

FABULOUS FINDS
IN
UTAH

U tah — the best of the West" is not an overstatement. There are few places like it on earth. From the aspen and pine-studded forests of the north to the immense sandstone canyons of the south . . . from the snow-covered slopes for skiers to the white-water raft thrills on the Green and Colorado rivers . . . from the old fur trappers to urbanites in Salt Lake City. Utah has five national parks, six national monuments, one national historic site, two national recreation areas, forty-three state parks, unlimited camping, fishing, hiking, skiing, swimming and some of the nicest people in the world.

When he viewed the Capitol Reef National Park, government geologist C.F. Dutton wrote: "The colors are such as no pigments can portray. They are deep, rich and variegated; and so luminous . . . the light seems to flow or shine out of the rock rather than be reflected from it." Much earlier, the Navajos named it "Land of the Sleeping Rainbow." The sandstone bridges and domes, monoliths and pinnacles and sheerwalled cliffs rival the sphinx in Egypt.

Nature did some of her most awesome work in San Juan and Grand counties. These small counties feature more national parks than most of the U.S. The world's largest concentration of natural stone arches is found in Arches National Park. Canyonlands National Park is unbelievably rugged with monumental stone pinnacles, plunging canyons and a mighty river that provides rapid transit when you run it on a rubber raft. Western River Expeditions (7258 Racquet Club Dr., Salt Lake City, UT 84121; (800)453-7450 and in Utah (801)942-6669.

At Natural Bridges National Monument, hundreds of tons of solid rock reach across deep canyons, forming the largest natural bridges anywhere. Rainbow Bridge National Monument's inside span is so high that the nation's capitol could fit under it.

U.S Deputy Surveyor T.C. Bailey tried to describe Brice Canyon . . . "thousands of red, white, purple and vermillion rocks resemble sentinels on the Walls of Castles; monks and priests with their robes, attendants, cathedrals and congregations . . . deep caverns . . . spires and steeples, niches and recesses, presenting the wildest and most wonderful scene."

☞ **FOR MORE INFORMATION**

Write for the brochure called *Utah National Parks and Monuments* from the Utah Travel Council (Council Hall/Capitol Hill, Salt Lake City, UT 84114; (801)533-5681). The photos are good enough to frame, and they certainly supply the color and grandeur that a written description cannot.

Fabulous Finds in . . .

DRAPER

VF FACTORY OUTLET CENTER

Thousands of square feet of bargains. They say, "We sell clothing you'd enjoy buying anywhere.

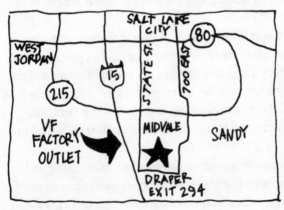

DIRECTIONS

Traveling North or South on I-15, take Exit 294 to the VF Factory Outlet.

Traveling East or West on I-80, take I-15 South, then take Exit 294 to the VF Factory Outlet.

But, since you're getting the products directly from the manufacturer, you pay just half the ticket price."

LOCATION: 12101 S. Factory Outlet Dr. I-15, exit 294; (801)572-6440.

STORES: **A Crafty Place.** Silk flowers, plants, craft hoops, aida cloth, knitting needles, wood and related products for tole painting, supplies for doll making, craft accessories.

American Tourister Factory Outlet. Hardside and softside luggage, business cases, totes and travel accessories at 40-70% off the suggested retail.

B.J. Spectrum. Fashion sportswear and contemporary apparel in children's, junior, misses, full-figure and maternity sizes.

Banister. The 40 Brand shoe outlet—Capezio, Pappagallo, Mushrooms, Liz Claiborne, Freeman, French Shriner, Reebok.

Bon Worth. Contemporary ladies' apparel coordinates, separates and fashion activewear.

Carter's Childrenswear. A manufacturer of fine children's wear for more than 100 years; nationally advertised brands of children's wear featuring Carter's—layette, infants, toddlers, boys and girls.

Mushrooms Factory Store. Women's shoes— Cobbies, Mushrooms, Red Cross and Selby.

New England Classics. Skyr & Catcher coordinated sportswear, with an emphasis on sweaters and turtlenecks.

The Paper Outlet. Gift wrap and gift wrap accessories, party goods, party decorations, office products, greeting cards, books, puzzles and games.

Polly Flinders. Girl's hand-smocked dresses, size newborn to girl's 14, for up to 60% less than retail.

Prestige Fragrance & Cosmetics. Men's and women's fragrances, toiletries, cosmetics and related accessories at 25-60% off suggested price.

Van Heusen Factory Store. Save 25-60% on first-quality, in-season fashion apparel for men and women.

The Wallet Works. Men's and women's first-quality leather wallets, clutches, key cases, accessories, briefcases, luggage and travel gifts at 25-75% below retail.

Windsor Shirt Company. Women's shirts and sweaters, men's sport and dress shirts — including big and tall sizes — sweaters, ties and other accessories.

Your Toy Center. Toys and games — Fisher-Price, Mattel, Coleco, Playskool, Milton Bradley, Matchbox and others.

Fabulous Finds
in
Vermont

Factory Outlets had their beginning in the New England States including Vermont. Dexter Shoe and Dunham Shoe have many stores scattered around New England. The factory outlets functioned like little roadside stores targeted directly at the tourists. It still works that way. There are numerous little clusters of outlet retailers scattered without rhyme or reason.

If you get that close to Fur Country, think about ordering a brochure from the Leather Ranch: "Manufacturers and Designers of the most exclusive garments on this planet at unbelievable prices." If you want "to buy leather direct," call the Leather Ranch head office in Toronto at (416)597-0151 or their Montreal store at (514)849-5111. Their brochure is outrageous. If the company delivers the merchandise shown in their brochure, and the price is right, please share your experiences with other Fabulous Finds shoppers.

A taste of old New England awaits you in the Green Mountain state. Enjoy the wealth of activities, events, scenery, folklore, back roads and world-class museums, granite quarries and a castle. Of course, skiing is a huge attraction to the Granite State. Mention the word "Killington" and you will have the attention of the skiers. With one hundred trails and seventeen lifts, you could spend a whole week and never ski the same trail twice. Within the Killington region, there are 115 places to stay, ranging from cozy country inns to contemporary condominiums. For reservations call (802)422-3711; if you want the latest ski report, call (802)422-3261. Killington is located in central Vermont at the junction of US 4 and Vermont 100 in Sherburne.

If Killington isn't for you, write to the Vermont Chamber of Commerce, Dept. of Travel and Tourism (P.O. Box 37, Montpelier, VT 05602) or call (802)223-3443 for more ski information. This phone and address is also good for Vermont country inns. And Vermont knows how to make you feel pampered in its country inns.

Nearly everyone knows how good pure maple syrup tastes on hot buckwheat pancakes or ice cream. But how many really know what maple syrup is, where it comes from, and how it's produced? If you're going to Vermont, get some information from the New England Maple Museum (Rte. 7 in Pittsford, P.O. Box 1615, Rutland, VT 05701), or call (802)483-9414. Be sure to bring home a supply of the maple syrup.

Vermont State Craft Center at Frog Hollow (Middlebury, VT) 05753; (802)388-3177) offers you Vermont's finest crafts. Sounds good.

Fabulous Finds in . . .
BRATTLEBORO
THE OUTLET CENTER
LOCATION: At exit 1E off I-91 on Canal St. If you need help, call (802)254-4594.
STORES: Marcraft Handbag Manufacturer, Kids Port USA, Manhattan Factory Outlet, Barbizon Lingerie, Amherst Sportswear Factory Outlet, Dunham Footwear Outlet, Van Heusen Factory Outlet, Jack Winter, Mary Meyer, Knitwits Factory Outlet and the Last Straw Outlet.

Fabulous Finds in . . .
MANCHESTER
MANCHESTER COMMONS
LOCATION: At the intersection of Rte. 7 and 11/30 and close to Bromlee and Stratton Mountain.

STORES: Ralph Lauren/Polo Factory Store, Boston Trading Co., Benetton Factory Store, Cole-Haan Company Store, Trader Kids, Samuel Roberts, Joan & David Shoes, ACA Joe and others.

Fabulous Finds in . . .
MANCHESTER CENTER

BATTENKILL PLAZA OUTLET CENTER

LOCATION: At the intersection of Rte. 11 and 30 (Rte. 7A); (914)949-5030.

STORES: First Choice for Escada, Anne Klein, Van Heusen, Kids Port USA, harvé benard, Sportswear Systems, Ellen Tracy . . . a very select group.

Fabulous Finds in . . .
RUTLAND

TENNYBROOK SQUARE

LOCATION: On Shelburne Rd. (Rte. 7). Call (802)775-2003 for hours and directions.

STORES: Bass Shoe Outlet, Van Heusen Factory Store, All Seasons Factory Outlet, Hathaway Factory Outlet, Swank Factory Store, Country Quilts, The Wood Carte, Formfit Outlet, Bed 'N Bath and a few little boutiques.

Fabulous Finds in . . .
WOODSTOCK

THE MARKETPLACE AT BRIDGEWATER MILL

A perfect example of how developers combine outlet stores and gift boutiques in the New England area.

LOCATION: 15 minutes west of the I-91 and I-89 intersection on Rte. 4 between Killington Mountain Ski Resort and Woodstock Center.

STORES: Dunham Footwear, Manhattan, Van Heusen, Prestige Fragrance & Cosmetics, The Outdoorsman Outlet Store, and about every small manufacturer in the state of Vermont— Vermont Canvas Products, Vermont Shaker Wood Products, Weston Bowl Mill, Bellflower Creations, Cameron's Casuals, Carbee Hill Collection, Deertan leather, Crafts of Vermont . . . and on and on.

FABULOUS FINDS IN VIRGINIA

Come walk golden beaches and follow mountain trails. Discover eighteenth-century towns and colonial plantations. Explore glittering caverns and fantasy worlds of fun. Visit historic cities and trace the steps of the famous and the great, back to America's beginnings. Come to Virginia. It's everything you love and a vacation you'll never forget." That is the invitation from Virginia State Travel Service (11 Rockefeller Plaza, New York, NY 10020; (212)245-3080).

Virginia is the oldest part of America. This is where the first battlegrounds and the first plantations are located. In 1607, America's first permanent English settlement was established on Jamestown Island. Colonial Williamsburg, the largest restored eighteenth-century town in America is located in the Tidewater area. Williamsburg commemorates America's beginnings with arts and crafts, costumed fife and drum corps, gardens and preserved architecture.

When the American Revolution began on April 18, 1775, there was little hope that the colonists could successfully resist the British. The ragtag army of farmers, artisans and shopkeepers gave up their homes and families to fight for the principles they held dear. Consider the impact on this area when General Lord Cornwallis arrived in Williamsburg with reinforcements that strengthened the British forces. Major General Marquis de Lafayette's troops defended the area against repeated assaults from the British.

To this day the Tidewater area is a fascinating display of the old plantation homes built along the James River. Some of the plantation homes are the ancestral or actual homes of former presidents.

Berkeley celebrated America's first Thanksgiving in 1619, a year before the Pilgrims landed at Plymouth Rock. In the Tidewater area, Virginia Beach is known to be one of America's outstanding ocean resort areas.

The Eastern Shore, a seventy mile long peninsula with hundreds of barrier islands, is a haven for snow geese and herds of wild ponies. Unspoiled beaches, quiet coves and lagoons slow the pace, allow time for seashelling. One side of the Eastern Shore faces the Atlantic Ocean and the other: Chesapeake Bay, which guarantees delicious seafood. Eastern Shore, like Key West, Florida, attracts the artists and craftspeople.

From the Tidewater area to the Highlands, Virginia is a land of history and beauty. You can see the beauty in the crafts displayed at festivals and fairs. The Blue Ridge, the Allegheny and the Cumberland mountains offer hiking trails, racing creeks and waterfalls, along with campgrounds and weekend homes for the lowlanders. You'll want to linger awhile in Virginia.

Fabulous Finds in . . .
FORT CHISWELL

FORT CHISWELL

LOCATION: Just outside Wytheville. At the junction of I-77 and I-81, take exit 25, then turn left onto the access road at Petro. If all else fails, call (703)637-6214.

STORES: Aileen, Banister Shoe, Bass, Campus, Fragrance World, Full Size Fashions, Kitchen Collection, Leather Loft, L'eggs/Hanes/Bali, Little Red Shoe House, Manhattan, Ribbon Outlet, Socks Galore, Toys Unlimited, Van Heusen, Wallet Works, Book Warehouse, Black & Decker and more to come.

Fabulous Finds in ...
FREDERICKSBURG

This historic town is just fifty miles south of Washington, DC. George Washington knew Fredericksburg well. Washington played in the streets as a boy, exploring its bustling waterfront. Others who figured prominently in the nation's early history came as well: Captain John Smith, Thomas Jefferson and other patriots. James Monroe practiced law here. Union and Confederate armies turned Fredericksburg and the surrounding countryside into a battleground. You can walk where the cannons roared and infantries charged. For more information write Visitor Center, P.O. Box FB, 706 Caroline St., Fredericksburg, VA 22401; (703)373-1776.

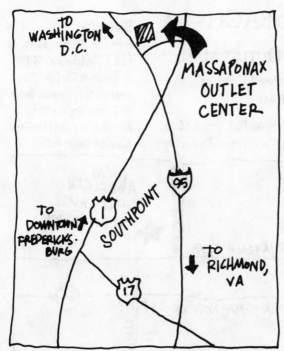

TO WASHINGTON D.C.

MASSAPONAX OUTLET CENTER

95

TO DOWNTOWN FREDERICKSBURG

1

SOUTHPOINT

TO RICHMOND, VA

17

DIRECTIONS
We're ¼ mile from Massaponax exit off I-95.

MASSAPONAX OUTLET CENTER

This factory outlet center recently opened but will be adding more stores. They are planning to include factory outlet retailers that you will like.

LOCATION: At Southpoint at the Massaponax exit off I-95 on the south side of Fredericksburg. The directions are easy and the traffic is manageable.

STORES: Fragrance World, Westport Ltd., harvé benard, Van Heusen, Cape Isle Knitters, Bass Shoe, Wisconsin Toy, Bruce Alan Handbags, Nilani, Aileen, S&K Menswear, Welcome Home, Rack Room Shoes, Springmaid Wamsutta, Corning/Revere and others opening soon.

Fabulous Finds in . . .
VIRGINIA BEACH

GREAT AMERICAN OUTLET MALL

LOCATION: On Virginia Beach Blvd. at Rosemont Rd., next to I-44.

STORES: Toy King, Amy Stoudt, Casual Male, Fieldcrest Cannon, Bare Necessities, Dress Barn,

DIRECTIONS
From I-64 North or South, or from I-264 take Rte. 44 East to Rosemont Rd. Take Rosemont north to Virginia Beach Blvd. Take Virginia Beach Blvd. west ½ mile to the Great American Outlet Mall.

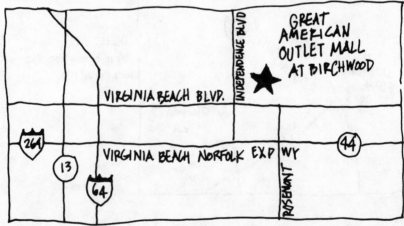

Old Mill, Famous Footwear, Legsense, American
Tourister, Shapes, Toy Liquidators, harve
benard, Nilani Outlet, Rolane, Palm Beach, Izod,
Acme Boots, Jordache, Piercing Pagoda, Fashion
Express, Aileen, Paper Outlet, Top of the Line
Cosmetics, Banister Shoe, Gateway Books, Kids
Port USA, Van Heusen, Leather Loft, Rack
Room, Jewelry Connection, Gold Factory,
Children's Bootery.

Fabulous Finds in . . .
WAYNESBORO

SHENANDOAH VILLAGE

Ellen Spence wrote, "On vacation, we visited the
new Shenandoah Village. It is in the beautiful
Blue Ridge Mountains of Virginia and has the
first Waterford crystal outlet I've ever seen. Wine
goblets that go for $40 were $18.50 a piece."
Thanks for the note, Ellen. Thanks for sharing
your opinions with the readers of *Fabulous Finds*;
hope to hear from you again.

LOCATION: On the Blue Ridge Parkway at the
intersection of I-64 and Rte. 340.

STORES: Housewares, Gitano, Banister, Jonathan
Logan, Manhattan, Ribbon Outlet, The Wallet
Works, Aileen, Van Heusen, Bass, Hanes
Activewear, Prestige Fragrance & Cosmetics,
Socks Galore & More, Fanny Farmer, Corning,
Barbizon, Leather Loft, Westport Ltd.,
Maidenform, American Tourister, Paper Factory,
Royal Doulton, Dansk, Petal Pushers, Book
Warehouse, Waterford/Wedgewood, harvé
benard, Liz Claiborne, Towle Silver, L'eggs/
Hanes/Bali.

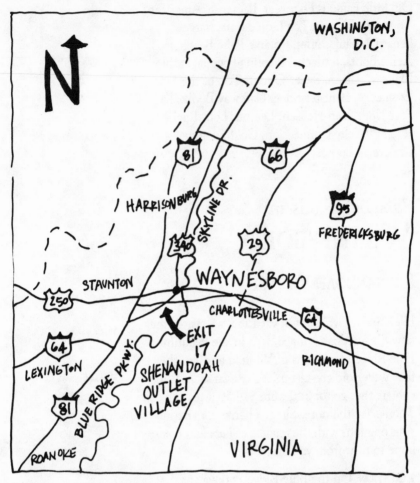

Fabulous Finds in . . .
WILLIAMSBURG

DIRECTIONS
I-64, Exit 17, left onto Rte. 340
South to Waynesboro, VA.

In Williamsburg, you can walk the streets where presidents walked. The giants of American history visited the taverns and state houses. The roll call is impressive: Thomas Jefferson, George Washington, James Madison and Patrick Henry debated the appropriate relationship between the American Colonies and the mother country. That debate ended in revolution. Williamsburg was at the center of the storm that became the American Revolution and that revolution cli-

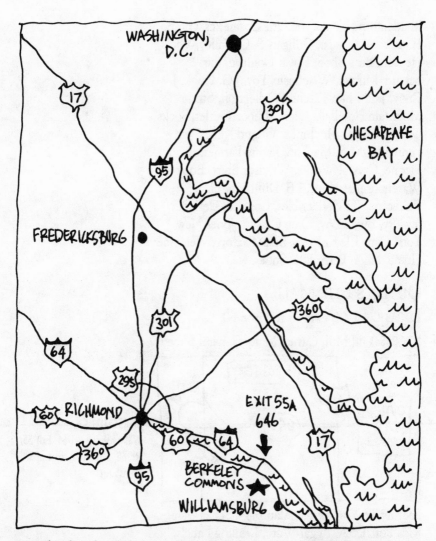

maxed only a few miles away from Williamsburg in 1781. For more information, write Colonial Williamsburg (P.O. Drawer B, Williamsburg, VA 23187) and ask for a vacation planner.

BERKELEY COMMONS OUTLET CENTER

LOCATION: Take the Lightfoot exit off I-64 one mile to Richmond Rd., a mile and a half from the Williamsburg Pottery Factory (listing follows).

STORES: Intimate Eve, Calvin Klein, Anne Klein,

DIRECTIONS

Located on Rte. 60 West. Richmond Rd. Three miles from historic Williamsburg, Va. From I-64—Take the Toano exit and turn right onto Rte. 60/Richmond Rd. Berkeley Commons is approximately 2 miles on the right.

Maidenform, Top of the Line Cosmetics, Gitano,
Hamilton Luggage, Gilligan & O'Malley, Van
Heusen, Bass Shoe, Royal Doulton, harvé
benard, Mikasa, Wisconsin Toy, J.G. Hook, J.
Crew, Jindo Fur, Kitchen Collection, Stone
Mountain Handbag, Lucia, Ribbon Outlet, Socks
Galore, Carole Hochman, Gitano Kids, Skyr,
Fenn Wright & Manson, Fanny Farmer, Evan-
Picone, Crystal Works, Windsor Shirt, Book
Warehouse, Argenti, I.B. Diffusion, Liz
Claiborne, JH Collectibles, Capezio, Designer
Jewelry, Bugle Boy, Oleg Cassini, Jones New
York, Cape Isle Knitters, Brass Factory, Welcome
Home, Nike, Perry Ellis Shoes.

OUTLETS LTD. MALL

LOCATION: I-64, exit 55 to Hwy. 60.

STORES: Old Mill, Casual Male, General Shoe

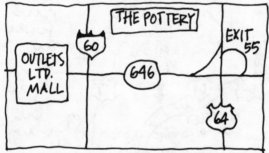

DIRECTIONS
Williamsburg — I-64, Exit 55/
Rt. 60, 5 minutes west of Wil-
liamsburg.

Factory To You, Bruce Alan Bags, Socks Galore,
Kids Port USA, Regal Ware, Leading Labels,
S&K Famous Brands, Dress Barn, Burlington
Brands, totes, Aileen, Paper Factory, Campus
Factory Outlet, Rack Room.

PATRIOT PLAZA

LOCATION: On Rte. 60 between historic
Williamsburg and the Williamsburg Pottery
Factory (see next listing).

STORES: Lenox, WestPoint Pepperell, Villeroy &
Boch, Leather Loft, American Tourister, Nettle
Creek, Ben and Jerry's famous ice cream.

WILLIAMSBURG POTTERY FACTORY

The innovator in this area. They started their factory outlet in 1938 with a pottery roadside shed on a half acre lot, where James E. Maloney started making eighteenth-century saltglaze pottery reproductions at his own wheel. His craft was so popular with the local citizenry and tourists who stopped by that he soon added china and glassware to his stock, discounting prices to keep customers coming back. That was the original Williamsburg Pottery. Almost half a century later the tempo has quickened. Today the original Williamsburg Pottery has grown to 130 acres, with another 196 acres under development. Thousands of Williamsburg Pottery bargains are available in more than thirty structures, including a solar building the size of eight football fields. In addition to pottery from all over the world, you will find elegant china, crystal, wines, cheese and from the Caribbean islands, woven baskets. From Mexico, onyx and brightly hued pottery. From the Far East, brass accent pieces, linens, gifts. They also have jewelry, glassware, gourmet foods, furniture, lamps, prints and frames, plants, gardenware, wicker, soap and candles, toys and games.

DIRECTIONS
Located at Lightfoot, Virginia, 5 miles west of Williamsburg. Take Exit 55A off I-64 and go south on Rt. 646. You'll see the signs.

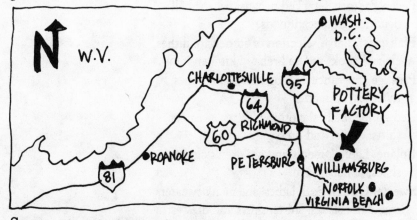

STORES: They also have outlet stores on the grounds and here is a partial listing.

Ann Michele Originals. Dresses, slacks, shirts, skirts and costume jewelry.

Banister Shoe. Both casual and dressy shoes for men, women and children—large selection of sportswear, shoes for the family.

Beacon Linens. Complete line of linens for bathroom, kitchen and bedrooms, bathroom accessory items and wall hangings.

Black & Decker. Tools, outdoor items, saws, drills, replacement parts for Black & Decker items—also, General Electric small appliances such as irons, toasters, skillets, broilers, hair dryers, mixers and can openers, radios and phones.

Boyd Brass Beds. Brass Beds, coat racks, lamps and brass finished tables.

Carter's. Children's clothing.

Kitchen Collection. Pots, pans, utensils, linens, small appliances.

Manhattan. Clothing for men and ladies, dresses, skirts, shirts, hosiery, slacks, sweaters, shorts both dressy and casual.

Oneida Silver. Flatware and holloware items.

Paul Revere Shoppe. Complete line of cookware, butcher blocks, utensils and other items.

Pecan Factory. Cracked pecans, pecan shell figurines and pecan foods.

Pfaltzgraff. Large selection of stoneware dishes, enamel cookware and related kitchen items.

Prestige Fragrance & Cosmetics. Perfumes, toiletries, cosmetics.

Red Horse. Ladies' clothing, skirts, sweaters, shirts; casual and dressy.

Rolane. Ladies', men's and children's clothing, shoes, handbags etc.

Sweater Outlet. Both ladies' and men's sweaters, and ladies slacks, shirts, skirts and dresses.

V.I.P. Yarns. Large variety of craft items and yarns.

WANTED

Interesting and unique lodgings, not chains—they are easy to find. Think of *Fabulous Finds* as the connecting link to thousands of other travelers and think what you would like to recommend to them.

Van Heusen. Men's and ladies' clothing both dress and casual.

You will find a food sales area and ice cream parlor on the grounds to rev up your energy so that you can shop, shop, shop.

Fabulous Finds in . . .
WOODBRIDGE

POTOMAC MILLS

Bantam Books proclaimed Potomac Mills the "best shopping mall" in the country in 1987. Potomac Mills features leading discounters such as IKEA, Sears Outlet, Waccamaw Pottery and Woodward & Lothrop Outlet Center. They also bring in manufacturer's factory-direct outlets, catalog outlets, brand name discounters, off-price retailers, and wholesale eliminators always offering quality brand names at 20-60% savings. If you think that this huge shopping center might be inhabited by an unseen colony of permanent twenty-four-hour shoppers, you might be right. A trip through the mall for orientation is advisable, particularly if you mark a mall brochure or these pages to guide you on the return shopping foray.

If you want to eat, you'll need to do it in the Potomac Mills almost like gassing up the car for a long trip. You will have a wide assortment of snack, cookie and sandwich shops, and bakeries.

LOCATION: Potomac Mills is easy to find and centrally located thirty minutes from downtown Washington, DC. If traveling south on I-95, take exit 52, Dale City (784 West). Stay to the right. At the stop sign, take a right onto Potomac Mills Rd. At the next stop sign, turn right onto Gideon. If you are traveling north on I-95, take exit 52 (west), which turns into Dale Blvd. At the first stoplight, turn right onto Gideon. For more information, call (703)643-1605.

NOTE: With this unique presentation of gigantic space and mixed retail concepts, the following list will help you to distinguish between the stores who proclaim themselves manufacturer's outlets and the stores who are sometimes called off-price or discounters. The primary difference between off-price and discounters is when and where the store was born. If the store was born in the eighties, it is probably called off-price. If the store was conceived in New York or New Jersey and is influenced by the old-time retail language, and if the store buys right and passes the discount along to the customer, it is probably called a discounter. This is a very murky area and that gives the manufacturer's outlet a competitive edge. Consumers tend to trust the producers of goods, or the roadside farmer, more than they trust the middleman/salesman. However, remember that manufacturers — the producers of goods — have also become the salesmen. Not all manufacturers sell at or near the wholesale price to the public. Some manufacturers sell with a small 20% discount and that can be misleading. Some manufacturer's sell a little bit of their merchandise and a lot of outside buys, but they call themselves a manufacturer's outlet. Look at the labels in the merchandise; if most of it belongs to the manufacturer whose store you are in, it's an outlet. If the manufacturer is located in a factory outlet center, the natural assumption is that you can expect savings of 40-50%. Don't assume anything, check the prices, the discounts/savings, and the quality of the merchandise. Even the best designers license their name and sometimes that name appears on some undesirable goods. Whenever you shop or spend money remember: *Buyer beware.*

MANUFACTURERS' OUTLETS: ACA Joe, Adolfo Sport, Again Boutique (Guess), Aileen Factory Outlet, American Tourister, Laura Ashley, Banister/Mushroom Shoes, Benetton Outlet, Bugle Boy Outlet, Calvin Klein Outlet, Campus Factory Outlet, Carol Hochman Lingerie, Campus Factory Outlet, Carter's Childrenswear, Children's Bootery/Jumping Jacks Outlet, Creighton Shirt Makers, Crown Jewels (Monet), East Hampton Clothing (Sergio Valente), Famous Footwear, First Choice Fashions (Escada, Laurel, Crisca), L'eggs/Hanes/Bali Outlet, Flair Graphics Outlet, Galerie de France (Limoges), Gitano, Goouch Outlet, Hahn Shoes Outlet, Hilda of Iceland, Intimate Eve (St. Eve), Just Kids Outlet Store, Lady Footlocker Outlet, Maidenform Outlet Store, Manhattan Factory Outlet, New England Trading Co. (Cambridge Dry Goods), Newport Sportswear, Nike Outlet, Oriental Weavers, Pandora Sportswear/ Sweaters, Puma Outlet, Prestige Fragrance & Cosmetics, R.W.'s Sweater Outlet, Rodier Paris Factory Outlet, Royal Silk Outlet, The Sofa & Chair Place (Rowe Furniture), Specials Exclusively Levi Strauss, Sportswear Systems (Fenn Wright & Manson), Stephanie Kay, Toy Liquidators, Van Heusen Factory Store, Westport Ltd., Windsor Shirt Company.

OTHER STORES: Hamricks, Adler's Art & Frame, Door Store Outlet, Galerie de France, Cargo Outlet, Ikea (and you will love that store), Kemp Mill Records, Lamp Factory Outlet, Linens 'n Things, New York Electronics, Piece Goods Shop, Record World, Sears Outlet, Waccamaw Pottery (it is huge!), Wall to Wall Sound & Video, Waxie Maxie Warehouse Store, Woodward & Lothrop Outlet Center, Books-A-Million, Break Point, Brewster Glassmith, Bud's Deep Discount, Central Newsstand, Cosmetics & Sculptured Nails, Dollar Bills, Elm Tree

Hallmark, Everything's a $1.00, Georgetown
Leather Design Outlet, The Hair Cuttery,
Hamilton Luggage, Inkadinkado, The Invention
Store, J.C. Clintons, Jewelry Vault, Keyworks,
LensCrafters, The Main Event, Package Pros,
The Paper Factory, Potomac Sports Factory,
Riggs National Bank, Ritz Camera & Video
Outlet Center, Show-Stoppers, Tract Software,
Sterling Super Optical, Vitamin World, The
Warehouse, Daffy's Clothing Bargains for
Millionaires, Freddy's Zoo, The Stuffed Animal
Kingdom, Kid's Barn, Ross Dress For Less, The
Toy Works, Toys and Gifts Outlet, Young Land,
The Answer, Busy Bodies, Custom Design Tee-
shirts, Coat World, Corner House, Sportswear,
Dress Barn Outlet, Fashion Express, The Fur
Place, Lady Bug Outlet, Lady Footlocker Outlet,
Lady Leslie, L.J. Fashions, Melons, Merry Go
Round Outlet, Potomac Sports Factory, The Pro
Image, Raleighs Clearance Center, Sassafras,
Stephanie Kay, Sweats Etc., Ten Below, T.H.
Mandy, $9.99 Stockroom, Casual Male, Casual
Male Big & Tall, Chess King Garage, Coatworld,
Compare Menswear by Ted Louis, Contemporary
Man, Sportswear, Men's Market, Potomac Sports
Factory, The Pro Image, Ross Dress for Less,
S&K Famous Brands, Webster Warehouse,
Beautiful Impressions, Best Jewelry, Bijou Catrin,
Busy Bodies, Crown Jewels, Dina's Discount
Boutique, Famous Footwear, Helen's Handbags,
International Diamond Cutters Exchange, J.C.
Clinton's, Jewelry Outlet, Leaves & Shells, Lord
Charles Quality Jewelers, Loves, Olympic Outlet
Featuring Adidas, Price Jewelers, Puma Outlet,
Rack Room Brand Shoes, Secaucus Handbags,
Shell Factory, Shoe-town Outlet, SneaKee Feet,
Top of the Line Cosmetics.

FABULOUS FINDS IN WASHINGTON

The explorers who sailed along Washington state's rugged Pacific Coast and into Puget Sound in the eighteenth century found spectacular scenery and native cultures that were already thousands of years old. Today's travelers can see the same "lofty snow mountains" and "innumerable pleasing landscapes" that delighted the British explorers George Vancouver and Peter Puget in 1792. You'll also find a record of Indian lives that goes back twelve thousand years, to a time when mastodons still inhabited the Olympic Peninsula.

After the glaciers of the last Ice Age retreated, coastal Indians turned to hunting whales and seals in ocean-going canoes, and netting salmon by the thousands in the rivers. The Makah Cultural and Research Center presents the record of this traditional life in amazing detail. Other good places to see native art and artifacts include the Thomas Burke Museum on the University of Washington campus in Seattle, the Yakima Nation Cultural Center on the reservation near Toppenish and the Museum of Native American Cultures in Spokane.

During the last Ice Age, the first people ever to reach Siberia arrived from Asia. When they reached the area that is now Washington, waves of migrations that lasted for thousands of years, left their mark on history.

The Museum of History and Industry sponsors many exhibits, and you may want to plan half a day learning about your ancestors. Call (206)728-0888 for information, or write Museum of History & Industry, (2700 24th Ave. E., Seattle, WA 98112).

Don't forget Mount St. Helens: It is still an awesome sight. Find a flying service or bush pilot and fly near the still-smoldering dome. See the destruction caused by the raging flood when 140,000 acre feet was thawed out by the heat of the volcano. The water, mud and ash flows carried trees, homes and logging equipment.

☞ **FOR MORE INFORMATION**
Other useful addresses: Washington State Office of Archeology and Historic Preservation (11 W. 21st Ave., KL-11, Olympia, WA 98504; (206)754-5600). Tourism Division of Destination Washington Project (101 General Administration Bldg. AX-13, Olympia, WA 98504-0613; (206)586-2088 or (206)586-2102).

Fabulous Finds in . . .
BURLINGTON
PACIFIC EDGE OUTLET CENTER
LOCATION: 65 miles north of Seattle.
STORES: Liz Claiborne, Fashion Flair, Gant, Maidenform, Jindo Fur, The Ribbon Outlet, Wallet Works, Van Heusen Athletic Sneaker & Apparel, Gitano, harvé benard, Leather Loft, Manufacturer's Jewelry, American Tourister, Evan-Picone, I.B. Diffusion, Socks Galore, Cape Isle Knitter, Prestige Fragrance & Cosmetics, Wisconsin Toy, Corning/Revere, Welcome Home, Tanner Factory Outlet, Aileen, Argenti, Kitchen Collection, Barbizon, Mikasa, Bugle Boy.

PLACES TO EAT AND SLEEP
The Washington Bed and Breakfast Guild (2442 N.W. Market St., Seattle, WA 98107) describes a couple of dozen places to eat and sleep in a brochure; write, or call (206)432-1409 or (206)384-3205. Bed and breakfast accommodations information for the beautiful, green Whidbey Island can be obtained from Whidbey Island Bed & Breakfast Association (P.O. Box 259, Langley, WA 98260; (206)321-6272.

Fabulous Finds in . . .
CENTRALIA
CENTRALIA FACTORY OUTLET CENTER
LOCATION: At exit 82 off-ramp in either direction is an outlet town. Centralia is about

eighty miles from either Seattle or Portland, Oregon, and the factory outlet stores love the location.

STORES: Oneida, Buffalo China, Wicker Factory, London Fog, Gitano, Banister Shoe, Ribbon Outlet, American Tourister, Mushrooms, Prestige Fragrance & Cosmetics, Leather Loft, Van Heusen, Corning/Revere, Fashion Flair, Aileen, Devon, Sperry Duffel and In-Sport, Old Mill, Manhattan Jewelry, Socks Galore, Cape Isle Knitters, Bass Shoe, Wisconsin Toy and Kitchen Collection. More stores coming.

Fabulous Finds in . . .
SEATTLE

The Olympic Peninsula has some of the most remote and least explored wilderness in this country. There are snow-fed rivers and mountain lakes, mystic rain forests, and the Olympic Mountains to explore. Along the seashore you will find rocky arches and islands carved by the Pacific's thundering waves, rocks ground smooth and round by the pounding surf, and giant redwoods washed down from higher elevations.

PAVILION MALL

If Seattle is the beginning and end of your trip to Washington state, shop in Pavilion Mall, possibly the best off-price shopping in the country. Luggage, apparel, cosmetics, linens and much more are priced right in Pavilion Mall.

LOCATION: At Southcenter Pkwy. and South 180th Tukwila one mile south of the 1-5/405 interchange.

Tillicum Village is an unforgettable experience of myth and magic presented with great taste. You can combine a delicious dining

THINGS TO SEE AND DO

Tillicum Village is an unforgettable experience of myth and magic presented with great taste. You can combine a delicious dining experience with the magic and folklore of a unique civilization; (206)443-1244 for arrangements.

The ferry from Anacortes (85 miles north of Seattle) will carry you to the enchanting San Juan Islands. Travel writers, tourists and natives alike have said that this cruise is one of the country's most scenic. This inland waterway is spectacular and the ferry system allows you to enjoy the islands and narrows for spare change. Call (800)541-WASH for information from outside Washington and (800)562-4570 if you live in-state.

experience with the magic and folklore of a
unique civilization; (206)443-1244 for
arrangements.

The ferry from Anacortes (85 miles north of
Seattle) will carry you to the enchanting San
Juan Islands. Travel writers, tourists and natives
alike have said that this cruise is one of the
country's most scenic. This inland waterway is
spectacular and the ferry system allows you to
enjoy the islands and narrows for spare change.
Call (800)541-WASH for information from
outside Washington and (800)562-4570 if you
live in-state.

FABULOUS FINDS
IN
WEST VIRGINIA

There are vineyards, battlefields, underground caverns, and lots more in West Virginia. Call (304)348-2286 or (800)CALL-WVA for information.

White water rafting is readily available. Call (304)658-5276 for an ultimate white water experience. Also try West Virginia River Runners (P.O. Box 78, Ames Heights Rd., Lansing, WV 25862; (304)574-0704).

Although glass manufacturing is a dying industry here, exploring a glass factory is exhilarating. Glassmaking is the commercial product of artists. Start with Blenko on Rte. 64 at the Milton exit (28), (304)743-9081 and you will find brochures to all the rest. Fenton Glass is in Williamstown (304)375-7772, and you will find many bus tours that will take you from factory to factory. For more information on West Virgina arts and crafts, call (800)624-0577 or (304)725-2055. For information on state parks and forests, call (800)624-9110 or (304)348-2764.

Fabulous Finds in . . .
MARTINSBURG

Martinsburg in Berkeley County is a historian's delight. The Tuscarora Indians did not exactly welcome the first white settlers and one of the first was George Washington. From 1755 to 1758 Washington defended the Jefferson County area against Indian attacks during the French and Indian War. Andrew Jackson was born to poor Irish immigrants at Big Springs, south of Martinsburg. In 1842 the Baltimore and Ohio Railroad came to the area and transformed this little village into a thriving industrial town.

Confederate Colonel Stonewall Jackson had his first encounter with Union soldiers near Martinsburg. The war raged throughout this area and many battles were fought here. By the turn of the century, Martinsburg became a manufacturing center with great mills locating in the town.

While you are shopping in the Blue Ridge Outlet Center (below), visit the information center just inside the main entrance. Trained staff will assist you with information regarding area attractions, restaurants, lodging, travel tips and directions. Martinsburg and the eastern part of the state provides recreational weekends for the city people in and around Washington, DC and Baltimore; consequently, this area has more than its share of resorts, restaurants and activities.

BLUE RIDGE OUTLET CENTER

Get set to enjoy yourself when you visit the Blue Ridge Outlet Mall. The stores are great, and the environment is perfect. The outlet center is located in an historic wool mill dating back to the turn of the century. You can save up to 70% on quality name brands from the nation's leading manufacturers.

LOCATION: 315 W. Stephen St.; (800)445-3993 or (304)263-SHOP, if you're calling from West Virginia.

PLACES TO EAT

Here is a partial listing of highly recommended restaurants.

Bavarian Inn & Lodge: "Award-winning cuisine and accommodations overlooking the Potomac River"; (304)876-2552. Mobil Guide four-star restaurant.

Boydville: This inn was spared burning during the "War of Northern Aggression" by the direct order of President Abraham Lincoln; (304)263-1448.

Mountain Village Inn: This inn is within an hour's drive of Back Creek Valley, Berkeley Springs Mineral Baths, Cacapon State Park, Thoroughbred racing at Charles Town Race Track, Harper's Ferry, white water rafting on the Potomac, and other interesting things to do. For reservations, call (304)735-6344.

In Harpers Ferry, try The Anvil at (304)535-2582.

Country Road Inn in Summersville (304)872-1620) has been recommended by *Southern Living*, Mobil Travel Guide, *Ford Times, Who's Who in America's Restaurants*, etc. Fort Savannah Inn (800)344-2507) near White Sulphur Springs.

The Country Inn in Berkeley Springs 103 miles from Washington, DC and Baltimore. Featured in *Country Inns and Back Roads*; (304)258-2210.

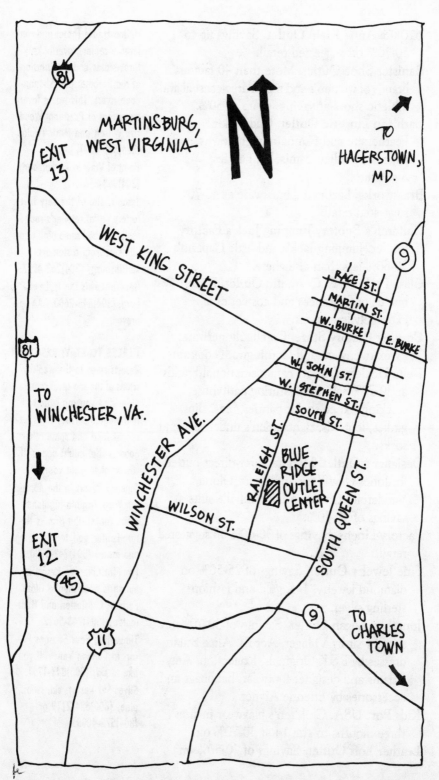

STORES: **Anne Klein Outlet.** Savings up to 50-70% off suggested retail.

Banister Shoe Outlet. More than 40 famous brands of women's and men's dress, casual and athletic shoes at savings of up to 50%.

Barbizon Lingerie Outlet. Cuddleskin, Featheraire and Flannaire nightgowns, and pajamas, teddies, camisoles, panties, nightshirts.

Brassworks. Lacquered brassware at 40-70% off suggested retail.

Children's Bootery/Jumping Jack's Factory Outlet. Jumping Jack's and little Capezio's 30-60% less than elsewhere.

Class Perfume & Cosmetic Outlet. Better brands of fragrances and cosmetics at extremely low prices.

Corning Factory Store. Corelle dinnerware, Pyrex ovenware and Corningware cookware.

Delta Hosiery Outlet. Famous national brands at 30-70% savings, featuring pantyhose, stockings, knee socks, panties, bras, slips, girdles, leotards, tights, men's underwear and socks.

Designer's Outlet. Manufacturer-direct outlet for Jones New York and Sport, Gloria Vanderbilt, Christian Dior, Saville suits at savings of 30-70%.

Factory Linens. Savings of 30-60% off suggested retail.

Fine Jewelry Outlet. Savings of 25-50% on diamond jewelry, 14K gold and fashion sterling silver.

Jonathan Logan Outlet. Savings of 30-70% on sportswear by Villager, Act III, Alice Stuart, dresses by R&K Originals, Kollection, Amy Adams and designer footwear, handbags and accessories by Etienne Aigner.

Kids Port USA. Children's playwear in sizes three months to size 14 at 30-70% off.

Leather Loft Outlet. Savings of 20-50% on

Hilltop House (hotel and conference center), overlooks three states and the junction of the Potomac and Shenandoah rivers. This was a favorite retreat of President Woodrow Wilson and Mark Twain; (304)535-6321.

Point of View in Parkersburg; (304)863-3366.

Jason's: site of the very first factory outlet retailer's roundtable, has had some high compliments from customers. In Martinsburg; (304)263-4997.

General Lewis Inn in Lewisburg; (304)645-2600. AAA approved.

PLACES TO STAY: RESORTS

Resorts cater to the wealthy scions of the sea-level communities and you can expect to find elegant surroundings, excellent food and some other goodies that might appeal if you want to treat yourself.

Oglebay Resort in the northern West Virginia highlands offers cabins, the Brooks Nature Center, golf, tennis, skiing and more; (304)242-3000.

Fox Fire Camping Resort in Milton is near Blenko Glass Factory, Charleston and Huntington; (304)743-5622.

Timberline Four Seasons Resort in Canaan Valley, if you like to ski; (800)843-1751.

Silver Ski Resort: ski, swim, dine; (800)624-2119 or (304)572-4000.

men's and women's leather goods: Edward Harvey, Gary's of California and ABA's.

L'eggs/Hanes/Bali Factory Outlet. Save 20-50% and more on slightly imperfects, closeouts and overstocks—hosiery, underwear, lingerie and activewear.

Manhattan Factory Outlet. Men's and ladies' apparel 25-60% below suggested retail prices; also, a big/tall department for men.

Misty Harbor Outerwear Outlet. 30-70% off Misty Harbor raincoats, jackets, slickers and outerwear accessories for men and women; activewear and swimwear by Rose Marie Reid, Bill Blass, Action Scene, Beach Party and other famous labels.

Nike Factory Outlet. Men's and ladies' apparel—save 25-60% on athletic footwear, sportswear, hosiery, sport bags and accessories for men, women and children.

The Paper Factory. Assortments of gift wrap and accessories, party goods and accessories, home and office supplies and books, games and puzzles—savings up to 50%.

Petals Factory Outlet Store. 40-70% off silk and dried flowers, plants, trees, custom arrangements, Christmas decorations, containers and gifts.

RevereWare Outlet. Save on irregulars priced 50-70% below retail.

The Ribbon Outlet. World's largest selection of ribbons—save up to 70%.

Royce Hosiery. Men's and ladies' socks.

The Sweater Outlet. Skyr turtlenecks, wool or cotton sweaters, coordinated sportswear, boiled wool jackets, cotton sleepwear, at 40-70% savings.

totes Factory Outlet. Save 50-70% on men's and women's umbrellas, outerwear, headwear, luggage, scarves, rubber footwear, etc.

Van Heusen Factory Store. Save 30-60% on Van Heusen dress and sportswear, Lady Van

The Woods: rustic pine rooms or luxury lodge rooms. dining, tennis, swimming, volleyball, hot tub and sauna and more; (800)248-2222.

Greenbrier: a world-famous conference center and retreat. Legendary food; (800)624-6070.

If you want information about Canaan Valley, Silver Creek, Snowshoe, Timberline, Winterplace, call (800)CALL-WVA.

Heusen and many other brands.

The Wallet Works by Amity. Wallets, money
   clips, travel kits, ladies' clutches, French
   purses, handbags, attachés, key cases,
   briefcases, portfolios, luggage and travel bags.

The Warnaco Outlet Store. 40-60% off White
   Stag, Geoffrey Beene, Warners, Olga,
   Spalding, Christian Dior, Speedo, Hathaway,
   Pringle, Albert Nippon, Chaps by Ralph
   Lauren, Hirsh Weis, Puritan and Thane.

West Virginia Fine Glass. Handmade glassware;
   save 20-60%.

MARTINSBURG FACTORY STORES

LOCATION: Just off I-81, Exit 13, King St.;
(304)263-6255.

STORES: Liz Claiborne Outlet Store, JH
Collectibles, American Tourister, Reebok,
OshKosh B'Gosh, harvé benard, Van Heusen,
Cape Isle Knitters and Oneida Factory Store.

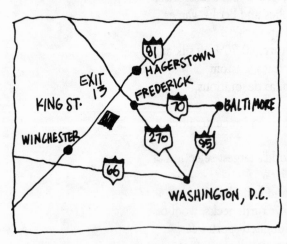

DIRECTIONS
Just off I-81, Exit 13, King St.
(at the Sheraton) Martinsburg,
WV.

FABULOUS FINDS IN WISCONSIN

Throughout the state, you will find fine roads, parks and vistas from which to view and enjoy the leaves and rolling hills. As you travel, treat yourself to the fine harvest of foods along Wisconsin's scenic routes. Wisconsin apples have a unique crisp, juicy quality and the honey is unbeatable. Cranberries, squash, pumpkins and of course several kinds of world-famous Wisconsin cheese make any fall trip enjoyable. And don't forget the seasoned sausage and bratwurst, wild rice harvested by hand, wine, beer, potatoes, veal, sauerkraut, pickles and a cornucopia of other farm products that will make your trip a real treat.

Wisconsin's variety is truly amazing. From rustic cabins to full-service resorts, elegant French restaurants to colorful beer gardens, folk art exhibits to works by the Masters.

The French explorer Jean Nicolet stepped off his boat at Red Banks, north of Green Bay, in 1634. He became the first recorded European to meet Wisconsin's Indians. The Chippewa/Ojibwa, Potawatomi, Winnebago, Onieda, Stockbridge-Munsee, Menominee and Brotherton are native Wisconsinites. Their art, music and crafts are living links to the past.

This is festival country and every month has a happening that could be fun.

☞ **FOR MORE INFORMATION**
Write to the Wisconsin Department of Development, Division of Tourism, (P.O. Box 7970, Madison, WI 53707), and you will get information on accommodations, car ferrying, golf courses, paper mill tours, restaurants and all the other happenings in Wisconsin.

Fabulous Finds in . . .
BELOIT

FREEMAN OUTLET MALL

LOCATION: On I-90 and 15 West. Look for the signs and call (608)364-1200 if you get lost.

STORES: Fieldcrest, Manhattan, Clothes Works, Kids Stop, Van Heusen, Freeman Shoe and Mr. G's Restaurant.

Fabulous Finds in . . .
KENOSHA

Kenosha is located on the shores of Lake Michigan and was named by the Potawatomi Indians. Kenosha means "pike or pickerel." You can discover the excitement of freshwater fishing on the Great Lakes while the family shopper exhausts the credit limits at the factory outlet stores.

FACTORY OUTLET CENTRE

Since opening in 1982, Factory Outlet Centre has enjoyed a history of success unparalleled in the outlet shopping center industry. Factory Outlet Centre continues to offer nationally recognized manufacturers a profitable means of marketing directly to value-oriented consumers. The enduring success of Factory Outlet Centre has led to the development of four new additions. Throughout the expansions, Factory Outlet Centre remained true to the outlet concept as

PLACES TO EAT AND SLEEP
Lots of specialty food restaurants and national chains nearby.

Milwaukee is so close to Kenosha that it should be on your list of places to eat and sleep and things to do. Call the Greater Milwaukee Convention and Visitors Bureau at (800)ESCAPES or (608)266-2161.

Milwaukee offers an unmatched variety of cuisine from wienerschnitzel to cabbage rolls to chateaubriand to bratwurst to beer.

Cheese factory tours are a must—you can get information by writing to Wisconsin Dept. of Agriculture, Trade and Consumer Protection (P.O. Box 8911, Dept AT, Madison, WI 53708).

Miller and Pabst Brewing Companies offer brewery tours. The beer-making process and the equipment used is quite interesting.

evidenced by a tenant mix comprised of 80% direct manufacturer outlets.

LOCATION: Situated on I-94 at Wisconsin Hwy. 50, five miles north of the Illinois/Wisconsin state line. 7700 120th Ave. Call (414)857-7961 for directions.

STORES: **Aileen.** Women's casual wear that works in any wardrobe.

Ambrosia Chocolate & Cocoa. Chocolate products for eating, baking and candymaking—fresh fudge, gift items.

American Tourister. High-quality luggage, sport bags, business cases and accessories at 40-70% off regular retail prices.

Athletic X-press. Brand name athletic shoes, clothing and accessories for the serious—or not-so-serious—athlete.

Aunt Mary's Yarn & Crafts. Wide selection of yarn and crafts for the entire family.

B.G. Chicago. Women's classic and contemporary coordinated sportswear, dresses, fragrances, jewelry, handbags, belts and samples.

Banister Shoe. Shoe bargains for men, women and children—dress, casual and athletic.

Barbizon Lingerie. Up to 60% off suggested retail on ladies' lingerie.

Bootery Outlet. Specializing in women's fashion footwear.

The Brighter Side. Oil lamps, lamp oil, outdoor oil lamps and flower rings.

Bristol County. Ladies' tailored American-made suits, skirts, slacks and blazers.

Brownberry Bakery Outlet. All natural breads, rolls, croutons, stuffings and other fine bakery products 30-40% off.

C.J. Chips. Ladies' fashions and men's regular, big and tall clothing and furnishings.

C.S.O. Junior fashions, sportswear, dresses,

coats, jackets, lingerie, accessories and more
at 20-70% off retail prices.

Cape Craftsmen. Gift and home decorating
items, including wood, brass, crystal, wicker,
the country look.

Carole Hochman Lingerie. Best of the best with
designer names that you will love.

Carter's Childrenswear. Newborn to size 14
girls and size 16 boys.

The Casual Male. Specializing in fashions for
men of all ages—fashions for the affordable,
contemporary, casual look.

Cheese Factory. Wisconsin's own fine cheeses,
sausage, honey, mustards, unique crackers.

Chicago Records. More than 8,000 cassettes,
more than 6,000 CDs, concert shirts and all
accessories.

Clothes-out. First-quality brand name
sportswear for men and women, also featuring
a complete line of Wisconsin Wear.

Clothes Works. Women's suits, blazers, skirts,
slacks and coordinating separates and
sportswear.

Clothing by Farah. Men's suits, sportcoats, dress
slacks and casual wear—boy's dress and casual
clothing, sizes 4-14 and husky sizes.

Cluett Factory Store. Arrow shirts, Gold Toe
socks, Sunday, Saturdays, R.P.M. Fashions,
children's wear and Arrow women's wear at a
40% savings—seasonal overruns, additional
savings on selected irregulars.

The Company Store. Down-filled coats, jackets,
vests, booties, European comforters and
accessory items.

Cookie Jar. Factory authorized, independently
owned Rippin' Good Cookie outlet, snacks,
crackers and more than 100 different cookie
jars at savings up to 65%.

Corning/Revere Factory Store. Corning and
Revere products, and discounts on first-
quality overstocks and discontinued items.

Cosmetic Outlet. Save up to 90% on brand name skin care products, perfumes and cosmetics.

Cost Cutters. Offering hair care services including styling and perm waving, hair care products, hair care and appliances.

Crazy Horse. Women's styles in natural fabrics.

Dickens Discount Books. *New York Times* bestsellers in hardcover and paperback, plus shelves of fascinating books—all at tremendous savings.

Draperies, Etc. Household linens, blankets, towels, sheets, kitchen accessories—made to measure draperies 35% off retail.

Dress Barn. 20-50% off department store prices on famous label sportswear, suits, dresses, coats and accessories.

Eddie Bauer. Fashions for the outdoor life-style, relaxed weekend wear and good-times apparel—just like the catalog fashions.

Fashion Flair. 40% off manufacturer's suggested retail on men's, women's and children's apparel, including Izod Lacoste, Ship 'n Shore and Monet.

Farberware. Farberware cookware at manufacturer's direct prices, well below the suggested retail.

Fieldcrest Cannon. Bed and bath linens, textiles and accessories.

Frame Warehouse. Direct factory outlet of photo frames, framed art, framed mirrors, etc.

Fuller Brush. The original Fuller Brush company—household mops, brooms, brushes, chemicals and personal care products at 25-50%.

Fureal. The Midwest's largest selection of men's and ladies' leathers, furs, motorcycle garments at 50-70% savings—men's and women's sizing, including big men to size 60.

Gentlemen's Wear House. Manufacturer of men's and ladies' clothing.

WANTED

Great restaurants—big or small, but not chains. When you eat in one chain, you've got the menu locked into your brain. Travelers are "strangers in town" and they need some objective guidance to good food and good service ... the kind that makes you want to tip!

The Genuine Article. Bib overalls in sizes six-months to sixty months — men's sportswear, sleepwear and workwear, plus children's shoes.

Gift Outlet. Giftware and home decor accessories, featuring brass, crystal, porcelain and more at 30-70% below retail.

Gitano. The modern look in casual clothes at affordable prices.

Great Midwest Craftmarket. Handcrafted gifts and decorative accessories in clay, metal, wood, fiber, paper, glass and leather — year-round Christmas Corner.

Hanes Activewear. A manufacturer's outlet featuring first quality and slightly imperfect Hanes activewear for men and women, and Hanes basic and fashion fleecewear, T-shirts and socks.

Helly-Hanson. Good-quality outerwear.

Houseware Outlet. Kitchen gadgets, cookware, bakeware, Wixon Spices, microwave, glassware, candles, woodenware, etc.

Jade Dragon. Chinese Cuisine from a four-star restaurant tradition; features Mandarin, Hunan-Szechuan and Cantonese regional cooking, offers soups, appetizers, entrees and many combination plates.

Jennifer's Cookies. Fresh-baked cookies.

Jockey. Great-quality underwear and other undergarments.

Jonathan Logan Outlet. Save 30-70% on famous label sportswear, dresses, activewear, suits, outerwear — misses, petites, juniors and women's sizes; famous brands include R&K Petites and Originals, Villager, Alice Stuart, Misty Harbor.

Julie's Jewelry. Unique costume jewelry and accessory items.

Kids Ca'pers. Children's wear — newborn to size 7; girl's — newborn to size 14.

Knits by K.T. Sweaters and other knits by

Kenneth Two and other famous labels.

L.A. Lifestyles. Complete line of the latest fashions for men, women and teens.

La Crosse Footwear, Inc. Manufactured in Wisconsin by La Crosse — sporting and work boots and protective footwear, athletic and casual footwear, winter fashion and moon boots.

Lamp Shade Outlet. Factory-owned-and-operated — brass, crystal, wood, stained glass, Tiffany-style lamps, table, dresser, desk, floor lamps; ceiling fixtures and swags.

L'eggs/Hanes/Bali. Save 20-50% or more on suggested retail prices on slightly imperfects, closeouts and overstocks — brand name hosiery, underwear, lingerie, socks, activewear and more.

Little Red Shoe House. Brand name shoes and accessories.

Loomcraft Textiles. Home-decorating fabric store, thousands of bolts in stock — Kirsch drapery hardware, upholstery, drapery supplies and foam.

Manhattan Factory Outlet. Men's designer shirts, slacks, ties, underwear and accessories, ladies' skirts, blouses, pants and more.

Maternity Wearhouse. Complete line of casual, career, play and after-five clothes, including lingerie for the mother-to-be, at 15-50% below manufacturers suggested retail.

Mid America Shoe Factory Outlet. Brand name shoes — athletics, dress and casuals, plus top-of-the-line work boots.

Mill City Outlet. Featuring Lee jeans for the entire family in both work and fashion styles — Lord Isaacs slacks, current junior and updated missy looks in tops and outerwear.

Mitchell Handbags. Save 40-70% on leather goods — handbags, attachés, and brand name luggage.

Munsingwear. Save at least 50% on men's

underwear and Grand Slam sportswear – plus, Vassarette intimate apparel.

Newport Sportswear. Savings of 50% on first-quality sportswear, dress shirts, heavyweights, sweaters, coats, activewear coordinates.

The Paper Factory. Gift wrap, party goods, school and office supplies and accessories.

Perfume Boutique. Men's, women's fragrance reproductions at 85% savings – plus balms, lotions, atomizers.

Rainbow Fashions. Junior and missy fashions, sportswear, dresses, jackets, accessories and separates, save 20-70%.

Regal Ware Outlet. Cookware, appliances and microwave ovenware, all factory direct – seconds, closeouts and refurbished items at 30-60% savings.

Ribbon Outlet. Ribbons and crafts materials.

Shapes Activewear. Activewear from famous American manufacturers at savings of 20-50% – leotards, tights, hosiery, leg warmers, socks, sweats, swimwear and accessories.

Socks Galore & More. Baby sleepers and the largest selection of quality socks in the country.

Sony. The guru of electronics selling deals you won't want to miss.

totes. Save 50-75% on umbrellas, raincoats, rainhats, folding luggage, scarves, rubber boots and more.

Toy King. Nationally advertised toys such as Nintendo, Fisher-Price, Mattel, Kenner, Little Tykes, Parker Brothers, and many more at discount prices.

Van Heusen. Men's and women's famous-maker fashions.

The Wallet Works by Amity. Wallets, briefcases, luggage, handbags and travel gifts.

West Bend Company. Electrical kitchen appliances, including skillets, woks, slow cookers, food processors, corn poppers,

percolators, urns, timers and specialty items—
seconds, closeouts and demonstrators, all at
discounted prices.

Whitewater Glove. Ski, casual, dress, work,
hunting gloves—also, jeans, belts, jackets.

Winona Knits. Men's, ladies' sweaters, Ragg,
Shetland, cotton, acrylic, tall man, men's,
women's shirts, pants, jackets, hats, scarfs,
socks.

... and more stores and kiosks.

LAKESIDE MARKETPLACE

LOCATION: On I-94 at exit 347. Two miles from
Hwy. 50, the route to Lake Geneva. 11211 120th
Ave.; (414)857-2101.

DIRECTIONS
We are located on I-94 at Exit
347, Hwy. Q.

STORES: Calvin Klein, Crystal Works, Anne
Klein, Gilligan & O'Malley, harvé benard,
Leather Loft, Jindo Fur, Bass Shoe, Van Heusen,
Fenn Wright & Manson, Maidenform, Prestige
Fragrance & Cosmetics, E.J. Plum, Gitano Kids,
American Tourister, Sassafras, Palm Beach, Liz
Claiborne, Wisconsin Toy, I.B. Diffusion, JH
Collectibles, That's Our Bag, Royal Robbins,
Fanny Farmer, J. Crew, Evan-Picone, Jones New
York, Kitchen Collection, Henson-Kickernick,
Benetton, Gitano, Cambridge Dry Goods, Just
Kids, Tanner Factory Outlet, Capezio, Argenti,

Mikasa, Crazy Horse, Cape Isle Knitters, Anko, Adolfo II, Au Pazazz!, Brass Factory, Etienne Aigner, Famous Brands Housewares Outlet, Fila, Galt/Sand, Geoffrey Beene, Great Outdoor Clothing, He-Ro Group Outlet, Jordache, Kristina K. Outlet, Linen Mill, Madeleine Fashions, Media Man, The North Face, OshKosh B'Gosh, Perfumania, Stone Mountain Handbags and Euro Cafe.

Fabulous Finds in . . .
OSHKOSH

MANUFACTURERS MARKETPLACE

A nice lineup of stores.

LOCATION: On US 41 near Wisconsin Rte. 44

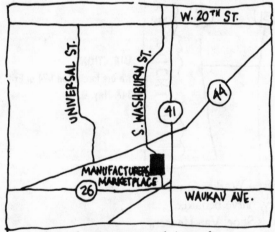

DIRECTIONS
We are located at U.S. 41 and Hwy. 44.

across from the Experimental Aircraft Association Air Adventure museum.

STORES: Shop Bugle Boy, Jordache, Dansk, New England Mackintosh, Newport Sportswear, Book Warehouse, Sports Factory, Nickels Company, Ideas, harvé benard, Euro Collections, Aunt Mary's Yarns, Swank, Wisconsin Toy, Famous Brands Housewares, Banister Shoe, Tanner Factory Store, Aileen, Barbizon, Little Red Shoe

House, Westport Ltd., Old Mill, L'eggs/Hanes/
Bali, Johnston Childrens, Gitano, Van Heusen,
Bass Shoe, Cape Isle Knitters, Royal Doulton,
Levi, Kitchen Collection, American Tourister,
Paper Factory, Manhattan, Welcome Home,
Leather Loft, Farah, Russell Mills, OshKosh
B'Gosh, Winona Knits, Fieldcrest Cannon, JH
Collectibles, Sweatshirt Company, Eddie Bauer,
Lands' End, Corning, Famous Footwear, Mikasa,
Fragrance World, Socks Galore & More, Wallet
Works, Ribbon Outlet and more coming.

Fabulous Finds in ...
PLOVER
(Near Stevens Point)

MANUFACTURERS DIRECT MALL & OUTLET CENTER

LOCATION: 101-17 Plover Rd., intersection of US
51 and Hwy. B.; (715)341-7980.

STORES: Van Heusen Factory Store, The
Genuine Article (OshKosh B'Gosh), Old Mill
Ladies' Sportswear Outlet, The Paper Factory,
Little Red Shoe House, Winona Knits, Aunt
Mary's Yarns & crafts and other off-price stores.

Fabulous Finds in ...
WEST BEND

WEST BEND FACTORY OUTLET MALL

LOCATION: 180 Island Ave., in downtown West
Bend at the intersection of Rte. 33 and Hwy. 45;
(414)334-3477.

STORES: Ambrosia Chocolate & Cocoa, The
Brighter Side, Can'da Fashions, The Card Stop,

The Cookie Jar Outlet, Houseware Outlet Store, Little Red Shoe House, Manhattan Factory Store, Maus Jewelry Imports, Newport Sportswear, The Paper Factory, Rainbow Fashions, Regal Ware Outlet, Sausage Plus, Trinkets 'n Treasures, The West Bend Company Store, Winona Knits.

Fabulous Finds in Canada's Provinces

There are a few things that every shopper needs to be aware of before embarking to the great north. Remember, Canada is a "foreign" country even though the U.S. and Canada enjoy the hospitality of the longest unprotected international border in the world. Here are a few pointers to keep you and your fabulous finds in good legal standing with both countries:

No passport is required to travel between the U.S. and Canada going either way, but you should always carry identifying documents (birth certificate, marriage license, etc.) to have concrete proof of citizenship, especially if you are a naturalized citizen.

You must stay in the country at least forty-eight hours before any purchased items can enter the U.S. duty free.

You can bring in, duty free, items in value up to four hundred dollars. And it is amazing how fast that four hundred adds up.

You are allowed only four hundred dollars of duty-free goods every thirty days. And they do keep records.

Plants, fruits and vegetables are restricted on both sides of the border — check to make sure you can take it home with you before you buy.

These are just a few of the most obvious things you need to know to enjoy a hassle-free shopping vacation in Canada. For more details contact your local U.S. Customs Service, listed in the white pages of your telephone directory under U.S. Government, Treasury Department, U.S. Customs Service. These are often located at the nearest international airport. The U.S. Customs duty officers can tell you everything you need to know.

☞ **FOR MORE INFORMATION**

If Canada is your destination, send $4.95 for a booklet with over 250 manufacturer's outlets in Ontario. This is the most comprehensive booklet of outlet operations available in Canada. Canada is a conduit for French and European fashions, and they differ from fashions available in the U.S. Order from: Oliver Enterprises, Box 2173, Cambridge, Ontario, N3C 2V8, Canada.

Fabulous Finds

in

British Columbia

Fabulous Finds in . . .
Burnaby

Pennington's Wearhouse
Location: 3355 North Rd., (604) 420-0118.
Items: Offers outerwear, day wear, sleepwear and intimate apparel in larger ladies' sizes.

Fabulous Finds in . . .
Vancouver

Jantzen Factory Outlet

They say they have great prices and I believe it. If the Vancouver store is anything like the ones in California, shopping will be great fun. Can someone give a shopper recommendation?

LOCATION: 2600 Main St., corner of 10th and Main; (604)872-3210.

ITEMS: Savings up to 75% on Jantzen factory surplus and seconds of men's and ladies' sportswear, sweaters and swimwear.

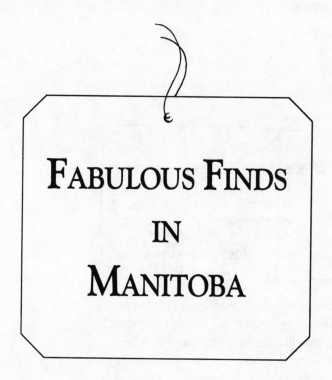

FABULOUS FINDS IN MANITOBA

Fabulous Finds in . . .

WINNIPEG

ARROW FACTORY OUTLET

LOCATION: 19-200 Meadowood Dr. in the Dakota Park Plaza; (204)257-9908. (See map on facing page.)

ITEMS: Imperfect, name brand men's and ladies' apparel. Men's dress and leisure shirts, sweaters, pajamas, men's underwear, ladies' lingerie. Great brands, great prices.

THE WORK STORE

LOCATION: 300 Princess St.; (204)943-6531.

ITEMS: Casual cotton and denim clothing for the

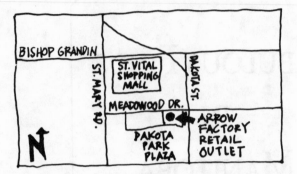

entire family at "unbelievable prices" . . . so good
in fact, the store owner says, "he can't advertise."
That sounds like the best of all worlds; 50% of
the merchandise is brand name, with discounts
of 60%-90%.

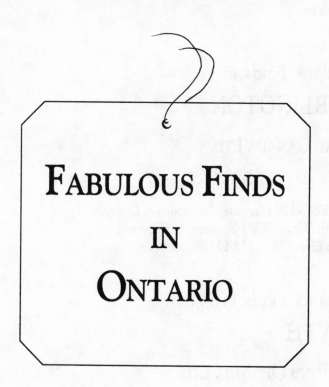

FABULOUS FINDS

IN

ONTARIO

Fabulous Finds in . . .

BELLEVILLE

SAMPLES & SECONDS SHOPPE LTD.

LOCATION: Two and a half kilometers east of Belleville on Hwy. #2 at Elmwood Dr., (613)968-6583.

ITEMS: Save 30-50% on suggested retail prices on quality sportswear, Canadian-made outerwear, Viyella shirts, ties and socks, wool and blend sweaters, famous-maker coats, ladies' coordinates and blouses, fleecewear, men's sport shirts and pants. Exchanges only—no refunds, so try before you buy.

Fabulous Finds in . . .

BURLINGTON

YOUNG CANADA LTD.

Canada's largest supplier of toys and gifts.

LOCATION: 4129 Harvester Rd., south of Queen
Elizabeth Way (QEW) between Appleby and
Walker Lines; (416)333-1115.

Fabulous Finds in . . .

BLYTH

BAINTON'S OLD MILL LTD.

A family-owned business specializing in leather
and wool. Low cost, high quality.

LOCATION: 140 Westmoreland St., in downtown
Blyth; (519)523-4740.

ITEMS: Products made from leather and wool.
Jackets, coats, shirts, pants, moccasins and much
more.

THE OLD MILL

A remarkable store filled with natural products
made from leather and wool. The Old Mill developed from the sheep industry and an in-house
tannery.

LOCATION: One mile south of Blyth; (519)523-
4595.

ITEMS: Leather and wool jackets, skirts, purses,
pants, sheepskin rugs, babycare lambskins,
blankets, etc.

Fabulous Finds in . . .
CAMBRIDGE
LEN'S MILL STORE

One of Canada's largest factory outlets. Save 20-70% off regular retail.

LOCATION: 215 Queen St. W., just east of Hwy. 401; (519)658-8182.

ITEMS: Family clothing, yarns, fabrics and upholstery fabric by Harvey Woods, Playtex, Paton's & Baldwins, Sea Queen, Stanfields, Trimfit, Levis and Buster Brown.

FLORSHEIM CANADA

They have other Florsheim Factory Outlets in London and Hamilton.

LOCATION: 19 Concession St. (519)740-4000.

ITEMS: Men's footwear, shoes, boots, casuals, athletic.

THE CAMBRIDGE WOODEN TOY CO.

LOCATION: 466 Franklin Blvd., north of Hwy. #8 (on Franklin); (519)621-0680.

ITEMS: Wood toys, trains, trucks and airplanes from Loony Banks and My Train. Average discount of 25% but can go as high as 40%. High quality at discount prices.

Fabulous Finds in . . .
COLLINGWOOD
BLUE MOUNTAIN POTTERY FACTORY OUTLET

Free factory tours, and they welcome bus tours.

LOCATION: Mountain Rd. and Hwy. 26, Collingwood W.; (705)445-3000.

ITEMS: Quality giftware at factory savings of 35-50%.

Fabulous Finds in . . .
GUELPH

JOHN RENNIE FACTORY STORE

Huge store with more than 20,000 shirts offers a great selection.

LOCATION: 420 Elizabeth St.; (519)822-3211.

ITEMS: Shirts, sweaters, ties, hose, pajamas by Bill Blass, London Fog, Eagle, Rennie at 35-50% off retail. First quality, some seconds.

LEN'S MILL STORE

LOCATION: Arthur and Ontario Sts.; (519)836-2412.

ITEMS: First-quality and some slight imperfects of family clothing, yarns, fabrics and upholstery fabrics.

BILTMORE

LOCATION: 139 Morris St.; (519)836-2770.

ITEMS: Dress felt, wool felt, straw, fabric hats; men's hats and caps in many styles including western felt. Discounts of 20-50%.

LEATHER BY MANN OF CANADA

LOCATION: 389 Woodlawn Rd. W.; (519)822-4427.

ITEMS: They sell substandards of top-of-the-line leather garments, purses, attachés, portfolio wallets, luggage, briefcases. Remember that the better makers have very high standards for first-quality inspections. These brands will assure you that you're getting good merchandise: Renwick,

Samsonite, McBrine and Leather by Mann. Average discount is 25-50%. They have 4,000-5,000 square feet of assorted Canadian-made leather items.

Fabulous Finds in ...

HAMILTON

SUPER STAR SPORT

LOCATION: 432 Main St. E.; (416)429-4711.

ITEMS: Sportswear and footwear from Champion, Umbro, C.C.M./Starter and more. 50% of the merchandise is branded, and the average discount is 30%. This is a downtown location with current styles and colors.

CANNON KNITTING MILLS

Fabrics manufactured on the premises. Genuine factory outlet, good selection and discounts up to 70%.

LOCATION: 134 Mary St. and Cannon; (416)525-7275.

ITEMS: Knit fabrics, cottons, wools, polyesters and blends for ladies', children's and men's wear.

NOCTURNE APPAREL LTD., ROBERT STONE FASHIONS LTD.

Nocturne Apparel and half a dozen other factory stores. There are several factory outlets in this area so plan a day and treat yourself to lunch.

LOCATION: 41 Brockley Dr. — two lights east of Hwy. 20 off Barton St.

STORES: **Cluett Peabody's Arrow Factory Outlet.** Shirts, dress and leisure — sweaters, slacks, ties, socks, belts, ladies' wear, yard

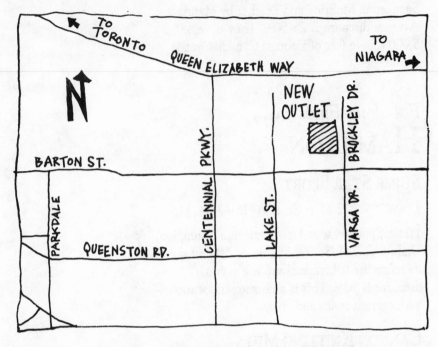

goods and more; first- and second-quality from Arrow and Cluett . . . their biggest discount is 70% and the least is 30% — now that is worthwhile; (416)578-0055.

Len's Mill Store. First-quality and some select imperfects of family clothing, yarns, fabrics and upholstery fabrics from Harvey Woods, Playtex, Paton's & Baldwins, Sea Queen, Stanfields, Levis, Trimfit and Buster Brown — save up to 70%; (416)560-5367.

Nocturne Apparel. Sleepwear and casual wear, ladies' day wear and children's two to sixteen years — they carry a great selection of first- and second-quality merchandise. They specialize in nursing gowns and hospital gowns at savings up to 70%; (416)578-7644.

Robert Stone Fashions Ltd. Name brand ladies' sportswear suits, separates and knits reduced 30-70%; manufacturer's samples, sub-standards, hosiery, jewelry and scarves, good quality and friendly service; (416)560-9223.

DIRECTIONS

Take QEW Niagara, exit at Hwy. 20 S. (Centennial Pkwy.), left at first light (Barton St.), left at second light (Brockley Dr.).

BEAUTY INDUSTRIES MILL OUTLET

LOCATION: On Sherman between Barton and Burlington Sts. Mill outlet next to the manufacturing plant; (416)549-1357.

ITEMS: First- and second-quality children's clothing. They also sell ladies' and men's colognes and fragrances. Beatrix Potter, Cute N Cuddly, British Sterling.

Fabulous Finds in . . .
HAWKESVILLE

LEN'S MILL STORE

Savings up to 70% on well-known brands. Great selection.

LOCATION: 9 Broadway St., northwest of St. Jacobs; (519)699-6140.

ITEMS: First-quality and some select imperfects of family clothing, yarns, fabrics and upholstery fabrics.

Fabulous Finds in . . .
KINGSTON

OFFPRICE SHOE CENTRE

LOCATION: 189 Princess St.; (613)542-9468.

ITEMS: Family footwear including boots at factory outlet prices. North Star, Vuarnet, Mickey Mouse, Weatherguard. Discounts range from 15-50% and about 30% of their merchandise is national brands.

Fabulous Finds in ...
KITCHENER

FACTORY SHOE LTD.

Factory Shoe is the largest discount store of its
type in Ontario, selling name brand and private
brands for the family at 20-60% off other store
prices.
LOCATION: 686 Victoria St. N., next to the
expressway; (519)743-2021.

BONNIE STUART FACTORY OUTLET

Bonnie Stuart Factory Outlet offers a wide selection of young children's and babies' footwear.
Their fit and quality has always been a strong
point.
LOCATION: 141 Whitney at the end of Cedar St.
near Courtland Ave.; (519)578-8880.
ITEMS: Leather children's shoes, athletics and
party shoes from Bonnie Stuart, Miss Magic,
Passport and Peaks. Savings from 45-75%.

CLUETT PEABODY CANADA ... THE
ARROW FACTORY RETAIL OUTLET

LOCATION: 112 Benton St.; (519)743-8211.
ITEMS: Men's and ladies' first-quality plus select

seconds casual wear, including talls and oversize. Arrow, Gotta Be Cotton, Bench Craft Leather. Customers like their quality and excellent prices.

NEW BALANCE CANADA INC.

LOCATION: 750 Fairway Rd.

ITEMS: Footwear and textiles in many sizes. Technologically innovative athletic shoes featuring quality and wide sizing. Fill your footwear needs at discounts from 50-75%.

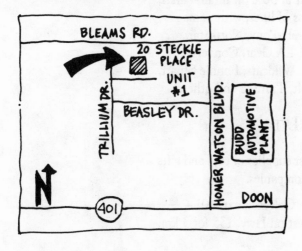

ROCKWAY GIFT FACTORY CLEARANCE OUTLET

Thousands of interesting gift items at low retail prices.

LOCATION: 20 Steckle Pl., Unit #1.; (519)748-2820. (See map above.)

ITEMS: Discontinued items, seconds, closeouts, wood giftware and novelties — thousands of items under $3. Rockway Wood, Forest Wood, housewares with discounts to 85% off retail.

Fabulous Finds in . . .
LONDON

FACTORY SHOE

More than 20,000 pairs of shoes on display.

LOCATION: 1700 Dundas St. E. near Canadian Tire.

ITEMS: Family footwear at 50% off retail—firsts, seconds, overruns, ends of lines, with name brands like Cougar, Greb, Pony, Northstar, Kamik, Weatherguard, LA Gear, Converse, Brooks, Buster Brown, Wildcats, Bonnie Stuart, HH Brown, Terra, Colt, Turntec and others.

YOUNG CANADA LTD.

This is Canada's largest supplier of toys and gifts to organizations and companies.

LOCATION: 187 White Oak Rd., ext. 401— Wellington Rd. N., west on Hwy. 135 for 3 km; (519)681-6666.

ITEMS: Wholesale prices and great selection on toys, gifts, games, crafts, paper supplies, novelties and books. The brands are easy to recognize: Fisher-Price, Lego, Mattel, Coleman, Golden at discounts to 75% off retail.

ITALIAN SHOE WAREHOUSE

Imported shoes for the whole family.

LOCATION: 186 'c' White Oak Rd.; (519)685-2996.

ITEMS: High-grade imported footwear from Fabiani, Quadrini and other makers at 10-40% below retail.

Fabulous Finds in . . .
MISSISSAUGA

JANTZEN FACTORY OUTLET

LOCATION: In the Dundas Tomkin Centre, at 966 Dundas St. near Tompkin; (416)238-1585.

ITEMS: Jantzen factory surplus and seconds of men's and ladies' sportswear, sweaters and swimwear. Savings from 45-75%, and their merchandise is 100% branded.

Fabulous Finds in . . .
NIAGARA FALLS

ONEIDA CANADA LTD.

LOCATION: 8699 Stanley Ave.; from Buffalo, New York, cross the Peace Bridge and take QEW to Lyons Creek Rd. exit east to Stanley Ave. and take a left; (416)356-9691.

ITEMS: Silverplated and stainless flatware, holloware and many other gifts. Stock consists of factory seconds, overruns and discontinued patterns.

Fabulous Finds in . . .
OTTAWA

MCINTOSH AND WATTS

LOCATION: 2417 Holly Ln. at the intersection of Walkley and Heron Rds.; (613)523-7240.

ITEMS: China, glassware, flatware, giftware, collectors' plates and bins full of dinnerware, stemware and giftware—all first quality from

WANTED
Information about the most interesting things to do in an area already listed in *Fabulous Finds*. Experiences that are memorable. Attractions that you can't forget.

Royal Albert, Johnsons, Noritake, Mikasa, Pfaltzgraff, Waterford, Oneida and other famous makers.

Fabulous Finds in ...
PORT CREDIT
CLEWS CLOTHING COMPANY LTD.

Clews features "livable clothes" — easygoing and stylish. They have natural fibers, especially cotton, denim and cotton/linen blend.

LOCATION: 155 Queen St. E. Approximately 30 minutes west of Toronto; (416)271-0830.

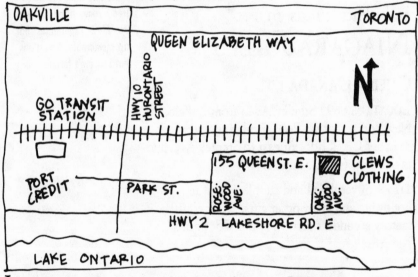

ITEMS: High-quality men's and women's dressy and casual sportswear exclusive lines designed and manufactured in Port Credit; belts, jewelry, cotton sweaters and handpainted sweatshirts.

Fabulous Finds in ...
PORT DOVER
LEN'S MILL STORE

LOCATION: St. George St. N. and Clifford by the Water Tower; (519)583-0800.

DIRECTIONS

Take the Gardiner Expressway from downtown Toronto and go west to the QEW (Hamilton). Go westbound on the QEW to Hwy. #10, Hurontario St. Exit Hwy. #10 South to Lakeshore Rd. Turn east and go four blocks to Oakwood. Turn north on Oakwood and go to the end of the street.

ITEMS: Family clothing, yarns, fabrics and upholstery fabrics at savings up to 70%. Harvey Woods, Playtex, Paton's & Baldwins, Sea Queen, Stanfields, Levis, Trimfit, Buster Brown.

Fabulous Finds in . . .
PRESCOTT

HATHAWAY FACTORY OUTLET

LOCATION: 707 St. Lawrence St.; (613)925-1530.

ITEMS: Men's dress, sport and knit shirts, ties, boxers, sweaters and ladies' shirts from Hathaway and Christian Dior—all of the merchandise is branded, with an average discount of 60%. This store accepts credit cards and personal checks. Let's hear from the shoppers—how do you like this store?

PORTOLANO OUTLET CENTER

LOCATION: 840 Walker St.; (613)925-4242.

ITEMS: Leather and dress gloves from Portolano. Savings of 25-70%.

Fabulous Finds in . . .
ST. JACOBS

DALYUN'S MILL OUTLET

In the charming town of St. Jacobs, this store offers quality men's wear at country prices. The store accepts credit cards and checks and makes exchanges. Casual men's wear with some dress clothing in a boutique environment.

LOCATION: Across from the silos at 7 Front St.

THINGS TO DO
Travelers in the Kitchener, Guelph and Waterloo area might want to include a trip to the Village of St. Jacobs. Call (519)669-2605 or (519)664-3518 for information. You can savor the aroma of fresh-baked bread and pastries, browse in the shops for locally handcrafted items, or take a quiet stroll along the Mill Race. In this unique village, the Mennonites have created a rich mix of history, homemade food, guest houses, crafts and authentic architecture. Quaint buildings lend a peaceful touch to the environment. You will also find Stockyard Farmer's Market where artisans create pottery, hand-blown glass, weave and more. Flea market on Thursdays and Saturdays.

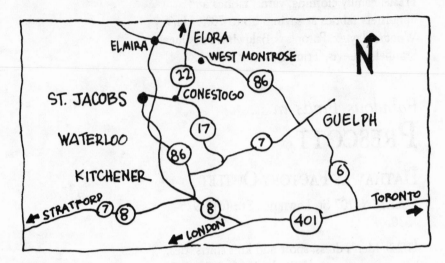

ITEMS: Brands include Arrow, Gant, Sperry and Ingo, in good-to-better men's wear.

Fabulous Finds in . . .

STRATFORD

SAMSONITE TRAVEL STORE

LOCATION: 753 Ontario St. at Burritt; (519)271-5040.

ITEMS: Luggage and travel accessories, softside and hardside luggage and business cases. They sell all styles of Samsonite luggage at regular retail, as well as discounted seconds and obsolete products. They have the best selection in Canada. Perhaps in the future, Samsonsite will have outlet stores selling only discounted merchandise.

Fabulous Finds in . . .

TORONTO

DOROTHEA KNITTING MILLS LTD.

This manufacturer saves on rent and commissions and passes the savings on to his customers.

PLACES TO EAT

Benjamin's Restaurant & Inn takes you into a time warp that puts life into perspective. In the same general area the Stone Crock, with their own bakery and delicatessen, serve up food fit for a king. Call (519)669-1521 for directions and information.

They say that their prices are right, they are friendly and not pushy. Sounds like a good place to shop.

LOCATION: 20 Research Rd., two blocks south of Eglinton NE, east off Brontclif; (416)421-3773.

ITEMS: Men's and women's sweaters, hats, gloves, scarves; ends of lines, overruns, samples, seconds, all Parkhurst brand—100% branded merchandise with discounts from 30-70%.

IRWIN TOY LIMITED

Don't miss this . . . they cater to bulk parties and functions for toys and will open on Saturday if requested for large groups.

LOCATION: 43 Hanna Ave. in the King Dufferin area; (416)533-3521.

ITEMS: Name brand toys, gift items, novelties, one-of-a-kind games, electronic games/cartridges. All kinds of sports equipment, discontinued items, end of lines at unbelievably low prices. Average 40% off regular retail on Irwin, Tyco, Worlds of Wonder, Ohio Ant, Sega, Cooper and more.

MACGREGOR FACTORY STORE

Canada's leading producer of quality socks provides "all kinds of socks for all types of feet" at their value-packed factory outlet in downtown Toronto. Broad selection and great prices.

LOCATION: 30 Spadina Ave.; (416)979-6760.

ITEMS: Men's, women's, boys' and girls'; sport, dress, casual and fashion socks including MacGregor, Weekender, Happyfoot, Christian Dior, Alfred—their goods are 100% branded. Savings average 50%, and they take credit cards.

YOUNG CANADA
WHOLESALE WAREHOUSE

See the London, Ontario, listing for more information. Accepts credit cards, returns and exchanges.

LOCATION: 5171 Steeles Ave. W., west of Hwy. 400 between Weston and Islington; (416)748-8888.

Fabulous Finds in ...
THE TORONTO
AREA

PENNINGTON'S WEARHOUSE STORES

Pennington has many stores located throughout Ontario. Rather than repeat a description fifteen times, this listing will contain one description for all the stores. Pennington's has up-to-the-minute large-sized ladies' fashions. Manufacturers clearances at reduced prices. Their average discount is 30% but can go as high as 75%. They take credit cards and checks.

Toronto (greater metropolitan):
    3112 Bathurst St.; (416)782-8463
    3003 Danforth Ave.; (416)691-7315
    Downsview, 3711 Keele St.; (416)630-3302
    Mississauga, 1225 Dundas St. E.;
    (416)276-4031
    Rexdale, 2267 Islington Ave.; (416)743-3737
    Scarborough, 1911 Eglinton Ave. E.;
    (416)755-2397
    Scarborough, 950 Brimorton Dr.;
    (416)431-1469
    Thornhill, 7691 Yonge St.; (416)889-7959
Toronto (outlying areas):
    Hamilton, 601 Upper Gage Ave.;

(416)388-3244
London, 4380 Wellington Rd. S.;
(519)681-6731
Oakville, 200 North Service Rd. W.;
(416)338-8311
Ottawa, 1444 Walkely Rd.; (613)526-3841
St. Catharines, 525 Welland Ave.;
(416)684-3322

Fabulous Finds in . . .
TRENTON
BATA FACTORY OUTLET
They say that customers like them because of price, variety, and a large selection of winter footwear. They do accept credit cards, returns and exchanges.
LOCATION: 43 Carrying Place Rd.; (613)392-0958.
ITEMS: North Star, Vuarnet, Mickey Mouse, Weatherguard.

SOCK STORE & MORE
LOCATION: Two stores: one is 1 mile south of Hwy. 401 at Glen Miller exit. The other is at Belleville, south of Towers on Hwy. #2. Both have the same inventory; (613)966-7725.
ITEMS: Socks, sweats, jeans and underwear. Excellent towel selection and excellent savings on Penmans, Blue Boy, Wallabee, Kodiaks and others. Least discount is 80% . . . and that is great. Mostly branded, some not, brought to you by Vagden Mills Ltd.

Fabulous Finds in . . .
WALLACEBURG
LIBBEY ST. CLAIR FACTORY OUTLET
LOCATION: On Forhan St.; (519)627-2271.
ITEMS: Glass tableware from Libbey Glass, Raven

Head and others. Libbey stemware, decorated
and plain glasses. Decorated cannisters, gift
items. Savings of 20-40% and they have
hundreds of items such as tumblers, stemware,
floral glassware, terrariums and wine, brandy,
beer and bar ware.

Fabulous Finds in . . .
WATERLOO

RAINBOW FASHION

Factory Outlet store offering a good selection of
high-quality, private-label sportswear for women,
children and men.

LOCATION: 625 Colby Dr., cross street Northfield
Dr. and Hwy. 86; (519)884-2140.

ITEMS: T-shirts, sweatwear and team garments.
Discounts average 30% but can run as high as
75%.

LEN'S MILL STORE

One of Canada's largest factory outlets.

LOCATION: 130 Moore Ave. at South and Union;
(519)743-4672.

ITEMS: Family clothing, yarns, fabrics, upholstery.
Savings averaging 50% on Harvey Woods,
Playtex, Paton's & Baldwins yarns, Sea Queen,
Stanfields, Levis, Trimfit and Buster Brown.

VICTORY FACTORY OUTLET

LOCATION: 115 Bridgeport Rd., corner of Weber
and Bridgeport Rds.; (519)742-1888.

ITEMS: Family, men's, ladies' and children's sweat
shirts and ski wear. Mostly branded merchandise.

Fabulous Finds in . . .

WOODSTOCK

PAQUETTE FACTORY SOCK OUTLET

This is a small outlet inside the actual factory that manufactures socks from raw yarn. Quality is high, and the price is right.

LOCATION: 311 Dundas St.; (519)537-3476.

ITEMS: Hosiery for men, ladies, infants, boys and girls . . . all sizes at 50% of regular retail.

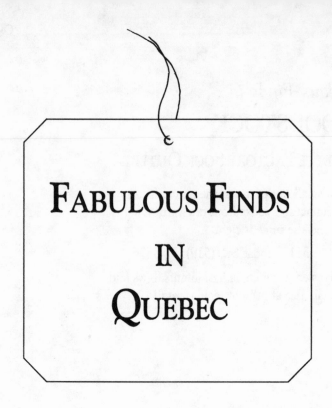

FABULOUS FINDS IN QUEBEC

Fabulous Finds in . . .

MONTRÉAL

PENNINGTON'S WEARHOUSE
1154 Beaumont Ave.; (514) 739-3538.

ITEMS: Ladies' wear in larger sizes. Outerwear, day wear, sleepwear, intimate apparel with discounts up to 75% off regular retail.

MORE
FABULOUS FINDS
OUTSIDE THE U.S.A.

If you want to shop factory outlets in Germany and Austria, buy this book: *Shopper's Guide to Germany*, Penn Books, 2280 E. Zermatt Circle, Sandy, UT 84093 . . . $10.95 ppd. or call (801)943-3175. This comprehensive directory has maps, store names, addresses, phone numbers and good product descriptions. The author also includes tours for crystal, porcelain and dolls. If you want to shop in Germany, this guide is a must.

Here are some other addresses that may interest you.

Hummel Figurines and Hutschenreuther china
Michael Kuchenreuther Porcelain
Sonnen Str. 22
8000 Munich 2
West Germany

Royal Copenhagen figurines/china
Royal Copenhagen Porcelain
Amagertorb 6
TK 1005
Copenhagen K, Denmark

English china
Royal Doulton Room
Army and Navy Store
101 Victoria St.
London, SW1E6QX, England

Belleck and Spode china and Lladro figurines
Austin Adams
54 Market St.
Cootehill, County Cavan
S. Ireland

If Great Britain is your shopping destination, order this set of books — which has good maps, descriptive information about the countryside and of course listings for factory outlets — direct from the authors:
Gillian Cutress and Rolf Stricker, 34 Park Hill, London SW4 9PB, England. Titles and prices are as follows:

Northern England Factory Shop Guide — 2.50£
Leicestershire Northamptonshire Guide — 2.75£
Wales Factory Shop Guide — 2.50£
Derbyshire Nottinghamshire Factory Guide — 2.75£
Staffordshire & The Potteries Guide — 2.75£
Western Midlands Factory Shop Guide — 2.50£
Yorkshire Humberside Factory Shop Guide — 2.75£

YOU ASKED FOR IT ...
YOU'VE GOT IT

W hen I was preparing my *SOS Directory*, Debbie Plaugher of Stevensville, Maryland, wrote: "Is there a way to be put on the mailing list of all the outlet stores? ... Maybe you can put their zip codes in the directory, and their phone numbers." Here is the list, Debbie — for the factory outlet retailers and manufacturers that you say you love. You and numerous others asked for home addresses and phone numbers for the factory outlet retailers; you've got it now in *Fabulous Finds*.

These retailers normally sell to department and specialty stores. This list is for shoppers who appreciate value. When using the list, you might want to request a company brochure from your favorite outlet retailer so you have up-to-date information between editions of *Fabulous Finds* directory. Or you may want to know when the company will open an outlet near you. Remember that manufacturing retailers are generally inexperienced in dealing with consumers directly. Whatever your request, remember to be specific when asking for information. (The listings tell you what the retailer sells if its name is not generally known.)

Only chains of factory outlet, catalog clearance stores and importer's outlet stores are listed. Off-price, discount, warehouse and liquidation stores are *not* listed unless they offer overpowering values to consumers. Factory outlet shopping is recreational retail, whereas off-price, discount, membership, warehouse and liquidation stores are alternatives to conventional retail. There is a big difference.

The word "outlet" is abused by discount retailers and shopping center developers, but if a store is listed in this section, you can be certain it is an outlet (or if it is a different concept, it will be designated as such). Single stores or two-store outlet chains aren't on this list because it isn't practical to travel across country to shop freestanding stores. However, some of these smaller stores are worth a stop if you are going to be in the area anyway. Single, freestanding outlets or very small outlet chains will be included in future editions, designated as "gems."

If you doubt the authenticity of a store called "outlet," look at the brand names it carries. If at least 75 percent of the merchandise, or if all the brand names, belong to one manufacturer, you are in a manufacturer's outlet. If any store on this list looks like a discount store and the store uses "outlet" in its name, let us know; we will be happy to check it out for you. Discounters and off-pricers are legitimate retail concepts, but when you think you are shopping in a factory outlet center, the stores in the center should indeed be manufacturers' outlets.

The following factory outlet retailer listings include condensed comments from customers. These comments are the printed version of word-of-mouth referrals that made shopping fun when people had more time to shop! You have personal opinions and Fabulous Finds gives you a forum to express those opinions.

If you like a retailer's stores, the quality of its brand names, the savings it offers in the outlet stores and in displays, write to Fabulous Finds. Your opinions, comments and information will be added to the factory outlet retailer's record. For your convenience, there is a recommendation form in the back of the book that you can photocopy and use. Be specific and fair; your comments will guide other shoppers to these legitimate manufacturing retailers. We will quote you unless you specifically request that your comments not be used.

Each new edition of *Fabulous Finds* will include new outlet retailers to give you a guide to stores you will want to shop.

ABSORBA INFANTWEAR
1333 Broadway
Suite 1200
New York, NY 10018
(212)947-6024

ACA JOE FACTORY STORE
148 Townsend St.
San Francisco, CA 94107
(415)546-0558

ACCESSORY FACTORY/LEATHER SHOP
152 Commonwealth Ave.
Concord, MA 01742
(508)369-9178

ACME BOOT COMPANY
1002 Stafford /
Clarksville, TN 37040
(615)552-2000, ext. 4303

ADOLFO/DESIGNERS ONLY
55 Triangle Blvd.
Carlstadt, NJ 07072
(201)939-6363
"I love their beaded knit sweaters!" — Lynda Hand, Nashville, Tennessee

ADRIENNE VITTADINI KNITS
1441 Broadway
New York, NY 10018
(212)921-2510

AILEEN FACTORY OUTLET

P.O. Box 248
Edinburg, VA 22824
(703)984-4181
"Practical, useful casual wear at the right price." —M. Smith, Ohio

"Anyone can find something to buy in this store."
Janice Colegrove

ALESSI AND BOURGEAT COOKWEAR

10 Wheeling Ave.
Woburn, MA 01801
(617)933-1930

ALEXANDER JULIAN MENSWEAR

21st Floor
8 W. 40th St.
New York, NY 10018
(212)382-3700
"My husband almost always buys this brand and he finds it in the S&K Men's Stores. Fabulous finds when the price, quality and service are all in the package." —Iris Ellis

ALEXON LADIES CAREER

3649 Browning Lane
Bethlehem, PA 18017
(215)867-6096

ALL SEASONS

(family clothing)
516 Shelburne Rd. S.
Burlington, VT 05401
(802)864-5777

ALLEN EDMONDS SHOE FACTORY OUTLET

201 E. Seven Hills
Port Washington, WI 53074
(414)284-3461

ALPS SPORTSWEAR

5 Franklin St.
Lawrence, MA 01840
(508)683-2438

AMBROSIA CHOCOLATE CO.

P.O. Box 23430
Milwaukee, WI 53223
(414)354-4334

AMERICAN TOURISTER LEATHER/LUGGAGE

91 Main St.
Warren, RI 02885
(401)245-2100

AMHERST SPORTSWEAR FACTORY

Box 578
Amherst, NH 03031
(803)889-8818

ANKO FASHIONS WOMEN'S WEAR

731 Franklin Sq.
Michigan City, IN 46360

ARGENTI WOMEN'S WEAR

55 Hartz Way
Secaucus, NJ 07094
(201)319-1222

ASTA COOKWARE

112 Broad St.
Box 2170
Flemington, NJ 08822
(201)782-1735

AUNT MARY'S YARNS

Ave. E and Second St.
Rochelle, IL 61068
(815)562-4121

B.G. CHICAGO WOMEN'S WEAR

4745 N. Ravenswood
Chicago, IL 60640
(312)/334-1800

BACOVA GUILD LTD.

(gift items)
Bocova, VA 24412
(703)839-5313

BALLY SHOES

1 Bally Pl.
New Rochelle, NY 10801
(914)632-4444

BANISTER SHOE OUTLET

18 Perimeter Park
Suite 100
Atlanta, GA 30341
(404)458-6252
"I always find something that I need when I shop the Banister store and the values are very good." —J. Lanning, Michigan

BANNER HOUSE WOMEN'S WEAR

40 Coxe Ave.
Asheville, NC 28801
(704)253-2043

BARBIZON FACTORY LINGERIE OUTLET

8 Stiles Lane
Pinebrook, NJ 07058-0736
(201)575-7290

BASS SHOE OUTLETS

P.O. Box 6804
Piscataway, NJ 08854
(201)885-5000
"I have worn Bass Shoes for the past forty years and I enjoy your prices in your factory outlet stores as much as I enjoy your shoes." —Jean Smith, Georgia

BEARS 'N THINGS

P.O. Box 275
Townshend, VT 05353
(802)365-7793

BEAUMONT GLASS

P.O. Box 803
Morgantown, WV 26505
(304)292-9401

BELDOCH PEPPER KNITS

1411 Broadway
New York, NY 10018
(212)869-9000

BENCH CO. LTD.

(women's fashions)
401 Second Ave. S.
Suite 505
Seattle, WA 98104
(206)622-6660

BENETTON ITALIAN KNITS

1234 Wisconsin Ave. NW
Washington, DC 20007
(202)333-9792

BENNINGTON POTTERS, INC.

324 County St.
Bennington, VT 05201
(802)447-7531
"Visit the factory store and you won't leave empty-handed." —Iris Ellis

BEST OUTLET STORE/MURJANIE LTD.

(Sergio Valente)
1411 Broadway
18th Floor
New York, NY 10018
(800)223-2680

BIKE ATHLETIC

P.O. Box 666
Knoxville, TN 37901
(615)546-4703

BLACK & DECKER
401 Riverfront Dr.
Reading, PA 19602
(215)373-5255

BLENKO GLASS CO.
P.O. Box 67
Milton, WV 25541
(304)743-9081
"If you like classy glass, go to the factory, buy direct and see the process of glassblowing . . . you will never forget it." —*Janice Carol, Ohio*

BLEYLE/EURO COLLECTIONS
14 Johnson Circle
Shenandoah, GA 30265
(404)577-3905

BOSTON TRADERS KNITS
315 Washington St.
Lynn, MA 01902
(617)592-4603

BOYD'S CRYSTAL ART
Box 127
1203 Morton Ave.
Cambridge, OH 43725
(614)439-2077

BRAHMIN LEATHER WORKS
189 Elm St.
S. Dartmouth, MA 02748
(508)994-4000

BRANDED SHOE OUTLET/CLARK
520 S. Broad St.
Kennett Square, PA 19348
(215)444-6550

BRIGHTER SIDE DECOR
4900 N. Lilly Rd.
Menomonee Falls, WI 53151
(414)784-5440

BRUCE ALAN BAGS AND PURSES
21-15 Rosalie St.
Fairlawn, NJ 07410
(201)794-6240

BUGLE BOY
96 Main
Andover, MA 01810
(508)475-2102

BURLINGTON HANDBAGS
112 Orange Dr.
Elon College, NC 27244
(919)222-0170

C'EST SIMONE/SWAN INDUSTRIES
16135 Harper Ave.
Detroit, MI 49660
(313)885-8028

CALVIN KLEIN
50 Enterprise Ave. N.
Secaucus, NJ 07094
(201)330-8500
"Designs are casual and elegant." —*B. Wilson, Maryland*

CAMBRIDGE DRY GOODS
269 Grove St.
Newton, MA 02166
(617)965-7080
"Classic women's clothing at good savings." —*D. Johnson, Massachusetts*

CAMPUS FACTORY OUTLET
(men's and children's)
807 N. Ninth St.
4th Floor
Reading, PA 19604
(215)378-4840

CANDLES BY ANITA
P.O. Box 457
Helen, GA 30545
(800)358-4130

CANTERBURY OF NEW ZEALAND

(men's active and outerwear)
P.O. Box 3425
Pinehurst, NC 28371
(919)295-1777

CAPE ISLE KNITTERS

10 Knightsbridge Rd.
Piscataway, NJ 08854
(201)885-1121

CAPTREE/VANDERBILT OUTLET

P.O. Box 851
Asheville, NC 28802
(704)255-8637

CARDINAL SHOE CORP.

468 Canal St.
Lawrence, MA 01840
(508)686-9706

CARLOS FALCHI

320 Fifth Ave.
New York, NY 10001
(212)594-2900
"Fashion forward handbags." — Iris Ellis

CAROL LITTLE FASHIONS

102 King Blvd.
Los Angeles, CA 90011-2699
(213)232-3100, ext. 258
"Fabulous find in women's clothing. I buy more Carole Little than any other brand." — Iris Ellis

CAROLE HOCHMAN LINGERIE

135 Madison Ave.
New York, NY 10016
(212)725-1212
"I saw Dior labels when I shopped this store." — D. Kinoff, Georgia

CAROLINA ENTERPRISES, INC.

P.O. Box 15085
Asheville, NC 28813
(704)254-0794

CARON KNITTING YARNS

350 W. Kinzie
Chicago, IL 60610
(312)222-0266

CARROLL REED CLEARANCE

(women's apparel)
510 Congress
Portland, ME 04101
(207)775-7421

CARTER'S FACTORY OUTLET

First Shelton Pl.
1000 Bridgeport Ave.
Shelton, CN 06484
(203)926-5000
"Mothers love Carter's clothing for the youngsters. They last and last." — Iris Ellis

CATALINA OUTLETS

(women's wear)
6015 Bandini Blvd.
City of Commerce, CA 90040
(213)726-1262

CHALK LINE SPORT WAREHOUSE

P.O. Box 38
Anniston, AL 36202
(205)238-1540

CHAMPION/OXFORD BRANDS, LTD.

(Family Clothing)
1908 Forge St.
Tucker, GA 30084
(404)491-1373

CHAUS WOMEN'S FASHIONS

800 Secaucus Rd.
Secaucus, NJ 07094
(201)863-4646
"Wonderful, wearable women's clothing that will stay with you to be worn year after year." — Iris Ellis

CHOCOLATE SOUP CHILDREN'S APPAREL

6515 Railroad St.
Raytown, MO 64133
(816)356-8080

CHRISTA FURS

601 S. Lindbergh
St Louis, MO 63131
(314)991-3877

CLUB USA/KAREN ANNE MANUFACTURING

(luggage)
P.O. Box 5120
Fall River, MA 02723
(617)674-0860

COACH LEATHERWARE

516 W. Thirty-Fourth St.
New York, NY 10001
(800)444-3611

COLE HAHN SHOES

N. Elm St.
Yarmouth, ME 04096
(207)846-3721

"It's been fun to travel with SOS but the outlet situation has certainly changed. My personal quest is to find out where Ferragamo shoes go to die. Cole Hahn is a good brand too." — C. Stanton, Florida

COLE OF CALIFORNIA

5110 Pacific Ave.
Los Angeles, CA 90058
(213)587-3111

COLEBROOK CLASSICS

30 E. Park Ave.
Sellersville, PA 18960
(215)257-2069

COMPANY STORE

500 Company Store Rd.
La Crosse, WI 54601
(608)783-6646

CONVERSE SHOES AND ACTIVE WEAR

1 Fordham Rd. N.
Reading, MA 01864
(508)664-0194

CORNING DESIGNS/REVERE OUTLET

HP-E-1
Corning, NY 14831
(607)974-8369

CORNWALL INDUSTRIES

(woodenware)
P.O. Box 1234
155 Commerce Dr.
Hauppauge, NY 11787
(516)273-3300

CRAFTEX CREATIONS INC.

(Gilligan O'Malley lingerie)
P.O. Box 245
Highway 301 N.
Latta, SC 29565
(803)752-5324

CRAZY HORSE SPORTSWEAR

810 Moss St.
Reading, PA 19604
(215)378-0960

CREIGHTON SHIRTMAKERS

P.O. Box 1797
One Industrial Dr.
Reidsville, NC 27320
(919)349-8275

CRISA TABLETOP
125 Ocean View Blvd.
Pacific Grove, CA 93950
(408)649-5727

CROWN CLOTHING CORP.
425 Providence Hwy.
Westwood, MA 02090
(617)329-6300

CRYSTAL BRANDS RETAIL
626 Bernard Ave.
Knoxville, TN 37921
(615)546-8106
"With Ship 'n Shore, Evan-Picone and Izod labels, you can't go wrong." — Iris Ellis

CRYSTAL FROM NACHTMANN
11 River Run
E. Greenwich, RI 02818
(401)885-0282

CURRENT CARDS AND STATIONERY
P.O. Box 2559
Colorado Springs, CO 80901
(719)594-4100

DALZELL/VIKING
(handblown glass)
P.O. Box 459
802 Pkwy.
New Martinsville, WV 26155
(304)455-2900

DAMON CREATIONS
(shirts and suits)
16 E. Thirty-Fourth St.
New York, NY 10016
(212)683-2465

DAN HOWARD MATERNITY
710 W. Jackson Blvd.
Chicago, IL 60606
(312)263-6700

DAN RIVER FABRICS
1001 W. Main
Danville, VA 24541
(804)799-7256

DANSK FACTORY OUTLET
(cookwear and tabletop)
Radio Circle Rd.
Mount Kisco, NY 10549
(914)666-2121, ext. 152
"Everybody loves the Dansk Brand, why don't they open more stores?" — J. Fear, Canada

DANSKIN EXERCISE ETC.
(leotards and exercise wear)
P.O. Box M-16
305 State St.
York, PA 17404
(717)846-4874

DESIGNER OUTLET (JONES OF NEW YORK)
Rtes. 11 and 30
Manchester, VT 05255
(802)362-3836

DEXTER SHOE FACTORY
Railroad Ave.
Dexter, ME 04930
(207)924-7341

I.B. DIFFUSION
(women's wear)
170 Apparel Ct.
Chicago, IL 60654
(312)836-4477
"Diffusions is a terrific store for career women." — R. Gunderman, Indiana

DONNKENNY INC.
(women's apparel)
P.O. Box 554
Wytheville, VA 24382
(804)228-6181

DOONEY & BOURKE
(Handbags and Accessories)
1 Regent St.
Norwalk, CN 06855
(800)243-5598
"My idea of a classy bag." — *G.L., Arizona*

DOWN OUTLET
(Pennfield sportswear)
P.O. Box 451
1 Tara Blvd.
Nashua, NH 03061
(603)888-8200

DOWNFILL COUNTRY U.S.A.
1455 S. Lipan
Denver, CO 80223
(303)839-1238

DUCHESS FOOTWEAR
3 Norten St.
Salem, MA 03908
(207)384-2207

DUNHAM SHOE FACTORY OUTLETS
P.O. Box 813
Brattleboro, VT 05301
(802)254-2316

EAGLE'S EYE
(women's and children's apparel)
1001 Washington St.
Conshohochen, PA 19428
(215)941-3700

ELFMODE CHILDREN'S OUTLET
P.O. Box 1804
Athens, GA 30601
(404)548-3176

ELLEN TRACY WOMEN'S APPAREL
165 Toledo Ave.
Lyndhurst, NJ 07071
(201)935-4210

EMBASSY FURS
363 Adelaide St. W.
Toronto, Ontario
Canada M5H 1Y2
(416)596-6767

EMERSON RADIO
1 Emerson Ln.
Secaucus, NJ 07094
(201)854-6600

ENDICOTT JOHNSON SHOES
1100 E. Main St.
Endicott, NY 13760
(607)757-4000

ENTENMANN'S BAKERY
55 Paradise Lane
Bay Shore, NY 11706
(212)880-5000

ESPRIT WOMEN AND GIRLS
127 E. Ninth St.
Los Angeles, CA 90015
(415)648-6900

ESTEE LAUDER, THE BEST THINGS
101 N. Fifth St.
Reading, PA 19601
(215)374-2209
"One of a kind." — *Iris Ellis*

ETONIC TRETOM AND PUMA
(athletic clothing and shoes)
147 Center St.
Brockton, MA 02403
(617)583-9100
"Spectacular store for those free and easy weekends and vacations." — *Peggy Stafford, Illinois*

EUROSPORT MEN & WOMEN
55 Tower Office Park
Woburn, MA 01801
(617)938-0450

EVANS FURS
36 S. State St.
Chicago, IL 60603
(312)855-2121

EVERFAST MILL STORES
P.O. Box 203
Walnut Rd.
Business Park
Gail Lane
Kennett Square, PA 19348
(215)444-9700

F. SCHUMACHER & CO.
(high-end fabrics)
1325 Cooch's Bridge Rd.
Newark, DE 19711
(302)454-3335

FACTORY LINENS
(Shen Manufacturing Co.)
40 Portland Rd.
W. Conshohocken, PA 19428
(215)825-2790

FACTORY OUTLETS INC.
P.O. Box 506
Salley, SC 28137
(803)258-3426

FACTORY TO YOU SHOE OUTLETS
P.O. Box 1090
Nashville, TN 37202
(615)367-7362

FALL RIVER KNITTING MILLS
69 Alden St.
Fall River, MA 02723
(617)678-7553

FANNY FARMER SHOPS
5885 Grant Ave.
Cleveland, OH 44105
(216)883-9700

FARAH INC./VALU SLACKS
P.O. Box 9519
8889 Gateway W.
El Paso, TX 79985
(915)593-4379

FARBERWARE
1500 Bassett Ave.
Bronx, NY 10461
(212)863-8000

FASHION FLAIR
(men's and women's clothing)
13th and Rosemont Blvd.
Reading, PA 19604
(215)921-5508
"This must be an Izod store — most of the labels were Izod." — A. *Summer, Alaska*

FASHION SHOE OUTLET
P.O. Box 5
2 Harbor Park Dr.
Port Washington, NY 11050
(516)621-2300

FASHIONS OF SEVENTH AVENUE
(Anne Klein label)
1589 Reed Rd.
West Trenton, NJ 08628
(609)737-6880
"Anne Klein store is a Fabulous Find. Elegance at the right price is my kind of shopping." — J. *McAfee, Florida*

FENN WRIGHT & MANSON SPORTSWEAR SYSTEMS
500 Seventh Ave.
New York, NY 10018
(212)704-9922

FENTON GLASS
700 Elizabeth St.
Williamstown, WV 26187
(304)375-6122

FIELDCREST CANNON OUTLET STORE

P.O. Box 107
Highway 14
Eden, NC 27288
(919)627-3444 STORE
"We have more letters in our files commending Fieldcrest than for any other retail operation." — *Iris Ellis*

"Best quality, best prices." — *Betty Jo Smith*

FILA SPORTSWEAR

821 Industrial Rd.
San Carlos, CA 94070
(415)595-1750

FIRST CHOICE/ESCADA

(women's apparel)
1466 Broadway
Suite 706
New York, NY 10036
(212)869-8424

FITZ & FLOYD

2055 Luna Rd.
Carrollton, TX 75006
(214)484-9494

FLEMINGTON CUT GLASS

156 Main St.
Flemington, NJ 08822
(201)782-3017
"One of a kind and worth whatever it takes to shop this store." — *(name withheld by request)*

FLEMINGTON FURS (COAT WORLD)

8 Spring St.
Flemington, NJ 08822
(201)782-2212

FOOT-JOY

144 Field St.
Brockton, MA 02403
(617)586-2233

FORECASTER OF BOSTON

37 Strafello Dr.
Avon, MA 02322
(508)586-1848

FORMFIT OUTLET

136 Madison
New York, NY 10016
(212)685-3900

FOSTORIA GLASS/LANCASTER GLASS

37 W. Broad St.
Columbus, OH 43215
(614)224-7141

FRANCISCAN

(Waterford/Wedgewood)
P.O. Box 1454
Wall, NJ 07719
(201)938-5800

FREEMAN MANUFACTURER'S SHOES

1 Freeman Ln.
Beloit, WI 53511
(608)364-1200

FROG POND FOR KIDS

747 Miami Circle
Atlanta, GA 30324
(404)239-2263

FRYE BOOT OUTLET STORE

84 Chestnut St.
Marlboro, MA 01752
(617)481-0600

GARMENT WORKS JEANS

P.O. Box 907
Portland, IN 47371
(219)726-7151

GENERAL SHOE FACTORY TO YOU

Genesco Inc.
P.O. Box 941
Room 672
Nashville, TN 37202
(615)367-8291

GENERRA SPORTSWEAR

278 Broad St.
Seattle, WA 98121
(206)728-6888

GENTLEMEN'S WEAR HOUSE

(men's and women's apparel)
194 Riverside Ave.
New Bedford, MA 02746
(508)997-4508

GENUINE ARTICLE

P.O. Box 300
Oshkosh, WI 54902
(414)231-8800
"My best buys come from OshKosh B'Gosh.
Kids love 'em, I do too." — B.B., *Texas*

GEORGE BARRY FURS

600 Meadowland Pkwy.
Secaucus, NJ 07094
(201)330-1820

GEORGES BRIARD FACTORY OUTLET

(ice buckets and such)
205 Chubb Ave.
Lyndhurst, NJ 07071
(201)788-1918

GERBER OUTLET STORE

(baby products)
445 State St.
Fremont, MI 49412
(800)253-3155

GITANO IMPORTS, INC.

(family clothing)
250 Carter Dr.
Edison, NJ 08817
(201)248-1220

GLASGOW KNITWEAR

11222 I St.
Omaha, NE 68137

GLORAY FACTORY

E. Penn St.
Robesonia, PA 19551
(215)693-3131
"Fantastic sweaters from the manufacturer
and they make most of the top label knits.
Prices are fabulous finds." — *Iris Ellis*

GOLBRO JEWELER & DISTRIBUTOR

1823 First Ave. N.
Birmingham, AL 35203
(205)323-7785

GOOD SHOP LOLLIPOP

1807 Spring Garden St.
Greensboro, NC 27403
(919)274-0763

GRANITE MILLS

(athletic wear)
P.O. Box 383
Granite Quarry, NC 28072
(704)279-5526

GREAT OUTDOOR CLOTHING OUTLET

P.O. Box 398
Truckee, CA 95734
(916)587-4377

GUCCI
45 Enterprise Ave.
Secaucus, NJ 07094
(201)392-2630

GUESS JEANS
(men's and women's sportswear)
9152 Alden Dr.
Suite 8
Beverly Hills, CA 90210
(213)747-8115

HAMILTON CLOCK & WATCHES
P.O. Box 3008
941 Wheatland Ave.
Lancaster, PA 17604
(717)394-7161

HANES HOSIERY
(hosiery and active wear)
P.O. Box 2760
Winston Salem, NC 27102
(919)744-8284

HART SHAFFNER MARX
101 N. Wacker
Chicago, IL 60606
(312)372-6300

HARTSTONE POTTERY
P.O. Box 2626
Zanesville, OH 43701
(614)452-9000

HARTSTRINGS CHILDREN'S WEAR
821 Lancaster Ave.
Strafford, PA 19087
(215)687-6900

HARVÉ BENARD
225 Meadowland Pkwy.
Secaucus, NJ 07094
(201)319-0909
"Impulse shopping got a new meaning when I visited the harvé benard Store." —J. Prichett, West Virginia

HEIRLOOMS WOMEN'S WEARABLES
511 Old Lancaster Rd.
Berwyn, PA 19302
(215)251-0733

HENSON LINGERIE LOBBY
P.O. Box 1026
Greenville, TX 75401
(214)455-1434

HICKEY FREEMAN
(ultra men's wear)
1155 Clinton Ave. N.
Rochester, NY 14621
(716)467-7240

HILDA OF ICELAND
212 Washington Ave.
Bridgeville, PA 15017
(412)257-3110

HYALYN LTD
(pottery)
P.O. Box 2068
581 11th St.
Hickory, NC 28601
(704)322-3400

IDEAS WOMEN'S APPAREL
P.O. Box 5225
Miami Lakes, FL 33014
(800)231-1030

INTIMATE EVE SLEEPWEAR
180 Madison Ave.
New York, NY 10016
(212)684-4684

J. CREW MEN & WOMEN
625 Avenue of the Americas
New York, NY 10011
(212)886-2539

297

J.G. HOOK
1300 Belmont Ave.
Philadelphia, PA 19104
(215)477-9600
"All-time favorite for most of the women I
know." — *Betty Berg, Pennsylvania*

JACQUE COHEN SHOES
20 Enterprise Ave.
Secaucus, NJ 07094
(201)867-9270

JAEGER OUTLET
(women's silks and cashmere)
818 Madison Ave.
New York, NY 10021
(212)794-0780

JAYMAR-RUBY MEN & WOMEN
5000 S. Ohio St.
Michigan City, IN 46360
(219)879-7341

JERELL INC. MULTIPLES
1240 Titan Dr.
Dallas, TX 75247
(800)527-5815

JINDO FURS/IMAGE INC.
165 Chubb Ave.
Lyndhurst, NJ 07071
(201)507-5300

JOAN & DAVID SHOES
4 W. Fifty-Eighth St.
New York, NY 10019
(212)371-8250
"Very popular brand, priced right. Nice selection." — *D. Foreman, Illinois*

JOAN VAS DESIGNER EXTRAS
P.O. Box 4296
Manufacturers Rd.
Chattanooga, TN 37405
(615)266-2175
"Their soft knit dresses have a quality look
for easy living." — *R.R., Ohio*

JOCKEY MENSWEAR FACTORY OUTLET
2300 60th St.
Kenosha, WI 53140
(414)658-8111 ext. 347

JOHNSTON INC.
(children's wear)
P.O. Box 310
Wylie, TX 75098
(214)455-8895

JOHNSTON & MURPHY SHOES
Genesco Real Estate #672
P.O. Box 941
Nashville, TN 37202-9832
(615)367-7401

JOLENE CHILDREN'S FACTORY OUTLET
7878S 1310W
West Jordan, UT 84084
(801)566-6671

JONATHAN LOGAN
3200 Liberty Ave.
N. Bergen, NJ 07047
(201)867-2020 ext. 265

JOSEPH & FEISS CO.
P.O. Box 5968
Cleveland, OH 44101
(216)961-6000

JUDY BOND BLOUSES
E. Rankin St.
Brewton, AL 36426
(205)867-2724

JUMPING JACKS
(children's shoes)
100 Fifth St.
Monet, MO 65708
(417)235-3122

JUNIOR HOUSE OUTLET CORP.
(collectibles)
4930 S. Second St.
Milwaukee, WI 53207
(414)744-5080

JUST COATS LTD.
11 Rowan St.
E. Norwalk, CT 06855
(203)866-8622

JUST KIDS OUTLET STORE
P.O. Box 9
Mauldin, SC 29662
(803)288-5450

KARLWOOD MANUFACTURING
220 E. Athens St.
Winder, GA 30680
(404)867-3111

KENNEDY BROTHERS WOODENWARE
11 Main St.
Vergennes, VT 05491
(802)877-2975

KIDS PORT USA
(Health-Tex)
1 Wholesaler Way
Cranston, RI 02920
(401)334-3900

KIDSWEAR PEACHES & CREAM
P.O. Box 405
Mebane, NC 27302
(919)563-5521

KILWIN'S CHOCOLATES
355 N. Division Rd.
Petoskey, MI 49770
(616)347-3800

KITCHEN COLLECTION
71 E. Water St.
Chillicothe, OH 45601
(614)773-9150
"Fun place to shop." —C. Kennedy, Canada

KNITS BY K.T.
1407 Broadway
Suite 703
New York, NY 10018
(212)354-1525

THE KNITTERY
Cambridge Rd.
White Horse, PA 17527
(717)768-3892

KNITWITS FACTORY OUTLET
Rte. 30
Bondville, VT 05340
(802)297-1800

KOMAR WOMEN'S FASHIONS
1715 Rte. 35 N.
Middletown, NJ 07748
(201)615-0800

KOSTA BODA
(crystal)
233 W. Pkwy.
Pompton Plains, NJ 07444

L.E. SMITH GLASS CO.
1900 Liberty St.
Mount Pleasant, PA 15666
(412)547-3544

L.L. BEAN
Freeport, ME 04033
(800)221-4221
"There really is an outlet in Freeport and in other locations for this catalog retailer." — *Iris Ellis*

LA ROCHERE INC.
201 S. Main
Lambertville, NJ 08530
(609)397-0149

LANDS' END
(catalog closeouts)
2317 N. Elston Ave.
Chicago, IL 60614
(312)693-0520

LARK FACTORY OUTLET
127 W. Washington
Osceola, IA 50213
(515)342-6145

LAURA ASHLEY
1300 McArthur Blvd.
Mahwah, NJ 07430
(201)934-3000

LE CREUSET STORES INC.
(kitchen enameled ware)
P.O. Box 575
Yemassee, SC 29945
(803)589-6211

LEADING LABELS UNDERWEAR
P.O. Box 2760
Winston-Salem, NC 27102
(919)744-8284

LEATHER LOFT STORES
(importer)
P.O. Box 1070
Exeter, NH
(603)778-8484

LEATHER SHOP INC.
152 Commonwealth Ave.
Concord, MA
(508)369-9178

L'EGGS/HANES/BALI
(underclothing)
P.O. Box 2495
Winston-Salem, NC 27102
(919)744-8284

LENOX CHINA
Coastal Rte. 1
Kittery, ME 03904
(207)439-0713
"Extremely popular outlet store. People like to buy presidential china at a discount. The entire line is elegant." — *Iris Ellis*

LESLIE FAY CO.
P.O. Box D
Rte. 315
Wilkes-Barre, PA 18773
(717)824-9911
"Some of America's most popular brands for women, Leslie Fay has always been known for quality." — *N.G., Michigan*

LESPORTSAC
(bags)
320 Fifth Ave.
7th Floor
New York, NY 10001
(212)736-6262
"Shop till you drop in these stores — the assortment is staggering." — *Cheryl Smith, Tennessee*

LEVI STRAUSS & CO.
(specials)
Chestnut Hill Plaza
1244 Boylston St.
Chestnut Hill, MA 02167
(617)739-6722

LILLIAN VERNON CATALOG CLEARANCE
510 S. Fulton Ave.
Mt. Vernon, NY 10550
(914)699-7698

LION UNIFORM
2735 Kearns Ave.
Dayton, OH 45414
(513)278-6531

LITTLE RED SHOE HOUSE
Worldwide Wolverine
9341 Courtland Dr.
Rockford, MI 49341
(616)866-5612

LIZ CLAIBORNE
1 Claiborne Ln.
N. Bergen, NJ 07047
(201)662-6000
"Everyone loves the Claiborne label. When will they open a store near me?" — *Deb Werner, New York*

LONDONTOWN FACTORY OUTLET
Londontown Blvd.
Eldersburg, MD 21784
(301)795-5900
"I shop outlets whenever I travel for my company and London Fog has the best buys." — *Gregory Linkendorf, Texas*

LUCIA WOMEN'S FASHIONS
P.O. Box 12129
Winston-Salem, NC 27117
(919)788-4901

MACGREGOR SPORTING GOODS
P.O. Box 297
East Rutherford, NJ 07073
(201)935-6300

MACKINTOSH OF NEW ENGLAND
(women's coats, suits)
638 Quequechan St.
Quality Factory Outlet
Fall River, MA 02721
(617)674-6640

MAIDENFORM LINGERIE
154 Avenue E
Bayonne, NJ 07002
(201)436-9200
"I remember Maidenform brand from my teens and they are as good as ever. It is nice to be able to buy at a savings." — *Norma Jean Lakes, Ohio*

MANHATTAN FACTORY OUTLET
Division of Salant Corp
P.O. Box 2907
Paterson, NJ 07410
(201)447-2000
Brands: Perry Ellis, Henry Grethel, John Henry, Big & Tall, Manhattan Shirt, Yves Saint Laurent, Anne Klein New Aspects, Michael Volbracht, Vera Sportswear, Peter Ashley and other famous brands.

MARCRAFT HANDBAG STORE
Canal St.
Brattleboro, VT 05301
(802)254-4594

MARISKA SHOES
79 Main St.
Flemington, NJ 08822
(201)788-3835

MARUSHKA PRINTS
P.O. Box 246
Grand Haven, MI 49417
(616)846-1451

MICKI CLASSIC FASHIONS
(women's wear)
638 Quequechan St.
Fall River, MA 02724
(508)672-0572

MIGHTY-MAC
(boat wear)
15 Union St.
Lawrence, MA 01840
(508)689-3317

MIKASA FACTORY OUTLET
1 Gilbert Dr.
Secaucus, NJ 07094
(201)867-9210

MIKASA, TABLE TOP
American Commercial Inc.
20633 S. Fordyce Ave.
Carson, CA 90749
(213)636-2300

MONET GOLD 'N VALUE
P.O. Box 1024
65 E. Elizabeth Ave.
Bethlehem, PA 18016
(215)691-0437

MUNSINGWEAR FACTORY
OUTLET
(men's and women's clothing)
P.O. Box 1369
Minneapolis, MN 55440
(612)340-4750

NAPIER JEWELRY
1231 E. Main St.
Meriden, CT 06450
(203)238-3087 Store

NATORI LINGERIE
40 E. Thirty-Fourth St.
New York, NY 10016
(212)532-7796
"The lingerie that men buy for their
women."—D.L. Young, California

NAUTICA SPORTSWEAR
10 W. Thirty-Third St.
8th Floor
New York, NY 10001
(212)947-4041

NETTLE CREEK CORP
P.O. Box 9
2200 Peacock Rd.
Richmond, IN 47374
(317)962-1555
"Top-of-the-line bed linens."—Molly
McLymon, Oklahoma

NEW BALANCE
(athletic shoes and clothing)
38 Everett St.
Boston, MA 02134
(617)783-4000

NEW MAN CLOTHING
2 Depot St.
Freeport, MA 04032
(207)865-3066

NEWPORT SPORTSWEAR
(men's and some women's sportswear)
P.O. Box 420
Wilmington, NC 28402
(919)762-4474

NIKE
5999 120th Ave.
Kenosha, WI 53142
(414)857-7747

NILANI WOMEN'S FASHIONS
100 Enterprise Ave.
Secaucus, NJ 07094
(201)319-1542

9 WEST OUTLET
9 W. Broad St.
Stamford, CT 06902
(203)324-7567

NORTH FACE
(athletic wearables)
999 Harrison St.
Berkeley, CA 94710
(415)527-9700

OLD MILL WOMEN'S WEAR
P.O. Box 769
Easton, PA 18042
(215)258-9143

OLEG CASSINI
30 Enterprise Ave.
Secaucus, NJ 07094
(201)330-1800

ONEIDA SILVERSMITH
(silverware)
Kenwood Ave.
Oneida, NY 13421
(315)361-3000
"Does everyone in the whole world own a
piece of Oneida? It is a quality product in a
time when shoddy merchandise is the
norm." —J. Smith, Ohio

OXFORD INDUSTRIES
P.O. Box 610
Gaffney, SC 29340
(803)489-7111

PACIFIC BEACH ACTIVEWEAR
684 Anita
San Diego, CA 92011
(619)423-3883

PANDORA KNITS
(women's and children's wear)
1407 Broadway
16th Floor
New York, NY 10018
(212)921-4200

PAPER FACTORY
(paper and party goods)
P.O. Box 2789
Appleton, WI 54913
(414)738-4377

PATAGONIA
(active wear)
P.O. Box 150
Ventura, CA 93002
(805)643-8616

PERRY ELLIS SHOES
730 Fifth Ave.
Suite 1102
New York, NY 10019
(212)956-4440

PETALS
1 Aqueduct Rd.
White Plains, NY 10606
(914)946-7373

PETITE BATEAU
(children's clothing)
P.O. Box 630
Newtown, PA 18940
(215)968-9606

PFALTZGRAFF OUTLET
140 E. Market St.
York, PA 17401
(717)848-5500

PINEHURST LINGERIE
P.O. Box 1628
Asheboro, NC 27204
(919)625-2153

POLLY FLINDERS FACTORY STORE
224 E. Eighth St.
Cincinnati, OH 45202
(513)721-7020
"Every little girl should have at least one
hand smocked dress from Polly Flinders and
every Grandma should buy it. I never saw so
many Grandmothers in a children's shop in
my life." —S. Bailey, Pennsylvania

POLO/RALPH LAUREN
590 Commerce Blvd.
Carlstadt, NJ 07072
(201)507-6650

PREGANTTI'S MATERNITY
33 Gazza Blvd.
Farmingdale, NY 11735

PRESTIGE FRAGRANCE & COSMETICS
60 Stults Rd.
Dayton, NJ 08810
(609)655-2929x207

PROPHECY CORP.
1302 Champion Circle
Carrollton, TX 75006
(214)247-1900

PUTUMAYO EUROPEAN COUNTRY
141 Wooster St.
4th Floor
New York, NY 10012
(212)995-9400

QUEEN CASUALS – STUFF TO WEAR
10175 Northeast Ave.
Philadelphia, PA 19116

QUODDY CRAFTED FOOTWEAR
1515 Washington St.
Braintree, MA 02184
(617)843-2226

RAMM STYLES UNIFORMS
330 Peters St., S.W.
Atlanta, GA 30313
(404)688-0839

RAWLING SPORTING GOODS
1859 Inter Tech Dr.
Fenton, MO 63026
(314)349-3500

READING CHINA & GLASS
739 Reading Ave.
W. Reading, PA 19611
(800)523-1818

REBECCA INC.
2435 Sand Ridge Dr.
Jackson, MS 39211
(601)948-3222

RED FLANNEL FACTORY OUTLET
73 S. Main St.
Cedar Springs, MI 49319
(616)696-9240

REEBOK INTERNATIONAL
Stougton Tech Center
Stoughton, MA 02072
(617)341-7353

REGAL WARE
1675 Reigle Dr.
Kewaskum, WI 53040
(414)626-2121
"Fantasy Land for people who like to cook." — Pat Conroy, Idaho

REVELATIONS
16 E. Thirty-Fourth St.
New York, NY 10016
(212)683-2600

RIBBONS & CRAFTS
3434 Rte. 22
W. Fox Hollow
Suite 10
Somerville, NJ 08876
(201)707-9800
"If you go through the door you will buy something." — C. Cappitoni, New York

RODIER CORP.
575 Fifth Ave.
New York, NY 10017
(212)599-6140

ROLANE
1006 Howard St.
Greensboro, NC 27403
(919)299-8831
"This is a something-for-everyone store. I stocked up for the coming year." —*M. Tumland, Washington*

ROYAL BELGIUM RUGS
1345 Hill Rd.
Anderson, SC 29621
(803)261-8307

ROYAL DOULTON USA
700 Cottontail Lane
Somerset, NJ 08873
(201)356-7880

ROYAL ROBBINS
(weekend clothing for men and women)
1314 Coldwell Ave.
Modesto, CA 95350
(209)529-6913
"If you want to see a great design on a man's shirt, write to this company for information. Their billy goat pants are beyond compare." —*Iris Ellis*

RUFF HEWN
(men's and women's clothing)
P.O. Box 4424
Rte. 4
Ridge Rd.
Spring Grove, PA 17362
(800)334-8716

RUSSELL MILLS/JERZEE'S
(athletic clothing)
P.O. Box 272
Alexander City, AL 35010
(205)329-4000

SADDLEMAKER MFG. CORP.
18 Grafton St.
Worcester, MA 01604
(508)752-4787

ST. GEORGE CRYSTAL LTD.
P.O. Box 709
Brown Ave.
Jeanette, PA 15644
(412)523-6501

SALEM CHINA
P.O. Box 876
1000 S. Broadway St.
Salem, OH 44460
(216)337-8771

SAMUEL ROBERTS ULTRA SUEDE
414 River St.
Haver Hill, MA 01810
(508)374-0475

SARA LEE
510 Lake-Cook Rd.
Deerfield, IL 60015
(312)405-0651
"If you have always wanted an opportunity to buy Sara Lee's scrumptious pastries, try them at their outlet stores and save money." —*Name withheld upon request.*

SAUCONY/HYDE ATHLETIC
Centennial Dr.
Peabody, MA 01960
(508)532-9000

SEMINOLE MFG. CO.
(men's apparel)
P.O. Box 391
Columbus, MS 39701
(601)328-1556

SKYR/NEW ENGLAND SPORTSWEAR
47 Peabody St.
Peabody, MA 01960
(617)729-4141

SLUMBERTOGS INC. & MISS DIOR

135 Madison Ave.
5th Floor
New York, NY 10016
(212)686-0560

SOCKS GALORE & MORE

220 Second Ave. S.
Franklin, TN 37064
(615)790-7625

SPRINGMAID/WAMSUTTA

1285 Avenue of the Americas
New York, NY 10019
(212)903-2073

STEPHANIE KAY LTD.

485 Seventh Ave.
Room 405
New York, NY 10018
(212)967-8088

STANDARD KNITTING MILLS

P.O. Box 360
Knoxville, TN 37901
(615)546-3211

STONE MANUFACTURING CO.

1500 Poinsett Hwy.
Park Place
Greenville, SC 29608
(803)242-6300

STONE MOUNTAIN HANDBAGS

P.O. Box 325
Conley, GA 30027
(800)241-6238
"Treat yourself to a nice handbag — visit one
of the Stone Mountain outlet stores and tell
them Fabulous Finds sent you." — *Iris Ellis*

SWANK LEATHER & JEWELRY

6 Hazel St.
Attleboro, MA 02703
(508)822-2527

SWEATER MILL

755 Heisters Lane
Reading, PA 19605
(215)921-2966

SWIRL LINGERIE FACTORY OUTLET

508 Greenville Rd.
Easley, SC 29640
(803)859-2400

TABLE LINEN FACTORY STORE

#6 John St. Ext.
Clinton, CT 06413
(203)669-5975

TAHARI FOR WOMEN

501 Broad Ave.
Ridgefield, NJ 07657
(212)921-3600

TANNER WAY STATION

P.O. Box 1139
Oak Springs Rd.
Rutherfordton, NC 28139
(704)287-4206

THOMASTON MILL STORES

115 E. Main St.
Thomaston, GA 30286
(404)647-6611

TIMBERLAND FACTORY OUTLET

11 Merrill Dr.
Hampton, NH 03842-5050
(603)926-1600, ext. 7271
"Yummy store with irresistible buys for men
and women. If someone loves the outdoors,
they need this store." — *E. Sams, Massachusetts*

TOP OF THE LINE COSMETICS AND FRAGRANCES

515 Bath Ave.
Long Branch, NJ 07740
(201)229-0014

TOTES
(umbrellas and accessories)
10078 E. Kemper Rd.
Loveland, OH 45140
(513)583-2300

TOWLE SILVER
MANUFACTURING CO.
262 Merrimack St.
Newburyport, MA 01950
(508)462-7111

US SHOE CORP.
1 Freeman Lane
Beloit, WI 53511
(608)364-1200

US SHOE CORP.
1 Eastwood Dr.
Cincinnati, OH 45227-1145
(513)527-7540

UNITOG FACTORY OUTLET
101 W. 11th St.
Kansas City, MO 64105
(816)474-7000

VAKKO RETAIL, INC.
225 W. Thirty-Seventh St.
10th Floor
New York, NY 10018
(212)221-6275

VALMODE
P.O. Box 281
Bridgeton, NJ 08302
(609)455-4234

VAN HEUSEN RETAIL DIVISION
P.O. Box 6804
Piscataway, NJ 08855-6804
(201)885-1121, ext. 442

VANITY FAIR
Hill Ave. and Park Rd.
Wyomissing, PA 19610
(215)378-0408
"A cousin lived in the Reading, Pennsylvania,
area and took us to Vanity Fair Outlet. Vanity
Fair Complex means quality, and my daughter
was thrilled when she saw how much further
our money went." — *Laurel Petty, Bermuda*

VILLROY & BOCH
P.O. Box 2330
Flemington, NJ 08822
(201)788-2785

VIOLA SPORTSWEAR
5115 El Paso Dr.
El Paso, TX 79905
(915)779-3831

WACHTERSBACH USA INC
8300 NE Underground
Kansas City, MO 64161
(816)455-3800

WALK-OVER SHOES
31 Perkins St.
Bridgewater, MA 02324
(508)697-6104

WALKER SHOE STORE
P.O. Box 1167
Asheboro, NC 27203
(919)625-1380

WALLET WORKS
(Amity Leather Products Co.)
735 S. Main St.
West Bend, WI 53095
(414)338-6601

WARNACO/OLGA/HATHAWAY/
WHITE STAG
325 Lafayette St.
Bridgeport, CT 06601
(203)579-8100

WEMCO
966 S. White St.
New Orleans, LA 70125
(504)822-3700

WEST BEND MANUFACTURER STORES
400 Washington
West Bend, WI 53095
(414)334-2311

WESTPOINT PEPPERELL
P.O. Box 609
Lanette, AL 31833
(404)645-7784

WICKER FACTORY
226 Nut Tree Rd.
Vacaville, CA 95687
(707)449-8063

WILLIWEAR LTD.
209 W. Thirty-Eighth St.
New York, NY 10018
(212)869-1380

WINDSOR SHIRT CO. INC.
601 S. Henderson Rd.
King of Prussia, PA 19406
(215)337-3474

WINONA GLOVE FACTORY OUTLET
416 E. Second St.
Winona, MN 55987
(507)452-6973

WINONA KNITTING MILLS
1200 Storr's Pond Rd.
Winona, MN 55987
(507)454-3240

WISCONSIN TOY LIQUIDATOR
(unique for toys)
80 Beckwith Ave.
Patterson, NJ 07503
(201)279-9518
"Wisconsin Toy was grandfathered in because the store is so wonderful that this liquidator needed to be listed. If you do not agree after you shop the store, tell me." — *Iris Ellis*

WOOLEN MILLS
1500 Second Ave. NW
Faribault, MN 55021
(507)334-6444

WOOLRICH OUTLET STORE
Park Ave.
Woolrich, PA 17779
(717)769-6464

WRANGLER
P.O. Box 21488
Greensboro, NC 27420
(919)373-5564

THE YARN OUTLET
P.O. Box 6392
Providence, RI 02940
(401)722-5600

YOUNG GENERATIONS
(women's and children's wear)
P.O. Box 2060
I-26 at US 64
Hendersonville, NC 28793
(704)697-2162

CUSTOMER COMMENT AND RECOMMENDATION FORM FOR UNLISTED STORES

This form can be used for factory outlet stores in factory outlet centers and for retail "gems" such as F. Schumacher's or Sak's or Lord & Taylor's clearance stores. Any comment or any retail concept that you want to share is welcome. Retail "gems" will be inserted in our next issue of *Fabulous Finds*. Please use the format below for your information collecting. Photocopy this page when necessary to research additional factory outlet stores. Use back of form for additional comments.

Store Name: _____

Address: _____

City/State/Zip: _____

Center Name (if applicable): _____

_____

Approximate percentage of savings: (Circle One)

        30%   40%   50%   60%   70%   more

Brands available: _____

_____

What you like about the store: _____

_____

What you don't like: _____

_____

Why should this center go in *Fabulous Finds?* _____

_____

Why is this store special? _____

_____

Additional information: _____

_____

_____

Your Name: _____

Address: _____

City/State/Zip: _____

Mail to: Fabulous Finds, Inc.
       9109 San Jose Boulevard
       Jacksonville, FL 32257

HERE'S YOUR CHANCE

Have you ever visited a factory outlet shopping center and thought "Wow! This is great!" or "Gee! This is awful!"? Did you want to tell someone about it afterward? Now you can. The form below is designed to evaluate shopping centers. The results of these survey forms will be tabulated and organized into a comprehensive report that will be used by retailers and developers who want to upgrade these centers. This is your chance to cast your vote for the type of retail you will or will not support. Don't miss this opportunity to speak up! (Photocopy form as needed.)

SHOPPING CENTER EVALUATION FORM

Shopping Center Name: _____

_____

Address: _____
City/State/Zip: _____

1. How did you find out about the shopping center? _____

_____

_____

2. Did you have any difficulty locating it? ☐ Yes ☐ No

3. Was access and parking adequate? ☐ Yes ☐ No

4. Did the shopping center have ☐ architectural and aesthetic appeal, or was it ☐ just another place to shop?

5. Was the number of stores and selection of merchandise adequate for you to find what you were shopping for? ☐ Yes ☐ No

6. Did you feel the values here were better than a traditional mall?
☐ Yes ☐ No

7. Did the stores have ☐ continuity of quality, or were ☐ some high-end and some low-end?

8. Were you satisfied with the way you were treated by the sales help in the stores? ☐ Yes ☐ No

9. Were convenience facilities such as restrooms and seating areas adequate? ☐ Yes ☐ No

10. Were the facilities for food adequate? ☐ Yes   ☐ No

11. Would you recommend this shopping center to a friend?
☐ Yes   ☐ No   Why? _____

_____

_____

12. What would you say the average savings were (e.g., 30-40%, etc.)?

_____

13. Was your experience in this shopping center
☐ irritating ☐ boring ☐ satisfying ☐ exciting

14. Did the area surrounding the shopping center
☐ add to ☐ detract from ☐ not affect your shopping experience?

15. On a scale of 1 to 10 (10 being most exciting), how would you rate
this shopping center? _____

16. How many times have you shopped there? _____

17. Will you shop there again? ☐ Yes   ☐ No

18. Why did you pick this particular shopping center to evaluate? _____

_____

_____

19. Do you have any additional comments to make about this shopping
center? _____

_____

_____

20. Other than purchasing necessities, please tell us how you feel about
shopping. _____

_____

_____

_____

*Will you please complete this section of the survey so that we can see who has
answered the survey.*

I am: ☐ Male   ☐ Female

I am: ☐ Under 21 ☐ 21-30   ☐ 31-40   ☐ 41-50
       ☐ 51-60   ☐ 61-70   ☐ Over 70

My education level is:

    ☐ Less than High School   ☐ College Degree
    ☐ High School Graduate   ☐ Professional Degree

The number of people with full-time employment in my household is:

_____

I take several mini-vacation or long-weekend trips each year:
☐ Yes   ☐ No Average number: _____

I shop when I travel: ☐ Yes   ☐ No   ☐ Sometimes

My family income is:
    ☐ Under $10,000/year   ☐ $30,000-$40,000/year
    ☐ $10,000-$20,000/year   ☐ Over $40,000/year

I live in: (City/State) _____

Optional, but preferred:

Your Name: _____
Address: _____
City/State/Zip: _____

Retailers respond to customer support. Integrity and value can be encouraged in factory stores if you express your opinions. Without your feedback, diminishing discounts and dilution of the outlet concept will destroy the viability for factory outlet shopping centers.

Thank you for your insights. This information will be available to both developers and to the stores in the center. They want your business and they want feedback from you. This is one way to know what you want, what you like, and what will bring you back.

Mail to: Fabulous Finds, Inc.
             9109 San Jose Boulevard
             Jacksonville, FL 32257

WANTED

Ihope you have read the wanted notices scattered throughout *Fabulous Finds*. We want your feedback. Become a Super Shopper.

Why are Super Shoppers necessary? Feedback from customers will help to direct the growth of retail in the future . . . just as it did in the past. They are discriminating and share their information with others.

The new format in *Fabulous Finds* offers outlet shopping centers with twenty to forty factory outlet stores in a festive environment. In future editions, we will research along with our readers to identify the factory outlets and reader's gems and include only the best for your shopping fun. We'll supply information about places to eat and sleep and how to enjoy the surrounding area too.

Your reward for information will be the gratitude of every traveler that follows your recommendations and walks away satisfied. Please send a brochure or at least enough detail to assist research efforts for *Fabulous Finds'* customers. Put yourself in their place and send the information that you would want if you knew nothing about the event, attraction, lodging or restaurant.

We can network this information and eliminate unpleasant surprises if *Fabulous Finds* researches the outlets and you report your good travel experiences. *SOS* was a good friend to every good shopper and *Fabulous Finds* will be even better with your help.

Send information to:
Fabulous Finds
9109 San Jose Boulevard
Jacksonville, FL 32257

Photocopy these tickets to send good news to your friends!

Personal Referral To Fabulous Shopping

I enjoyed this store/center: _____

Address: _____

City/State/Zip: _____

Phone or directions: _____

_____

_____

Hope you like it too. _____
  sign your name when you refer an outlet store/center

Place additional comments on back of ticket.

Personal Referral To Fabulous Shopping

I enjoyed this store/center: _____

Address: _____

City/State/Zip: _____

Phone or directions: _____

_____

_____

Hope you like it too. _____
  sign your name when you refer an outlet store/center

Place additional comments on back of ticket.

Personal Referral To Fabulous Shopping

I enjoyed this store/center: _____

Address: _____

City/State/Zip: _____

Phone or directions: _____

_____

_____

Hope you like it too. _____
  sign your name when you refer an outlet store/center

Place additional comments on back of ticket.

INDEX